OF MYTHS AND MOVEMENTS

Rewriting Chipko into Himalayan History

HARIPRIYA RANGAN

VERSO
London • New York

First published by Verso 2000
© Haripriya Rangan 2000
All rights reserved

Verso
UK: 6 Meard Street, London W1V 3HR
USA: 180 Varick Street, New York, NY 10014–4606

Verso is the imprint of New Left Books

ISBN 1–85984–783–8
ISBN 1–85984–305–0 (pbk)

British Library Cataloguing in Publication Data
A catalogue record for this book is available from the British Library

Library of Congress Cataloging-in-Publication Data
Rangan, Haripriya, 1960–
    Of myths and movements : rewriting Chipko into Himalayan history / Haripriya Rangan.
    p. cm.
Includes bibliographical references and index.
    ISBN 1–85984–305–0 (pbk.)—ISBN 1–85984–783–8 (cloth)
    1. Chipko movement—History. 2. Forest conservation—India—History. 3. Forest
conservation—Himalaya Mountains—History. I. Title.
SD414.I5 R36 2000
333.75′16′095496—dc21

00–043709

Typeset in 10pt Bembo by SetSystems, Saffron Walden, Essex
Printed by Biddles Ltd, Guildford and King's Lynn

For my family of relatives, friends, critics, and beloved
who encourage and challenge my work

and

in memory of S. Ramaswamy (1921–90),
my uncle and member of CPI, who introduced me to
a carnivalesque understanding of Marx and political economy
in my tender years

CONTENTS

Acknowledgements   ix

Preface   xiii

1   Myth and Marginalisation   1

2   Passages from History to Nature   13

3   Naturalised Himalaya   43

4   Himalayan Backwardness   66

5   Biogeography of Control   97

6   Development in the Margins   136

7   Chipko's Movements   153

8   Regional Questions and Sustainable Development   175

Notes   196

Bibliography   241

Index   269

LIST OF MAPS
AND FIGURES

Garhwal and Kumaon Himalaya   67

Forest Categories and Access Regimes   118

Forest Reclassifications in Garhwal and Kumaon, 1865–1975   129

Distribution of Vegetation within Resource Control Regimes   131

ACKNOWLEDGEMENTS

It has taken me close to ten years to write this book. This may seem an embarrassing admission in an age when the motto 'publish or perish' directs the fate of academic life in seats of higher learning. But I am happy to admit that these years spent in field research, teaching, and writing articles about regional development, social change, and resource management in the Indian Himalayas have been both necessary and worthwhile in shaping the ideas contained in this book. Ideas, like good wine, require a great deal of rigorous and critical testing to develop character and maturity before being offered for consumption by discerning audiences. The past ten years of testing have been carried out in the process of working on my doctoral degree in urban and regional planning at the University of California-Los Angeles, postdoctoral research at the University of California-Berkeley, and teaching at the University of Kentucky, the Royal Melbourne Institute of Technology, and Monash University.

My research on the Garhwal Himalaya has benefited from several funding sources. Preliminary fieldwork and travel were supported by grants from the Taraknath Das Foundation, Centre for South Asian Studies, Columbia University, New York, and the Graduate Division of the University of California-Los Angeles (1990). The major source of funding for dissertation field research was the Junior Fellowship Program of the American Institute of Indian Studies, Chicago and New Delhi (1990–91). Subsequent field trips to Garhwal (in 1993, 1994, and 1997) were supported in large part by the S.V. Ciriacy-

Wantrup Postdoctoral Fellowship in Natural Resource Studies at UC-Berkeley and personal funds.

Field research in Garhwal was enriched by the lively interest, generosity, and assistance of a number of people living in the villages and towns of the region, and by conservators and officers of the Uttar Pradesh Forest Department in various divisions of the Yamuna, Bhagirathi, and Garhwal Forest Circles. My life in Dehra Dun would have been lonely and dull had I not been welcomed into the homes and families of Raja Devendra Singh and Rani Anjali Singh of Sahanpur; Mr and Mrs Y.K. Dhand; Umeshwari Singh, a dear friend and sister who is no more; and Harish Virmani, K.V. Singh, Chandra Raj Singh Tomar, Bharatendra Singh, Savita Dhand, and Rajjo. My travels in the mountains were made delightfully unpredictable by Benson, my favourite taxi driver, who told fabulously improbable stories as he cheerfully screeched his way around hairpin bends. No one else I know shares his rare ability to keep a person vastly entertained while making her profoundly aware of impending mortality.

John Friedmann, Susanna Hecht, Francesca Bray, Judy Carney, Margaret FitzSimmons, and Michael Watts have been academic advisors and friends through these years, and continue to encourage and challenge me to think in new ways. I have also learned a great deal from a number of friends who, at various moments in time and place, have been colleagues, critics, or students with similar research interests and political commitments. Yuko Aoyama, Brigitta Bode, Jacque Chase, Preeti Chopra, Stuart Corbridge, Yaakov Garb, Carole Gallagher, Mary Gilmartin, Rebecca Glasscock, Richard Gordon, Charles Hadenfeldt, Gillian Hart, Isabel Herguera, Sally Hubbard, John Paul Jones, Michelle Knight, Balaji Parthasarathy, Rae Porter, Chella Rajan, Sumanta Ray, Jesse Ribot, Joyce Rieman, Sue Roberts, Scott Salmon, Satinder Singh, Eric Vander Woude, and Richard Walker have shared their ideas and the pleasures and frustrations of pursuing careers in academia and the creative arts. Alexander Cockburn and Robin Bloch have provided their distinctive forms of humour and support over most of these years.

Bharat and Mala Dave, Nicolina Franchesci, Raju Gokhale, Marcus Lane, Jane Jacobs, Julian Golby, Leonie Sandercock, Jim and Sue Sawaya, Sanjay Seth, Paolo Tombesi, and many others have made Melbourne a wonderfully convivial place for intellectual engagement and everyday life. Vanita Seth has routinely rescued me from the difficult patches in writing, dragging me to cafés for discussions, helping me realise that Melbourne remains the undisputed haven for connoisseurs of fine coffee, introducing me to the versatility of Australian slang, and expanding my knowledge of G.W.F. Hegel, Sir William Jones, and Count Buffon. Francesca Bray, Tony Corbett, Margo Huxley, Kevin O'Connor, and Patrick Wolfe have been enthusiastic and critical supporters, providing comments on style and substance. David Harvey has been a wonderful long-distance (and, at times, exasperated) comrade, arguing, criticising, advising, and encouraging me along the way. I am also grateful to Jane Hindle and Judith Ravenscroft at Verso for offering valuable editorial comments and help in readying the manuscript for publication.

My parents, sister, and brother, maintain a remarkable amount of faith in me and my abilities. I can only hope they will find no reason to question this faith as I continue my career in teaching and research. I have learned a great deal from their experiences and abilities to appreciate the charm and aesthetics of story-telling without losing sight of the rich texture of realities that are integral to any good narrative.

I have drawn on published and about-to-be published articles in a variety of publications. The original sources include "The Political Ecology of Sustainability and Forest Management: Reflections on Contemporary Theories and Material Practices", in F.P. Gale and R.M. M'Gonigle (eds), *Nature, Production, Power: Towards an Ecological Political Economy* (Cheltenham, Glos.: Edward Elgar, forthcoming, June/July 2000); "State Economic Policies and Changing Regional Landscapes in the Uttarakhand Himalaya", in A. Agarwal and K. Sivaramakrishnan (eds), *Agrarian Environments: Negotiating Conflicts over Identities and Resources in India* (Durham, NC: Duke University Press, forthcoming, August/September 2000); "Bitter-Sweet Liaisons in a Contentious Democracy: Radical Planning through State

Agency in Postcolonial India", *Plurimondi*, 1: 2 (1999): 47–66; "Indian Environmentalism and the Question of the State: Problems and Prospects for Sustainable Development", *Environment and Planning* (A), 29: 12 (1997): 2129–43; "Property vs. Control: The State and Forest Management in the Indian Himalaya", *Development and Change*, 28: 1 (1997): 71–94; "From Chipko to Uttaranchal: Development, Environment, and Social Protest in the Garhwal Himalayas", in R. Peet and M.J. Watts (eds), *Liberation Ecologies: Environment, Development, Social Movements*, London: Routledge, 1996, pp. 205–26. I would like to thank the editors and the referees of these pieces for their comments and suggestions. They have proved invaluable in the process of sharpening some of the theoretical arguments in the book.

PREFACE

I never fail to be amazed by how Chipko has found a niche in the imaginations and memories of numerous scholars I have encountered in North America, Europe, Australia, or Asia. It appears, without fail, in conversations that centre on sustainability, the Himalayas, deforestation in India, or social movements in poor regions of the world. I wait for that moment when I will inevitably be asked the question, "Do you know of Chipko, the movement to save trees in India?"

Each time someone invokes Chipko as an exemplar within environmental discourse, they are also, consciously or otherwise, making statements, assertions, and assumptions about how humans influence the world around them, the organisation of social life and material practices, the use and management of resources, the nature of government, the relationships between states, markets, and civil societies, the powers of social agency and their discursive strategies for social transformation. This book uses the Chipko movement as the means to explore each of these themes.

Chipko's fame has proved a mixed blessing. On the one hand, it attracts a wide audience of anthropologists, sociologists, ecologists, political economists, environmental scientists, social and environmental historians, geographers, political scientists, social theorists, cultural theorists, postcolonial theorists, activists, planners, foresters, and policy-makers – all of them interested in questions of sustainability in its varied aspects. On the other hand, it makes my task here more difficult because I must speak to the interests and concerns of each of these disciplines. It requires me to draw on their vocabularies and concepts in ways that recognise the disciplinary conventions and traditions of each, to make my arguments cogent and plausible to not just one, but to all groups comprising this knowable community. It is the complicated experience of speaking to and *translating between* this diverse and interested audience that forms the central task of this book.

I choose the phrase 'translating between' consciously, and use it in two interrelated ways. The word 'translate' is derived from Latin and means 'bearing across'; it carries with it a sense of change. It is possible to think of ideas and people that move from one place to another – migrants, refugees, travellers, metaphors – as translated beings. People often say that something is always lost in translation, but I disagree. I steadfastly share Rushdie's belief that a great deal is gained through the process. The second dimension of translation is, as James Boyd White says,

> the art of facing the impossible, of confronting unbridgeable disconti-
> nuities between texts, between languages, and between people. As
> such it has an ethical as well as an intellectual dimension . . . It requires
> one to discover both the value of the other's language and the limits
> of one's own . . . It is a word for a set of practices by which we learn
> to live with difference, with the fluidity of culture and with the
> instability of the self . . . The activity of translation in fact offers an
> education in what is required for this interactive life, for, as I have
> suggested, to attempt to "translate" is to experience a failure at once
> radical and felicitous: radical, for it throws into question our sense of
> ourselves, our languages, of others; felicitous, for it releases us momen-
> tarily from the prison of our own ways of thinking and being.[1]

Translation of an idea into a coherent narrative within a single disciplinary tradition is a difficult task in itself. It becomes formidable when it is about a variety of narratives – familiar and unfamiliar – of a social movement that holds symbolic meaning for so many people belonging to different disciplines. I have sought to overcome these challenges by focusing the book on certain themes that are of common interest to all and of special interest to some disciplines.

The first chapter uses Chipko as an exemplar to show how history and myth interact and how historical events are transformed into myth through narratives. The second chapter focuses on narratives, and Chipko narratives in particular, to explore the ways in which they are constructed so as to gain power and authority to influence political processes and change material practices. The third chapter explores the ways in which interactions in the Himalayas between humans and nature are represented through social and ecosystem models, discusses their strengths and limitations, and provides an alternative theoretical approach for understanding and employing the analytical framework of political ecology. The fourth chapter focuses on facets of 'the state' – precolonial, colonial, and postcolonial – in Garhwal and Kumaon Himalaya and argues for the need to examine the historical contexts within which forms of governance, dominant policy phases, and actions of different state agencies are shaped within particular spatial and political configurations. The fifth chapter, focusing on forestry and the activities of the Imperial Forest Service, reexamines concepts of property, access, and control in Garhwal, all of which inform contemporary discourses of sustainability and sustainable management of natural resources. It reinterprets the ways in which differentiated means of institutional control over access to resources shape both the biogeography and economic opportunities for various social classes within the region. The sixth chapter explores the ways in which concepts of development, nationalism, and democracy have been imbued with new meanings in postcolonial India, and how the interactions of these contextually translated concepts reproduce or transform social and economic processes occurring within the existing political and spatial configurations of the region and nation. The seventh chapter, returning to Chipko, discusses the role of social movements – old and new – in reshaping the relations of power and material practices. It provides an alternative understanding of social movements by focusing on the ways in which popular mobilisation occurs through discursive strategies that link the identities of individuals with particular social roles. It shows how successful discursive strategies may, in some fortuitous instances, bring widespread recognition to social movements but simultaneously fail to deliver the material and institutional changes desired by their participants. The final chapter brings all these themes together to examine the concept of sustainability and sustainable development. It discusses the problems of presenting sustainability as global-local discourse, and argues instead for the need to view sustainability as a regional question that seeks possible ways and means for ensuring accessibility of resources for all social classes within regions. It offers an alternative perspective on sustainable development as a regional process in the continuing present where institutions of state and civil society are coupled in a bitter-sweet liaison that requires constant negotiation, adjustment, and reworking of their mutual commitment to substantive democracy and accessible development.

I have written this book with the hope of showing that diverse disciplines with overlapping interests may need to find new ways of conversing with each other as they work towards a shared sense of purpose, which, in this case, is in or may involve promoting sustainable development in various regions of the world. Interdisciplinary research requires a new orientation towards concerns, experiences, and ideas while constantly testing the limits of existing conventions, skills, and abilities to effectively communicate between people and places. It involves translation, which, as I have pointed out, creates a sense of anxiety about one's abilities, about what might be lost in the process, but simultaneously offers possibilities for producing expanded and richer narratives that provide different understandings of processes and encourage new forms of action. It welcomes strangers into knowable communities of political and academic discourse by creating more room for manoeuvre and making them more accessible to new entrants. I hope this book will enable its readers to transcend disciplinary boundaries and rediscover familiar ideas and unfamiliar possibilities that reinforce their commitment to the long revolution of socially just and ecologically sustainable regional development.

Melbourne, 1999

ONE

MYTH AND MARGINALISATION

Chipko was a social movement that emerged nearly twenty-five years ago in the Garhwal Himalaya. Today, transformed by a variety of narratives, it exists as myth. Myths are made from narratives which – in their attempt to reshape human values and material life in particular places and moments – imbue particular social events or practices with meanings that appear to transcend both time and space. That is to say, myths are produced through narratives that render particular social events significant by transporting them from their geographical and historical contexts into the realm of pure nature. Having made the passage, as Roland Barthes says, from history to nature, myth

> does not deny things, on the contrary, its function is to talk about them; simply, it purifies them, makes them innocent, it gives them a natural and eternal justification, it gives them a clarity which is not that of an explanation but that of a statement of fact ... In passing from history to nature, myth acts economically: it abolishes the complexity of human acts, it gives them the simplicity of essences, it does away with all dialectics, with any going back beyond what is immediately visible, it organizes a world which is without contradictions because it is without depth, a world wide open and wallowing in the evident, it establishes a blissful clarity: things appear to mean something by themselves.[1]

It is in this sense that this book explores the transformation of Chipko from historical event to myth.

The purpose of writing the book is twofold. First, I want to illustrate how Chipko as myth, despite its powerful ability to fire the imagination of people in various parts of the world who employ it for their own struggles, has affected social and material life in the Garhwal Himalaya in ways that have been neither benevolent nor innocent. I wish to bring Chipko back from the realm of nature into geographical history to understand how this has happened. Second, in the process of escorting Chipko back to the Garhwal Himalaya, I want to explore new meanings and insights that can be gained from this journey: Chipko as prodigal myth returning home does not have to be imprisoned within its boundaries; it can (and will) still travel, but, it is to be hoped, with a little more geographical and historical baggage. The baggage will, I believe, be absolutely necessary if it is to continue to illuminate and usefully reshape the highly problematised and contested idea of sustainable development.

Why should a social movement like Chipko that emerged as it did from the Garhwal Himalaya – a region routinely characterised as marginal, backward, existing in the remotest margins of a country like India – be imbued with so much symbolic importance? And given that India, as V.S. Naipaul says in his characteristically elegant prose, is the land of a million mutinies – now,[2] why is it that of all the million mutinies constantly erupting in its cities and countryside the Chipko movement has become so deeply symbolic for so many environmental scholars and activists in India and across the world?

Perhaps it is because we live in a world that is rife with debates over impending ecological catastrophes emerging from deforestation, global warming, desertification, and floods that so many people are drawn to the Chipko movement with such faith and hope. Chipko as myth touches on all these problems in some way, it offers the possibility of arriving at solutions which seem, not abstract, but real: that change towards an ecologically sustainable world is possible through grassroots activism and social protest. It provides the symbolic weapons, the small ammunition, that fire the spirits of those who hope to save the earth, and who, perhaps, also nurture the romantic desire to see the meek inherit the earth one day. Indeed, it was the beguiling simplicity of the Chipko movement, as I encountered it a decade ago, that captured my attention and drew me to study the movement.

The Chipko story, as I then knew it, fascinated me for a variety of reasons, academic and personal. It was a movement that had emerged, not in the past, but relatively recently. It was a story about a movement that had emerged in a region of India that is commonly regarded as primitive and backward, and the people involved in it seemed to be on the margins of Indian society as well. It was mobilised by women, it was non-violent, and its participants argued against rampant economic exploitation of nature's resources. They successfully prevented logging by engaging in the simple act of tree-hugging when lumbermen arrived in the forests. The story spoke of the movement's remarkable success (I had rarely, if ever, come across similarly successful social movements in my limited experience as an academic and as a planner) in persuading the Indian state to completely acquiesce to its demands. It was heralded by its narrators as a movement that showed an alternative pathway to an ecologically sustainable development, which I saw as meaning, in its most positive sense, the reshaping of social and material practices so as to improve the conditions and opportunities of existence for all human and non-human life. I could not find any other movement that offered a similarly compelling vision worthy of deeper study.

There were personal reasons as well. I had spent most of my childhood and teenage years in various parts of the Himalayas; more importantly, I realised that Chipko had emerged during my high-school years in Dehra Dun, the largest town in the foothills of the Garhwal Himalaya. Looking back at that time, I felt a growing sense of excitement in discovering that, unbeknownst to me, Chipko had actually formed part of my personal history! The discovery, however, was also disconcerting, because I could not recollect being aware of the emergence of such a potentially historic social movement in the region. The lack of memory or awareness might, perhaps, have been attributed to the happy ignorance that middle-class teenagers adopt towards all things political, but this was not the case: I remembered most of the political events that had occurred during my high-school years, including the railway strike, the postal workers' strike, and Mrs

Gandhi's imposition of Emergency rule in the country. What confounded me most was that several of my friends at school came from families that owned timber businesses; I had known some of them and their families well enough to be aware of the rhythms of the annual timber-business cycle: their fathers and brothers travelling to inspect the quality of trees in felling sites demarcated by the Forest Department, the auctions that followed, the recruitment of labour for felling, the felling itself, which was carried out during the winter months, the anxieties shared by the households as the timber made its way to their wholesale yards in Dehra Dun, and the subtle changes in household expenditures and consumption as profits or losses were made from timber sales; all of this was familiar. But during those years, between 1973, which in some accounts is when the Chipko movement began, and 1975, the year I left Dehra Dun for college, I could not recollect any of my friends or their family members discussing potential threats to or drastic changes in the routines of the timber business. I thought, perhaps, that the movement had not yet made its way down from the mountains to the foothills. All in all, Chipko intrigued me for a variety of reasons, and I hoped to return to the Garhwal Himalaya to resolve this personal mystery through an academic exploration of events surrounding the social movement and its outcomes.

The Chipko story that I originally shaped from the accounts provided by Indian environmental activists, scholars, and journalists went something like this[3]:

There was once a time when the people of the Garhwal Himalaya – through centuries of isolation and learning from their surroundings – lived in harmonious and peaceful coexistence with nature. They tilled the land to produce what was necessary for life, and took from the dense forests the bounties that nature provided for their need – twigs and deadwood to light fires, timber to build and repair homes, fodder for animals – and fruits and nuts for seasonal enjoyment.

Then, more than thirty years ago, after India's war against China, this peaceful idyll was disrupted. The Indian government no longer wished to lose any more territory in the Himalayas and therefore resolved to bring its border regions firmly under its control. Roads began to be constructed, mining projects launched, and army bases established. The forests in Garhwal bore the brunt of this activity in pursuit of commercial gain. Timber merchants poured in from outside, bringing labourers with them to clear large forest tracts. Single-minded in their pursuit of profits, they soon left behind degraded and barren landscapes. During every monsoon season that followed, entire mountain slopes, villages, and terraced farmlands were washed away into the turbulent rivers.

Soon the people of Garhwal could bear this destruction no more. They spoke up against cutting down the forests, denounced the short-sighted practices of timber merchants, and urged government officers to act immediately. But their voices fell on indifferent ears. In 1973, they asked the Forest Department to allot them two ash trees for making agricultural implements. The Forest Department refused. It was then that the village people of Garhwal rose in anger and said, "These trees are like our brothers and sisters. We will not let them be harmed for the profits of the Forest Department and greedy timber merchants."

And so, the story goes on, the people got together and devised a plan. Each time the lumbermen were sent out to fell trees in the forest, people from nearby villages ran out to hug the trees and persuaded the labourers to go away. They gathered together at felling sites and chanted the question, "What do forests bear?"; the gathering gave the answering chant, "Soil, water, and pure air." They were successful each time. As news of these small victories spread across the neighbouring hill regions, more and more people from other villages went out to hug trees in nearby forests to prevent them from being felled. Soon this tree-hugging strategy came to be known as *chipko*, which means to stick to, or adhere to, in both Garhwali and Hindi.

Gradually, people from the cities – students, activists, and intellectuals – began hearing of Chipko. They rushed to support the cause, and spread the message of the movement across the country. They joined the leaders of the Chipko movement in their criticism of the Indian government's ecologically destructive forest policies. The government finally yielded to pressure and acknowledged the error of its ways. It praised the Chipko movement for acting as the conscience of the nation, for renewing the ancient traditions and environmental values of Indian civilisation, and promised Chipko's activists that preservation of the sacred and harmonious Himalayan landscape would henceforth be an honoured national duty. The Indian government issued orders banning timber contractors from exploiting the forests in Garhwal. In the years that followed, it passed several pieces of environmental legislation aimed at protecting forests across the country, particularly those in the Himalayas. Chipko was hailed as India's civilisational response to the ecological crisis and became an inspiration for numerous grassroots and environmental movements in other parts of the country and across the world. Its success had given rise to the proliferation of grassroots activities and the emergence of ecologically sensitive approaches to development in the Garhwal Himalaya.

I went to Dehra Dun in early 1990, anxious and excited, to begin my field research in Garhwal. My nervousness stemmed from a sharpened awareness of the fact that I was returning to the place of my childhood and teenage years, a place I had not visited for fifteen years: the past, as L.P. Hartley observed at the start of his novel *The Go-Between*, "is a foreign country: they do things differently there".[4] Yet there was the excitement too of looking forward to seeing familiar landscapes with a different purpose in mind, of exploring how Chipko had motivated people in Garhwal to nurture, as it were, the new and vigorous seedlings of sustainable development in their villages, towns, and communities. But as I began meeting people in Dehra Dun and travelled to the districts to organise my field research, it became apparent that Chipko rarely provoked the sort of unequivocal enthusiasm expressed by those who wrote about the movement for the world beyond Garhwal. The responses were startling, to say the least. More often than not, my attempt to refer to the movement in conversations evoked a blank stare which was quickly transformed into a small shrug that seemed to cast Chipko into a past teeming with inconsequential events. Those who remembered the movement dismissed it with a few derisive remarks, others spoke with anger and bitterness of how development in the Garhwal Himalaya had been held hostage by Chipko and its publicists. I was bewildered. I wondered how all those Chipko narratives, new and old – which celebrated the local communities and people of the Garhwal Himalaya as foot-soldiers of ecologically sustainable development at the grassroots – had overlooked, or failed to explain why such responses might emerge in the wake of a successful social movement.

In the eighteen months that followed, I proceeded to find every possible way of understanding the historical and geographical context from which Chipko had emerged, and what had since happened in the region. As I travelled to various parts of Garhwal, interviewing and conversing with forest officers and field staff, district administrators, elected village representatives, migrant labourers, and households, I found myself being enmeshed in a dense web of stories and emotions which added to my overwhelming confusion about the movement and its outcomes. How was I to make sense of all these narratives that spoke of visions of what had been lost or hoped for? How was I going to reproduce them into a structure that reflected thoughtful scholarship and erudition?

Towards the end of those eighteen months, I made one last visit to the northernmost reaches of Dehra Dun district and had the rare opportunity of a long conversation with Kalbali Khan, then 96 years old, who lived in a village within the Chakrata forest division and made his living by collecting firewood and selling it in the small town that also served the military cantonment nearby. He had watched me each time I visited the area, but rarely did I receive more than a nod acknowledging my presence. Perhaps he'd heard this was my last visit, and thus decided to spend a few hours one late afternoon telling me what he thought I needed to know. As we conversed about his life and experiences, I found the courage to ask him about the Chipko movement. What did he think it had achieved for the people of Garhwal? He spent the rest of the afternoon telling me what had gone wrong with Chipko, the problems it had created for people whose livelihoods had depended on selling products of the forests.

"But why, then, *Saheb*," I finally asked, "is the Chipko movement so famous around the world? Why is it claimed as such a success although you say it has failed the people of Garhwal?"

The sun dipped behind the mountain ridge, taking away its warmth with the last glimmer of light through the deodar trees.

"Poor people," he replied, in soft, clear, tones, "harvest the most fabulous myths from barren lands; when people have no food to eat they have no choice but to fill their bellies with myths."

Khan *Saheb*'s allusion to the link between myths and poverty proposed a haunting paradox. Until then, I had never thought of Chipko as a myth, and that was because I regarded myths in two, fairly conventional, ways. One way of viewing myths was to see them as fabulous, entertaining narratives that suffused people's lives but had little to do with everyday realities. They were legends of yore, imagined realms of narrative where humans and gods mingled with ease. Myths were fascinating because they revealed glimpses of the contradictions and absurdities that pervade human life on earth; taken to their functional limits, they might offer humans little insights, small lessons, to help them cope with the complexities of the world.[5]

From another viewpoint, myth, in the everyday usage of the term, implied unreality, a bright falseness that bordered on untruth. This meaning was often to be found in scholarly articles, books, and newspapers that spoke about one myth or other, and then proceeded to contrast it with reality: here is myth, here is reality, make your choice. In this sense, therefore, myths were invisible veils that had to be made visible, then stripped, uncovered, deconstructed, or taken apart, thread by thread, to reveal the nakedness that hid beneath. Truth, or Nature, or Reality – these words are often used inter-changeably – implies nakedness. Myths were the fabrics that humans wove to clothe it for various reasons, ranging from modesty – false or otherwise – deceit, power, basic human survival, fashion, or aesthetic pleasure. But we, as humans, have also routinely felt the need to strip off these clothes, to reveal the truth inherent in nakedness, in that particular state of nature that none of us can fail to understand in a visceral way. Nakedness may imply vulnerability, beauty, innocence, or savagery; but whatever the qualification, nakedness almost always implies Truth.

From the latter perspective, therefore, uncovering myth is serious business. It requires the right sorts of tools. In recent times the tools commonly employed for such acts of exposure have been called facts. Facts are those tangible minutiae that appear and surround us in various forms, like particles of dust or piles of human-generated litter (journalists and gossip-columnists, popular truth-seekers of our times, refer to much of their work as "getting the dirt"). They are carefully gathered in varying quantities, and then sorted, sifted, classified, and arranged, like surgical instruments in an operating theatre, to be purposefully used for dissection and exposure.

Khan *Saheb*'s reference to Chipko did not fit within these conventional ways of understanding myths. He wasn't implying that the movement had never occurred, because it had; nor was he stating that communities in Garhwal had not participated in acts of tree-hugging, that it was entirely fabricated, because there were plenty of people who freely admitted that they had done so themselves: these were facts. Chipko seemed to comfortably accommodate these facts – any number of available facts – and more, by merely floating, wallowing, even revelling in them: facts could be used to reveal Chipko as a women's movement, a non-violent movement, a peasant movement, an environmental movement. If, even for a fleeting moment, it appeared naked, it was in childlike simplicity, bathed in innocence, purified by facts. Chipko, in its nakedness, in its state of nature, was ultimately revealed as Chipko; it meant something by itself.

Over the years, as I have revisited Garhwal and written about its geographical history of regional development, forestry, and natural-resource management, I have come to recognise other ways of thinking about myth and myth-making. Exploring the scholarly writings on myth has made me realise that the word often seems to mean many things at once, yet escapes precise definition, at least in English. Elizabeth Baeten, for instance, says that myth is "a term used to describe what is 'other', what does not belong to the existential, intellectual, cultural, and historical position of the person applying the label 'mythical' ... Myth functions or works to identify and classify aspects of human existence that are foreign to the observer."[6] While such a definition might serve to illustrate how some people use the terms "myth" or "mythical", I find it difficult to understand why – if it indeed represents human experiences that are foreign and exotic to the observer – it is still seen by some as the means through which most people make sense of, familiarise themselves with, or come to terms with the complexities of their worlds.

The closest I have come to understanding what Khan *Saheb* may have implied is to recognise that myth is not merely a reference to fabulous legends, exotic experiences, or patent untruths, but an allusion to a particular type of narrative or form of communication, written, spoken, or visually conveyed through various kinds of image-making. Myth, in this sense, as Roland Barthes points out, is more than an object, a concept, or an idea; it is a mode of signification,[7] a process of image-making, of imbuing symbolic meaning to particular things, places, material life, and social practices. Myths are not just ancient tales of gods and heroes, of Elysium, Olympus, Arcadia, or the Golden Age, nor is their production an activity confined to "primitive" societies and religious-minded folk. William McNeill describes them as "general statements about the world and its parts, and in particular about nations and other human in-groups, that are believed to be true and then acted on whenever circumstances suggest or require common action."[8]

Myth-making occurs in the present, within rational, secular, and non-exotic worlds, and through contemporary modes of communication. These modes of communication, whatever they might be, employ narratives as the intermediaries, the agents for arranging marriages between particular forms and particular social actions or practices – we can call them functions – and, through this process, invest both form and function *and* their mutual relationship with meaning or significance. For example, a politician may exhort his or her audience to rebuild the "community", a form that is invested with meaning by linking it with descriptions of apparently mundane, "everyday" activities such as children playing football or cricket on the neighbourhood commons unsupervised by adults, families gathering round the dinner table, people joyously participating in religious or secular festivals. The "community" along with these social actions chosen from "everyday life" become symbols imbued with their own significance within the narrative. The process of linking them together produces a myth of "the community"; a family gathering around at the dinner table, children playing cricket, the neighbourhood commons, become symbolic acts and places that no longer need be linked to any one geographic location, or to actions that occur in a particular period or moment in time. They become timeless, placeless, and, by inference, self-validating.[9]

Myth does not always produce bucolic imagery. Having made the link between particular forms and functions, narratives choose to give distinctive meaning to the relationship itself; it may be a joyous union, on the verge of breakdown, sullen coexistence, pleasant indifference, or sundered by inexorable forces. The politician in the example may, after having described the ideal community, narrate its collapse by invoking images of latchkey children, of barricaded playgrounds and gang-ridden streets. These stark images come to symbolise "anti-community" but in so doing simultaneously reinforce the symbolic meaning of "the community"; the form may be represented as an outcome of selected functions, as in the positive description of "community", or given the negative description, be jeopardised by another set of chosen functions. Myth succeeds in transforming particular forms into symbols whose significance appears to transcend their historical and geographical contexts, time, and space.[10]

From this perspective, then, Chipko *as myth* is produced by narratives that have succeeded in transforming the movement into a symbol, a form that is self-validating, that appears to mean something by itself. Through these narratives, Chipko as myth is able to transcend both its geographical context of the Garhwal Himalaya and the context of its historical evolution. But in their eagerness to prove Chipko's transhistorical and transregional significance, its narratives have stripped the region and its communities of their histories. Geographical history belongs to the temporal and material world; it is the product of social, political, and economic practices in particular places over time. Places without history are playgrounds of the imagination, barren lands for humans, perhaps, but fertile spaces for myths.[11] People without history become humans who have been stripped, divested, or deprived of their social or political identities.[12] They can be represented, depending on the story-teller or academic scholar, as mythic humans who have no material needs or desires, or as poor creatures whose material practices and aspirations are insignificant or irrelevant. The link between poverty and myth may not be paradoxical at all; it can become an integral part of myth. Whether or not this is what Kalbali Khan implied in our conversation is a matter I leave readers to decide as they explore the narratives in this book.

TWO

PASSAGES FROM HISTORY TO NATURE

Some time during the early 1980s, an Australian scholar of politics visited the Indian Himalayas and met some of the leading activists of Chipko through his Gandhian friends and acquaintances. These meetings and interactions inspired him to write a book called *Hugging the Trees: The Story of the Chipko Movement*, which was published in 1988. Dedicating his book to "all those who have embraced the cause of a green earth", Thomas Weber began his narrative with the observation: "It does not take visitors to the Himalayan regions long to realize that ecologically something is very wrong. Guide books talk of the problems of deforestation and the bare hills and landslides are disturbingly visible."[1] Following on with descriptions of the ecological conditions of the Himalayas and the evolution of the Chipko movement, his narrative ends with these words:

> The Chipko *andolan* [movement] is becoming an inspiration for activists around the world, and whether its work in the Uttarakhand Himalayas is almost complete or not is to some extent irrelevant. Much of the rest of the Himalayan mountains are bare and in desperate need of friends. The Earth in general no less so. And at this stage these friends of the Earth would greatly benefit if Chipko continued to illuminate the path towards a green earth and a "true civilization".[2]

Weber's wishes appear to have been fulfilled. Grassroots activists in Canada and the Pacific Northwest region of the United States hug and chain themselves to trees, invoking the Chipko movement while confronting police officers sent to arrest them for engaging in such incomprehensible acts. In 1993, the *Canadian Dimension* carried an essay by Joan Kuyek, an environmental activist, who described how she derived courage for her work. "Last night", she wrote,

> I read an account of Chipko women in India, the women who circled the trees. The government sent in soldiers to shoot them but the soldiers lost their nerve. So they sent in army elephants to trample them. The women walked to the elephants and caressed them, stroking their trunks and legs, crooning to them. The elephants knelt and refused to budge.[3]

In England, Chipko made a curious appearance in a legal wrangle in 1989 – which had gone on for nearly thirteen years – over a horse-chestnut tree in the north London suburb of Islington. Yaakov Garb describes the unfolding of events:

> An accountant who had bought a house on St. Paul's Place complained to the local council that the tree was damaging the perimeter wall of his premises, and should be removed. While some of his neighbours had no objections to cutting the tree, which tempted children to scale their walls looking for chestnuts and playing conkers, others objected. The chestnut was, in the words of a reporter for the *Telegraph*, 'Magnificent. Tall and upright, with an expansive canopy of leaves and white blooms in season, it creates a kind of portal which half obscures the grassy area behind, and lends an illusion of quiet, rural mystery.' In addition to providing illusion and conkers, the tree apparently had also long served as a meeting place and 'a sheltered spot for evening trysts'.
>
> The Islington Council thought it important to keep the horse chestnut since it was one of the few old trees still remaining in a borough that has the least green space of any in the country. It offered to trim the tree and put a lintel over it, as well as rebuild the wall and maintain it in perpetuity. When the accountant refused many residents 'took up the cudgels, supported and encouraged by the local chapter of Friends of the Earth and other environmental groups' . . . In March of 1989 . . . years of legal battle had culminated in the London Court of Appeals ordering the reluctant Islington Council to carry out a prior lower court order to 'abate the nuisance of the tree'. As soon as

campaigners heard about this ruling they organized day-long shifts at the tree, intending to make felling impossible without injuring them.

On the day the Islington Council workers arrived to chop down the horse-chestnut tree, a local Friends of the Earth member had orchestrated a protest with children painting and drawing around the tree. There was also a man with a snake around his neck, and a group of women playing piccolos to the tree, while many people sat around singing and talking . . . a telephone call [was] received by a member of the staff of the Prince of Wales' office at Buckingham Palace. It was from an activist in the Hackney tree group who had spent several previous nights sleeping in the tree to prevent a surprise night-time attack by chainsaws to carry out the High Court order. Speaking on a portable phone from a string hammock twenty feet above the ground, the man who identified himself as David *Chipko* wanted to talk with Prince Charles about the importance of sparing the tree.[4]

Whether speakers of English are aware or not, Chipko has made its way into the language with the appearance of two commonly used, not always flattering, terms which refer to environmental activism and activists: 'tree-hugging' and 'tree-huggers'. Whenever Chipko is invoked in the English-speaking world, it is as a symbol of people – particularly women – hugging trees, a symbolic act that defies state power, and signifies a bond between humans and nature, and a commitment to nature's protection. While Chipko is inevitably used within the context of environmental debates that centre on forests, the people who use it as a symbol are not always 'tree-huggers'; Chipko has also been used to chastise the unseemly behaviour of particular kinds of environmental protestors. In an op-ed piece for the *Los Angeles Times*, an attorney for the Natural Resource Defense Council criticised EarthFirst!'s monkey-wrenching activities in the Pacific Northwest, while presenting Chipko as an alternative form of environmental defence that was respectful of the liberal values of democracy and private property.[5]

Chipko's status as a transnational icon for environmental action has emerged from a variety of narratives which have, through repetition and translation into contexts other than its place of origin

in the Garhwal Himalaya, spawned more versions and interpretations
of the movement. Chipko is brought into these narratives in distinctive ways: some of its baggage – particularities of place, social and
institutional structures, and ongoing material and social practices, all
of which are part of the movement itself – may be abandoned so that
narratives flow with efficiency and remain coherent for their particular audiences. The need to shed some of Chipko's baggage is not, by
itself, very surprising or suspicious; indeed, it appears eminently
practical. What is fascinating, however, and more complicated to
understand, is the process of decision-making which leads its narrators
to select the baggage that they think is essential, consciously leave
some behind, or forget other details that might have seemed necessary
to their narratives. Such acts of inclusion, exclusion, and elision are
not unique to Chipko narratives; they are a characteristic part of
narration, and are paradoxes inherent to the very form of narrative
itself.

NARRATIVES: NECESSITY AND PARADOX

Narrative is, according to William Cronon, a rhetorical activity "that
organises all representations of time into a configured sequence of
completed actions".[6] Simply put, it is the process through which a
number of facts, people, places, and events are linked together to tell
a story. Even though some scholars make a distinction between
'narrative' and 'story' – which is seen as a limited genre – both story-
telling and narrative, in their broadest sense, involve the activity of
organising facts, processes, and events into particular forms of
expression that usually have beginnings, middles, and ends.

Philosophers, historians, and literary theorists in recent decades
have critically examined the relationship between narrative and
history, drawing attention to the problems that emerge when narratives are used to reshape complex, dynamic social processes into fixed
structures of description and explanation.[7] A problem often emphasised is that the rhetorical exercise of narrative involves the process of
defining what is to be included and excluded, relevant and irrelevant.
As Cronon notes:

Narrative succeeds to the extent that it hides the discontinuities, ellipses and contradictory experiences that would undermine the intended meaning of the story. Whatever its overt purpose, it cannot avoid a covert exercise of power: it inevitably sanctions some voices while silencing others. A powerful narrative reconstructs common sense to make the contingent seem determined and the artificial seem natural.[8]

Despite the problems inherent in narratives, they nevertheless remain the fundamental means through which we, as humans, explain and understand the world. The paradox emerges from the fact that we are, quoting Graham Swift, "story-telling animals"; and, as Cronon adds:

Whatever may be the perspective of the universe on the things going on around us, our human perspective is that we inhabit an endlessly storied world. We narrate the triumphs and failures of our pasts. We tell stories to explore the alternative choices that might lead to feared or hoped-for futures. Our very habit of partitioning the flow of time into "events" with their implied beginnings, middles, and ends, suggests how deeply the narrative structure inheres in our experience of the world.[9]

Cronon goes on to suggest that the storied reality of human experience is what compels environmental discourse to consistently find its plots in nature, and also why those plots always centre on people. Nature cannot tell stories; nature knows neither memory nor history; but people do. Stories about nature, or environmental narratives, remain focused on people, he says, because what we care about in nature is its meaning for human beings. Events in nature have meaning because they stand as symbols for human actions. Human interests and conflicts create *values* in nature that in turn provide the moral centre for our stories. Cronon argues that instead of being paralysed by postmodern critiques of narrative, it may be necessary to embrace the challenges they offer without giving up the narrative form. To do so, he says, would require

telling not just stories about nature, but stories about stories about nature. I do so because narratives remain our chief moral compass in the world. Because we use them to motivate and explain our actions, the stories we tell change the way we act in the world ... In organizing ecological change into beginnings, middles, and ends – which from the point of view of the universe are fictions, pure and simple – we place human agents at the center of events that they themselves may not fully understand but that they constantly affect with their actions. The end of these human stories creates their unity, the telos against which we judge the efficacy, wisdom, and morality of human actions.[10]

Cronon's discussion provides a set of propositions and arguments which can be used as a starting point for understanding how narratives about nature emerge within contemporary debates around environmental issues.

First, environmental narratives are *fictions*, or particular forms of representation, in that they attempt to organise ecological change, or changes in the bio-geophysical world, into forms that have beginnings, middles, and ends.

Second, there is the fact that "nature does not tell stories"; but humans do. Hence environmental narratives about floods, soil erosion, population growth, desertification – despite their use of scientific language to impart a sense of objectivity and freedom from all 'ideology' – are fundamentally human stories which invest nature, or particular aspects of the bio-geophysical world, with values that emerge from human interests and conflicts.[11]

Third, environmental narratives are structured by moral ends often expressed in concepts such as "keeping nature in balance", "carrying capacity", "establishing harmony between humans and nature", "preserving community", "ecological sustainability", or "ecotopia". Rather than being unknown and indeterminate, the moral end, or telos, reflects human choice which may be shaped by social practices in particular places at particular times.

Fourth, a distinctive feature of environmental narratives is that they almost always are, in a sense, morality tales. The particular moral or telos of an environmental narrative remains constant over time. Consequently, an environmental narrative follows a path that travels through time and space, but inevitably reaches towards, or arrives at the moral position where it first began; it becomes a *teleological* form that links past actions to the present or a future which culminates or contains its telos.

Fifth, because they follow paths that begin and end with the moral concept of their choice, both the telos and teleological form invest environmental narratives with a kind of moral *authority*.

Sixth, narrators of environmental stories use the moral authority derived from their telos and teleological forms as the means for deciding what should be included or excluded from their narratives; that is to say, they act *authoritatively*, selecting some contextual facts, events, and experiences, and excluding those that do not fit within the teleological form, or which may seduce – in the literal sense of being led astray – the narrative from its telos.

Seventh, in the process of acting authoritatively, narrators of environmental stories *authorise* or *legitimise* some facts, events, and experiences, and in so doing render whatever has been excluded – consciously or otherwise – from their narratives as inauthentic or illegitimate.

Finally, these teleological exercises invest narrators with authority, authorise particular objects, facts, events, and experiences in relation to their telos, which, in turn, reinforce the *authenticity* of the narrators, their narratives, and the subjects of their narratives.

In short, environmental narratives are particular forms through which social power is gained, asserted, and reinforced by narrators in various spaces of political discourse. They are legitimate fictions about nature emerging from a morass of illegitimised social realities.[12] Each environmental narrative aims to reshape social and material life by authorising particular experiences, people, and events in relation to bio-geophysical processes, by seeing them as natural, as integral parts of nature and the natural world, and in so doing, dismissing other social practices and experiences by deeming them artificial, illegitimate, or inauthentic. A powerful environmental narrative gains power by convincing its audience to dismiss the existence of its illegitimized social realities *and* to make the act of dismissal seem perfectly natural. Or, alternatively, it gains power by presenting a fictive, moral world that asserts its authenticity by appearing to transcend place and time, to exist beyond the morass of social, material, and cultural practices in a simple, purified, and eternal state of nature.

The Chipko movement has been produced and authenticated in environmental and political discourses through such narrative processes. It has become an authentic, natural centre of meaning shaped by a variety of telos. It is the guiding light showing the path towards a "green earth and a true civilisation"; the symbol of "non-violent protest"; the vanguard for "ecologically sustainable development"; a nation's "civilisational response to the environmental crisis"; a symbol of "the feminine principle in nature".

But the question remains as to why Chipko should symbolise so many things at once; what is it about the movement, what sorts of people, processes, and actions did it bring together in events, that motivates its narrators to link Chipko to a plethora of moral ends?

CHIPKO'S MEANINGS

Chipko, in its literal sense, is a verb in both Hindi and Garhwali which means 'to adhere'. The word was used by village communities living near forested areas of Chamoli district in Garhwal in 1973 for a particular set of actions that involved people hugging trees.

Why did the villagers of Chamoli feel motivated to hug trees in nearby forests? All existing narratives seem to concur that this extraordinary act was carried out to prevent trees from being felled by lumbermen. They also agree that these acts of hugging trees were a form of protest against the Uttar Pradesh Forest Department which had auctioned felling coupes within its jurisdiction to contractors (the local short-hand for the commercial timber businesses from outside the region).

Who were the protestors and why did they protest against what appeared to be a perfectly normal part of the Forest Department's activities? This question is answered differently by the various Chipko narratives. Some state that the protestors were mainly women who were concerned with protecting the ecology of their areas; others state that small-scale timber extractors in the district wanted the contracts themselves, or that a petition made by a local artisanal cooperative was rejected by the Forest Department in favour of more lucrative contracts with timber merchants.

How did these localised acts of tree-hugging in Chamoli district come to be seen as a social movement? Most narratives indicate that, as each *chipko*-ing event succeeded in gaining the attention of government administrators and local media, village communities in other parts of Garhwal and other Himalayan districts of Uttar Pradesh adopted similar strategies to protest against the Forest Department and timber contractors. The replication of this tree-hugging strategy in two or three Himalayan districts of Uttar Pradesh led them to be collectively named as the Chipko movement. It is in this sense that the verb *chipko* came to be associated with social protests that emerged in Garhwal during the mid-1970s. Chipko's evolution from local acts of tree-hugging into an environmental movement is summarised with bureaucratic precision in a policy document published by the Government of India:

> Though the main demand of the Chipko movement in 1973 was an end to the contract system of forest exploration [sic] and allotment of raw materials for local, forest-based industrial units on concessional rates, since then there has been a basic change in the objective of the movement. It has developed into an ecological movement of permanent economy from a movement of short-term exploitative economy. The movement is striving to get the scientific truth accepted that the main products of the forest are oxygen, water, and soil.[13]

The question arising from this intriguing summary is: how did Chipko come to be transformed from a strategy of protest by groups demanding concessions for forest-based industrial development in Garhwal, into an "ecological movement of permanent economy" whose aim, presumably, was to convince the larger world of the scientific truth that forests yielded oxygen, water, and soil?

The explanations for its radical transformation may lie in the narratives that have been produced by the movement's leading activists, Chandi Prasad Bhatt and Sunderlal Bahuguna. They may also be found in the work of particular Indian scholars who have described and repeatedly invoked Chipko in their writings and engagements within the realms of environmental and political discourse: Vandana Shiva, an environmental scholar–activist, and Ramachandra Guha, a social historian. Both individuals bear national and international reputations as the definitive authorities on the Chipko movement. Their opinions are repeatedly sought and inevitably invoked in discussions of environmental issues and problems in the Indian subcontinent and less industrialised countries of 'the South'.

CHANDI PRASAD BHATT

Chandi Prasad Bhatt is a well-known Gandhian activist in Chamoli district and has been involved for many decades in community development, following Gandhian principles of self-reliance and the promotion of cooperative work and cottage industries.[14] He played a central role in helping village communities in Chamoli form a labour cooperative in the early 1960s and founding the Dasholi Gram Swarajya Mandal (Dasholi Village Self-Reliance Cooperative), the artisanal cooperative that initiated protests against the Uttar Pradesh Forest Department. Bhatt's involvement in these community-orientated projects emerged from his conviction that it was necessary to find occupational alternatives for young men in their own localities so that they would not be forced to migrate outside their villages to seek employment.

Bhatt founded the artisanal cooperative with financial assistance from the Khadi and Village Industries Commission, established on Gandhian principles by the Government of India during the 1950s. The cooperative set up a workshop for making wooden farm implements to meet local demand but soon found that this activity alone could not provide adequate income for its members. Bhatt and other members of the cooperative decided to concentrate on forest-based extractive activities. They competed with non-local firms at Forest Department auctions for timber and resin-tapping contracts. However, a persistent problem faced by such small-scale cooperatives was that they could rarely compete with non-local contractors – often from cities and towns, or successful local businessmen who had moved out of the region to cities in the plains – who had access to capital, credit, and marketing networks. Local cooperatives and small-scale extractors, therefore, depended heavily on quotas allotted at concessional (cheaper) rates by the Uttar Pradesh state government and its Forest Department. The scale of production in these units not only remained relatively low, but was also at the mercy of the Forest Department's production and management policies.

The very first tree-hugging event is said to have been inspired by Bhatt when he found out that the Forest Department had denied the Dasholi cooperative its request for an allotment of ash trees which were to be used for manufacturing agricultural implements by its woodcraft unit. The Forest Department had, instead, decided to auction the felling coupe to a firm in Allahabad that manufactured cricket bats. The cooperative had also been unsuccessful in its earlier attempts to compete against non-local contractors in bidding for resin-tapping contracts. Bhatt is reported to have announced, "Let them [the Forest Department and the contractors] know that we will not allow the felling of ash trees. When they aim their axes on them, we will embrace the trees."[15]

Bhatt's commitment to community development in the Garhwal Himalaya led him to view the contractor system as the key factor impeding local economies. He criticised the Forest Department for favouring commercial timber contractors from outside the region and thereby depriving locally based cooperatives of access to forest resources at concessional rates. Bhatt also criticised the Uttar Pradesh state government for building roads which, he claimed, were built with the aim of facilitating "extraction of timber wealth out of the region" by contractors.[16] He demanded that the contractor system be replaced by forest-labour cooperative societies in Garhwal so that local communities would benefit from forest-based extractive activities. He also argued for reassessment of forest rights held by village communities, for "rural industrial ventures based on forest resources in the region, involving local labour, industrial workers and villagers", and the need for incentives and assistance from the government in the form of "sufficient raw materials, finance, and technical know-how".[17]

Yet Bhatt's descriptions of Chipko rarely (or in a few instances, awkwardly) mention these economic demands. In one such account of the movement first published in English in 1987, he begins by drawing attention to the "fragile" Himalayan ecosystem, the delicate balance between nature and humans until the "unabated spate of callous exploitation of the jungles" threatened this harmony in the 1970s and 1980s. Rather than emphasising the ways in which households in this region participate in a larger money-based economy through small-scale extraction of products such as resin, timber, medicinal plants, and fuelwood from forests to earn cash incomes, Bhatt insists that forests are used for simple household subsistence rather than commerce: "the social, economic, and cultural milieu of this region has remained largely dependent on the forest which forms the main pivot of existence here. The forest has been chiefly catering for the needs of fuel, foods, and fodder of the local people."[18] The people of Garhwal exercised "this age-old right over natural resources" until the "increasing trend of uncontrolled exploitation of forest resources" in the 1970s and 1980s upset the delicately balanced Himalayan ecosystem and drastically altered their life ways. This led to

> the loss of traditional rights of the local folk over the forest wealth, and they had to escape to other regions in order to struggle for survival. This also amounted to a serious dearth of manpower in the region as the local talents left the region ... They left behind an innocent, humbler lot of people ... The hardships of life and the rising trend of natural catastrophes ultimately compelled the people to think seriously for their safety and security, finally marking the birth of *chipko*, a movement connotative of personal, regional, national and human interest.[19]

Bhatt's narratives emphasise that Chipko is a movement that "emerged as a humble, non-violent protest of the inhabitants of Garhwal against the atrocities launched by a distant 'bureaucratic set-up' at the life-giving trees".[20] He describes it as a "rural-mass movement" which arose from "practical and personal, not hypothetical" experiences, which motivated the village people to demonstrate against the state government; the uniqueness of Chipko is that "instead of being led by professional leaders and demagogues, it is guided by the common rural folk".[21]

Although most Chipko narratives observe that the Dasholi Gram Swarajya Mandal was involved in forest-based extraction, Bhatt chooses to describe it as "the parental body of *Chipko* [which] has been endlessly working with the support of the local people to achieve the high goals of agro-forestry and social forestry for the last five years in 25 villages". The Dasholi Gram Swarajya Sangh, he states,

> upholds the view of a 'development without destruction' and by creating a right atmosphere through public teaching and actual work for decorating the naked lands with the green garment of trees, it is engaged sincerely to nurse the Himalaya back to health.[22]

According to Bhatt, village women who were generally supportive of the cooperative's activities became more involved in the movement during an event that occurred in the forests of Reni (a village near the Indo-Tibetan border). It so happened that the menfolk in the village had been called to a meeting with district officials in a nearby town; "even the *chipko* representatives were not there as they had also been called to Gopeshwar for consultation [to the district administrator's office]". While they were away, the lumbermen arrived to begin felling in the demarcated tracts; "not caring for the odds against them, these women rushed to the forests and clung to the marked trees with angry tree-fellers threatening them with glistening axes".[23] Following this event, village women of the region became more active in the movement, engaging in numerous acts of tree-hugging and protest against the Forest Department; in some instances "women were so much inspired that they even disobeyed the male members of their own village". Matters were brought to a head at one such event, when a village *pradhan* (elected leader), "in deep anguish, served the *chipko* representatives a notice . . . stating

that they had illegally misguided the women folk of the village".[24]
By this time, however, village women had apparently developed
their own views regarding the protection of forests and were not
cowed by such reprimands.

Bhatt celebrates the "miraculous way in which Chipko spread
across the Himalayas", and reiterates that this has occurred through
humble acts of people's "resistance without any professional leadership". He ends with a poetic eulogy for the movement:

> Chipko bears a direct relevance to the life of local people and hence,
> it has hit the centre of their emotions. Chipko has germinated a
> devotional attitude among them towards trees which stand sentinel
> over troubled Nature. Today, chipko has ceased to be a movement
> and become the very incarnation of bliss and benediction which
> affords respectability and prosperity to the woodlands and the wood-
> landers of the region.[25]

The Chipko movement undergoes a fair amount of mutation
within Bhatt's narratives. It is gradually divested of demands for
forest-based industries and is represented as a movement that aims to
protect the simple subsistence needs of households in the Garhwal
Himalaya. The Dasholi Gram Swarajya Mandal is no longer an
artisanal cooperative engaged in forest-based extractive activities but
is represented as an institution committed to public education and
ecological service. These changes appear natural in themselves, and
as part of the natural life-cycle of the movement: Chipko is born, it
is nurtured, it matures and thrives in the Himalayas, it is married to
women's concerns and assists in their social liberation, it raises a
family of related issues through its senescence until it ceases its
temporal existence, finally merging into the transcendental state of
"bliss and benediction". They continue to alter, vanish, and reappear
in later writings by Bhatt;[26] yet, despite these mutations, Chipko's
people remain simple and natural; they embrace nature, they are
wedded to it with love, devotion, and mutual respect; they are
people who care for nature's wounds and nurse it back to health.
Chipko retains an essential, timeless form symbolising the perfect
union between humans and nature.

SUNDERLAL BAHUGUNA

Sunderlal Bahuguna entered the world of Indian politics in 1947 and was soon elected general secretary of the Tehri Garhwal branch of the Congress Party (which was the party in power at the time in India under the prime ministership of Jawaharlal Nehru).[27] He is said to have retreated from formal party politics in 1956, following which he founded an ashram on Gandhian principles, started a school, and organised a local cooperative aimed at securing road-building contracts in the region; his cooperative was also involved in small-scale timber extraction for some period of time.[28] In addition, he and his wife, Vimala, were committed to an anti-prohibition movement (another Gandhian project) which aimed to reduce chronic alcoholism among men in the region.

Despite moving away from formal party politics, Bahuguna has maintained an important presence in the regional politics of Garhwal during the five decades since India's emergence as an independent nation-state. Although he was not the first person to make a link between ecological crisis and poverty in the Himalayan region, Bahuguna is seen as one of the first to use the rhetoric of tree protection to challenge the prevailing system of commercial timber extraction in Garhwal.[29] Bahuguna issued a manifesto, which is not dated, but is likely to have been distributed in the districts of Tehri and Pauri Garhwal between 1969 and 1973:

> Since time immemorial, forests have remained the socio-economic basis of our lives. Protection of trees is our main duty and we solicit our birthright to get our basic needs and employment in forests and forest products. To maintain a loving relationship with forests, the basis of our happiness, it is essential that the treasure of the forests be used primarily for the needs of the inhabitants of this region. For this the material used in village industry and other daily needs should be made available to common-folk and small industries should be set up in the vicinity of forests for the processing of raw materials obtained there. Cooperative societies of forest labourers should be established and the contractor system should be done away with.[30]

Bahuguna's manifesto was primarily concerned with gaining greater concessions from the Forest Department, and the targets of his resentment were non-local timber contractors. His rhetoric linked the protection of trees to the promotion of local small industry by asserting that it "is our birthright to obtain basic needs and employment in forest and forest products". By referring to himself and his audience as "we", and "common-folk", Bahuguna's manifesto establishes a popular, collective identity and thereby avoids emphasising the interests of small-scale, forest-based extractors (such as his cooperative) within Garhwal, whose businesses were jeopardised by the existing system of competitive bidding for felling contracts.

Yet none of Bahuguna's Chipko narratives incorporates the economic demands made in his earlier manifesto. His descriptions of the movement are a skilful blend of Gandhian aphorisms, environmental doom-saying, populist critiques of "western" models of development (which, interestingly enough, employ the "western" rhetoric of universal improvement), and assertions about the spiritual relationship between humans and nature. He invokes the words of Sarala Behn, one of Gandhi's European disciples who, during her years of social work in Garhwal, had stressed the need for preserving ecological balance in the Himalayas:

> We must remember that the main role of the hill forests should not be to yield revenue, but to maintain a balance in the climatic condition of the whole of northern India, and the fertility of the Gangetic plain. If we ignore their ecological importance in favour of their short time economic utility it will be prejudicial to the climate of Northern India and will dangerously enhance the cycle, recurring and alternating floods and droughts . . . Every green tree standing on the hills is a sentry against the invasion of flood and famine. Felling it on any pretext is an encouragement to flood.[31]

The impetus for Chipko, Bahuguna asserts, emerges from India's ancient philosophies and cultural traditions: "One of the main gifts of Indian culture is to see God in nature – in rivers, mountains, forests and in all forms of life. It is a sacred duty to protect these."[32] He describes how this sacred duty has been performed since antiquity: a stone carving excavated from the ruins of an ancient township in Patan, Gujarat, which depicts a woman hugging a tree while an axeman stands nearby ready to fell it; rural women in sixteenth-century Rajasthan who died while protecting their trees from the axemen sent to cut them down by the Maharaja of Jodhpur. These acts are part of Chipko's prehistory. But the ancient and spiritual love for nature received a setback with the arrival of the British in India. The British

> took over the control of forests from village communities. This process started in the beginning of last century. But the forest dwellers, who regarded forests as their own, revolted against this. In Uttarakhand (the hill region of Uttar Pradesh) there were mass movements against the Government control and commercialization of forests, which culminated into an open revolt in the Yamuna valley of the erstwhile Tehri-Garhwal state (now Uttarkashi district).[33]

Chipko is "a revolt against the butchery of Nature. It is an attempt to re-establish the values of *aranya* [forest] culture by making spirituality the guide of science and technology for the well-being of all living beings."[34] Bahuguna describes how economic demands articulated during the early stages of the movement were transformed into broader ecological concerns as the women of Garhwal began to participate in protests.

> [I]nitially *chipko* was an economic movement. The activities planned with great enthusiasm [were] various economic programmes like setting up of small saw mills, working with forest labour cooperatives to fell the trees and extract resin from pine trees etc. But these are what men thought.

Women thought differently about Himalayan forests because they "were involved in the actual struggle for life". Garhwali men left their homes in the mountains to earn money in cities and towns in the plains, leaving women behind to manage their households and property. Women had to toil day after day in the fields, walk miles to fetch water from springs, collect fuel for cooking and fodder for cattle from forests to ensure the basic survival of their households:

They knew the reality, they knew the actual meaning of the struggle for existence. They knew the value of the forest because from the forest they got fuel, fodder, roots and fruits, their basic needs. They knew these and still know these through generations' experiences.

Garhwali men, who saw forests as a source of employment and economic gain, were forced to fundamentally change their way of thinking about forests when, on 5 December 1977, the women of Henwalghati in Tehri Garhwal

tied a sacred ribbon [known as *rakhi*, a north Indian ritual symbolising the ties of affection and love between brothers and sisters] around the trees marked and auctioned for felling by the Forest Department . . . they declared their firm determination to save these trees from contractors' axes at the cost of their lives. These became an eye-opener for the malefolk of the hill region who then started realising the actual value of the forest.[35]

Rather than battling against state government agencies (as Bhatt had attempted), Bahuguna directed his appeals to the national government. He succeeded in garnering the attention of politicians and bureaucrats in New Delhi by presenting tree protection as the means through which Himalayan nature and culture, and by extension, the nation's territorial integrity and cultural heritage could be defended. He described the devastating monsoon floods and ensuing mudslides and destruction of terraces, cattle, and crops along the watersheds of the Ganga and its tributaries in Garhwal (which occurred between 1970 and 1972) as disasters caused by reckless tree-felling by non-local timber contractors. Bahuguna pleaded for the need to protect the Himalayas, its forests, common folk, the nation, and Mother Earth, from the ruthlessness of commercial exploitation. These themes – the protection of Himalayan nature and defence of Indian territory and identity – were repeatedly woven together in Bahuguna's narratives, along with references to the plight of Garhwali women who toiled in fields and forests and struggled against formidable odds to preserve their life ways. "Everywhere in the hills," he proclaimed, women are the backbone of economic and social life. Their active participation in public life will go a long way in establishing a sane society which is free from exploitation of man and the exploitation of Mother Earth.[36]

Bahuguna's dexterous weaving of popular idiom and Gandhian aphorisms with the language of development (used by the Indian state) in his narratives has enhanced his public image as a charismatic saviour of the Himalayas, the authentic voice of its common folk, and as the leading representative of the Chipko movement. This image, in turn, not only invests his Chipko narratives with greater authority, but also allows him to speak authoritatively on a variety of environmental issues. He criticises conventional models of development which encourage life styles of affluence and excess; he condemns modern science and technology which lead to the unrestrained exploitation of resources: "every living being has a birthright to fulfill his basic need from the Mother Earth. Every one needs oxygen first, then water, food, clothing, and shelter." He calls for spiritually informed science and technology which can ensure that all living beings enjoy their birthright by giving

> top priority to the plantation of five "F" – food (nuts, edible seeds, oil seeds, honey), fodder, fuel, fertiliser, and fibre-trees. These trees, of course, should be good soil builders and soil improvers with greater capacity to conserve water, as soil and water are the two basic capital resources of mankind. This will re-establish the harmonious relationship between man and Nature – the relationship of Child with the Mother.[37]

Bahuguna's narratives draw on symbolic images that appear perfectly natural: Chipko emerges as a movement struggling to reestablish the link between humans and nature, analogous to that between a child and its mother, a biological and social bond necessary for the continuation of life on earth; this relationship is viscerally understood and defended by the village women of Garhwal when they embrace trees in the Himalayas. His narratives succeed in presenting Chipko as a struggle of simple hill folk, especially women, whose sole aim is to restore the link between mother (nature) and child (humans) that has been sundered by modernity, science, and commerce-driven technology.

VANDANA SHIVA

Vandana Shiva is the best-known Indian (and Third World) ecofeminist in the world today. It would be fairly accurate to say that her recognition as the spokesperson of Third World women and their relationship to nature derives, in large part, from her repeated and widespread narration of the Chipko story to environmental audiences in the English-speaking world. Shiva's initial encounters and later involvement with Chipko were through Sunderlal Bahuguna. Her narratives and representation of the Chipko movement (mostly published during the 1980s and 1990s) are based on his views and those that arose from the interaction between them and their individual ideas, rhetorical language, vocabularies, and narrative styles.

Shiva's narratives of Chipko centre on women. She draws the village women of Garhwal into her narratives by binding them to Himalayan forests and nature, not because they are their birthright, as Bahuguna might have said, but through the "feminine principle" which exists in both Woman and Nature. Nature is feminine; the Earth is Mother:

> Women in India are an intimate part of nature both in imagination and in practise. At one level nature is symbolised as the embodiment of the feminine principle, and at another, she is nurtured by the feminine to produce life and provide sustenance.[38]
>
> ... As an embodiment and manifestation of the feminine principle, it [nature] is characterised by a) creativity, activity, productivity; b) diversity in form and aspect; c) connectedness and interrelationship of all beings, including men; d) continuity between the human and the natural; and e) sanctity of life in nature.[39]

Thus the peasant women of Garhwal, imbued with the feminine principle, are at once providers, nurturers, and defenders of nature. Having inextricably bound together the village women of Garhwal with nature, Shiva presents them as exploited by colonialism and threatened by modernisation and economic development. When the British colonised India, she states,

> they first colonised her forests. Ignorant of their wealth and the wealth of knowledge of local people to sustainably manage the forests, they displaced local rights and reduced this primary source of life into a timber mine. Women's subsistence economy based on the forest was replaced by the commercial economy of British colonialism.[40]

This marked the beginning of colonial forestry which, she claims, was not based on any superior knowledge of forests or scientific management, but on military need and power. "Commercial forestry, which is equated with 'scientific forestry' by those narrow interests exemplified by western patriarchy is reductionist in intellectual content and ecological impact, and generates poverty at the socio-economic level for those whose livelihoods and productivity depend on the forest."[41] Contemporary approaches to economic development are, in effect, equivalent to maldevelopment, "a development bereft of the feminine, the conservation, the ecological principle".[42]

> The poverty crisis of the South arises from the growing scarcity of water, food, fodder, fuel, associated with increasing maldevelopment and ecological destruction. This poverty crisis touches women most severely, first because they are the poorest among the poor, and then because, *with nature*, they are the primary sustainers of society.[43]

Chipko is, for Shiva, a women's ecology movement, a resurgence of women's power. Women's environmental action in India, she states, preceded the UN Women's Decade as well as the Stockholm Environment Conference. "Three hundred years ago more than 300 members of the Bishnoi community of Rajasthan, led by a woman called Amrita Devi, sacrificed their lives to save their sacred *khejri* trees by clinging to them. With that event begins the recorded history of Chipko."[44] Embodying the feminine principle, Chipko women, like their historical forbears, went forth and hugged trees; being both of nature and intimately bound to it, they saw trees in the forests as their families, their brothers and sisters. Chipko women were against exploiting forests for timber because they valued forests for providing their simple needs, fruits, water, fodder, and fuel for simple subsistence; they did not care for economic gain. Forests, for them, provided soil, water, and pure air.[45]

Shiva's narrative portrays the village women of Garhwal as the real leaders of Chipko; Bahuguna and Bhatt are merely the "runners and messengers" of the movement.[46] In 1977, she states, the two paradigms of forestry, one life-destroying (commerce-orientated and masculine) and the other life-enhancing (subsistence-orientated and embodying the feminine principle), clashed, following which Chipko became "explicitly an ecological *and* feminist movement". Although women had always been part of the movement, local commercial interests had also participated in the resistance. But even after the movement had succeeded in "removing" non-local private contractors,

> and a government agency (the Forest Development Corporation) started working through local labour contractors and forest cooperatives, *the women continued to struggle against the exploitation of the forests.* It did not matter to them whether the forest was destroyed by outsiders or their own men ... Peasant women came out, openly challenging the reductionist commercial forestry system on the one hand and the local men who had been colonised by that system, cognitively, economically and politically on the other.[47]

Chipko thus emerges in Shiva's narratives as the natural expression of women's concern for nature, and as a movement striving to reveal the deep-seated feminine knowledge of nature's innate rhythms. Despite the fact that most Chipko narratives note that the majority of women in Garhwal depend on cash remittances by their kinsmen who migrate to other regions in search of employment,[48] Shiva asserts that Chipko women are against development, modernisation, and economic rationality; "they expect nothing from 'development' or from the money economy. They want to preserve their autonomous control over their subsistence base, their common property resources: the land, water, forests, hills."[49] Consequently, her narratives make no reference to the lack of alternative economic opportunities for men and women in the region. Garhwali men are represented as being peripherally involved in the household economy and in Chipko; demands for forest-based industrial development made during the early stages of the movement are invoked merely to illustrate how men were colonised by masculinist and reductionist ideology.

Shiva's narratives derive their authenticity by constantly reinforcing the link between Woman/Nature and women/Chipko.[50] Her rhetoric invests her – as woman-narrator – with the authority to speak on behalf of Feminine Nature, of Garhwali women, and for the poverty-stricken South; and it is by the constant insertion of "Chipko women", as she often calls them, into her other narratives that Shiva reinforces her authenticity as an ecofeminist in contemporary environmental discourse.

RAMACHANDRA GUHA

Ramachandra Guha is widely regarded as one of India's leading environmental historians. In his well-known book, *The Unquiet Woods: Ecological Change and Peasant Resistance in the Himalaya* (1989), Guha describes himself as a "sociologist trying to write history"; he claims that unlike most historians, he is "more consciously theoretical and comparative" in his approach.[51] The book "was originally conceived as a sociology of Chipko", but was transformed into a more historical study when he realised that "a sociological perspective significantly reveals that the most celebrated 'environmental' movement in the Third World is viewed by its participants as being above all a *peasant* movement in defence of traditional rights in the forest and only secondarily, if at all, an 'environmental' or 'feminist' movement." Seen from a historical perspective, Chipko is part of a "much longer tradition of peasant movements in the Himalaya". Hence his narrative "turned into a more general history of ecological decline and peasant resistance in this region, whose main focus is on recovering the history of forest-based resistance within which Chipko is a small though undoubtedly distinguished part".[52]

Guha outlines two existing paradigms that attempt to analyse social movements: the structural–organisational (S-O) and the political–cultural (P-C). He locates his analysis within the latter paradigm, which, while it accepts the importance of large-scale economic change, argues that resistance can be better understood by examining the

> systems of political legitimacy and the interplay between the ideologies of domination and subordination . . . the P-C paradigm is more likely to emphasize the expressive dimensions of social protest – its cultural and religious idioms. The significance of lower-class resistance, it argues, consists not merely in what the rebels accomplish or fail to accomplish, but also in the language in which social actors express their discontent with the prevailing arrangements.[53]

Having located Chipko within the P-C paradigm and along a historical continuum of peasant resistance in the Himalayas, Guha goes on to provide an account of "the mountains and their people", where he describes the region's precolonial (pre-British) history, the caste and class differentiation within agrarian structure, and systems of revenue collection. Garhwal's precolonial society, he observes, is different from the stratified villages of the Indo-Gangetic plains and closer to the

> peasant political ideal of a 'popular monarchy, a state without nobles, perhaps without churchmen, in which the peasantry and their kings are the only social forces' . . . The absence of class cleavages *within* village society, however, clearly owes its origins to the ecological characteristics of mountain society . . . In Uttarakhand, as in the Alps, Andes, and other comparable ecosystems, agrarian society has had a more or less uniform class structure, composed almost wholly of small peasant proprietors, and with a marginal incidence of big landlords and agricultural labourers. This distinctive class structure meshed nicely with the other ecologically determined hallmark of mountain society, the close integration of agriculture with forests and pasture.[54]

Uttarakhand society held the abundant Himalayan forests in great reverence. They identified with the forests through their myths and legends; "the inhabitants also exhibited a deep love of vegetation, often acting 'entirely from a sense of responsibility towards future generations' by planting species whose span of maturity exceeded a human lifetime." Its "hardy peasant communities" were primed for collective action:

> The absence of economic differences facilitated social solidarity, as did the ties of kinship and caste shared by villagers. In its democratic characteristics and reliance on natural resources Uttarakhand is representative of mountain societies in general, in which ecological constraints to the intensification and expansion of agriculture have historically resulted in an emphasis on the close regulation of the common property resources so crucial for the subsistence of individual households ... As Uttarakhand was virtually unaffected by external political forces in the millennia before the Gurkha invasion, these systems of resource use had become a seemingly permanent part of the social fabric.[55]

This apparently stable and harmonious state of existence within Uttarakhand was disrupted with the onset of British colonial rule. The introduction of "scientific forestry" led to a change from collective to individual use of the forests and fundamentally altered agrarian life in the region. "The erosion of social bonds which had regulated the customary use of the forests thus led to what can be described as an alienation of humans from nature." For Guha, this is the inevitable outcome when a social system based on colonialism and industrial capitalism replaces one that is based on craft production and subsistence agriculture. Forests and their products which had until then been "treated, as in other peasant societies, as a free gift of nature to which all had equal access" were brought under state monopoly which "ran contrary to traditional management practices ... Colonial forest law, which recognized only individual rights of user ... initiated the fragmentation of the community and erosion of social bonds, processes hastened by the commercialization and capitalist penetration of later years."[56]

Guha states that with this radical shift in the management of the Himalayan ecosystem, commercial forestry came into sharp conflict with those of the hill peasantry whose systems of resource management had been part of a tradition of several centuries. He describes the ways in which Himalayan peasants rebelled against the curtailment of resource use within forests by drawing on traditional forms of protest, ranging from symbolic appeals to their moral economy to passive resistance, non-cooperation, and challenging the authority of the colonial Forest Department through acts of poaching and arson. Peasants also sought the support of the burgeoning nationalist movement to challenge the forestry practices imposed on them by the colonial state.[57] In the decades following India's independence from Britain, state agencies continued to function within administrative structures that had been established during colonial rule. The management practices of the Forest Department remained unchanged. The growth of population pressure on the Himalayan ecosystem along with rampant exploitation of forest resources promoted by the Forest Department once again raised popular consciousness in Garhwal to "combat the social and ecological disintegration of hill society".[58]

Guha's traces the emergence of Chipko through various events, protests, and actions undertaken by the Dasholi Cooperative, Bhatt, and Bahuguna, and describes the ways in which the movement spread to different parts of Garhwal. He notes that Chipko's leaders and activists employed strategies that were used in earlier traditions of social protest "to obtain justice by bringing the wrongdoings of officials to the notice of heads of government".[59]

> Chipko is only one, though undoubtedly the most organized, in a series of protest movements against commercial forestry dating from the earliest days of state intervention. Different Chipko agitations have invoked the memory of past upsurges against the curtailment of customary rights. The continuity is also strikingly manifest in the moral idiom in which protest has been expressed . . . Essentially, the movement was in response to a perceived breach between the ruler and the ruled known as the 'moral economy' of the peasant.[60]

Guha argues that the formal ideology of Chipko as presented to the world outside Garhwal is not entirely consistent with the ideology of peasant actions. While Chipko may have involved women, adopted Gandhian non-violent strategies, and raised popular awareness towards environmental problems in the Himalayas, it is neither an environmental, nor Gandhian, nor feminist movement.

> Here it is useful to distinguish between the 'private' face of Chipko, which is that of a quintessential peasant movement, and its 'public' profile as one of the most celebrated environmental movements in the world. Thus while the last Chipko agitation in Uttarakhand occurred in 1980, the movement's activists have since been tirelessly propagating its message. Within the Himalaya, foot-marches and environmental camps are organized at regular intervals. There has also been a significant attempt to contribute to the environmental debate in India and abroad.[61]

For Guha, then, Chipko is a social movement with the "public" identity of an environmental movement and the "private" identity of a peasant movement. Chipko's participants are peasants who, like their forbears and counterparts in other montane regions of the world, belong to a homogenous class and share a common culture shaped by their ecological surroundings. Their main aim is to protect their subsistence agriculture, which, given the mountainous geography, is closely integrated with forests and pastures, and to restore the moral economy of hill society destroyed by the predatory forces of capitalism.

NARRATIVE WORLDS AND SOCIAL PRACTICE

Chipko's transformation into an "ecological movement of permanent economy" occurs within narrative worlds that are fashioned by its narrators through careful selection of particular elements and actors from a morass of facts, details, and events. The physical space of the Garhwal Himalaya – its forests and rivers, its rugged, remote, and elemental nature – shapes the hardy character of its inhabitants and the simplicity of material life. Isolated from the rest of the world, its hill societies consist of simple and guileless folk who desire little else than to subsist in harmony with nature in accordance with their age-old traditions and customs. Depending on the perspective of the narrator, these near-heroic yet humble social actors are peasants, women, or plain 'common-folk'. Their life of simple subsistence renders them natural; their desire to live in harmony with nature underscores the authenticity of their actions.

Chipko emerges from these narrative worlds as an act of collective resistance against the relentless advance of capitalism, "western" rationality, commercialisation, and timber contractors, which result in "maldevelopment" or the "butchery of nature". Chipko's actors struggle to restore the world they have lost; for the "humble, common-folk" in Bhatt's narratives, it is the age-old right to natural resources and the harmonious union between humans and Himalayan nature. Bahuguna's "forest-dwellers and hill-women" desire to rees-tablish the ancient values of forest culture through a spiritually informed science and technology. Shiva's "Chipko women" strive to restore the feminine principle in Woman/Nature destroyed by reductionist science, western rationality, masculinist ideology, and maldevelopment. Guha's peasants employ cultural traditions of pro-test so as to restore their customary rights and the moral economy of hill society.

Thus Chipko's varied incarnations, identities, and mutations become possible and entirely natural; its authentic cast of actors, elements, and events selected by its narrators can be combined through numerous permutations to produce an infinite variety of Chipko stories. It becomes relatively easy to 'borrow' or invoke Chipko as a symbol in other contexts, in Canada, California, or Islington.

One may ask, well, so what? All narratives attempt what these Chipko narratives have achieved, so why shouldn't they carry the authority and power inherent to any good story? Indeed, as some might counter, the wide range of Chipko narratives challenges the very notion that any single narrative can encompass the variety of possible interpretations of social actions and events. They may even provide useful correctives to any single narrative and allow different voices to be heard; facts and events omitted from any one narrative may be found in others. The solution may well lie in Cronon's suggestion that we "tell stories about stories".

All these are, no doubt, valid arguments. The point I wish to make, however, is that while telling stories about stories may provide a benign alternative to the overweening power of metanarratives, such efforts are only likely to result in banal observations regarding the complexity of social processes, the interrelatedness of places and events, exclamatory comments on the wondrous diversity of human opinion, or expressions of amazement regarding the ways in which "local–global" links occur. What I want to emphasise is that these Chipko narratives are persuasive *fictions* (legitimate or otherwise), which attempt to invest material and cultural practices occurring within a geographical and political configuration with particular meanings. They have been produced for social and political purposes. Their purposeful production and use intentionally aims to alter cultural and material practices and relations of power within that spatial and political context. As T.J. Clark points out,

> Society is a battlefield of representations, on which the limits and coherence of any given set are constantly being fought for and regularly spoilt. Thus it makes sense to say that representations are continually subject to the test of a reality more basic than themselves – the test of social practice.[62]

Narratives derive their structure and form from their telos, a chosen end that does not reside in external nature, but is a moral choice constructed from within the material realm of social practices and asserted as an absolute truth.[63] The telos is located in social actions, and these are what narratives ultimately aim to influence, to change or redirect in one way or another. Every narrative is an exercise in establishing a particular morality; and narrators often succeed (they are called charismatic or compelling when they do) when their narratives exercise a limited and limiting morality which renders most social and material practices, save their chosen few, as irrelevant, inauthentic, or illegitimate.

I do not wish to argue against the production and refashioning of Chipko narratives, nor against the borrowing of Chipko in other social contexts. I would, however, insist that these narratives be subjected to the test of social and material practices within the contexts they refer to. It is perfectly reasonable to ask if Chipko, which has most recently been described by Guha as a "decentralised, environmentally sensitive alternative to the present patterns of 'destructive development'",[64] has contributed to "bliss and benediction", or if not, to some measure of change that benefits communities in the Garhwal Himalayas. Have their economic and environmental problems been resolved, or have they simply disappeared in the wake of Chipko's fame and success?

Garhwal today remains a region in economic crisis. High unemployment still plagues the region, and young men continue to leave their homes in search of work elsewhere in India. Garhwal is now enveloped in political turmoil from protests that routinely erupt with intensified violence around caste and class conflicts.[65] Political groups within the region demand autonomy from Uttar Pradesh and the creation of a separate hill state of Uttarakhand which, they claim, will allow economic development to occur in the region; regional economic development, rather than environmental protection, is the core of their demands.[66]

One of Shiva's "Chipko women" from the Pindar Valley in Chamoli District, Gayatri Devi, bitterly states that the movement has made life worse in the valley: "Now they tell me that because of Chipko the road cannot be built [to her village], because everything has become *paryavaran* [environment] . . . We cannot even get wood to build a house . . . *our haq-haqooq* [rights and concessions] *have been snatched away.*" She adds, "I plan to contest the *panchayat* [village administrative body] elections and become the *pradhan* [village leader] next year . . . My first fight will be for a road, *let the environmentalists do what they will.*"[67]

THREE

NATURALISED HIMALAYA

I saw her crouched over a patch of rice paddy as we walked along the narrow path skirting the mountain-side. The plot stood at the middle of carefully crafted terraces that cascaded their way down to the bottom of the valley. She looked up from weeding as we came closer.

"Who is she?" she asked the forest guard accompanying me. He shot a nervous glance in my direction before replying. I waited to hear his introduction.

"She's a visitor," he offered tentatively, "a senior person inspecting the Forest Department here."

Not much help, I thought to myself, as I saw her look at me again with curiosity and disbelief. I gave it another try.

"I am not a government official, I'm a student from elsewhere."

"Where?"

"From America," I replied. They both stared at me in surprise.

"That's very far away," she pronounced, after a moment's consideration. "Why have you come here to study? There's no college around here."

"I have come to find out how people who live here make a living," I responded, "and to find out how they use the forests here and look after them."

She seemed satisfied with the reply, and rose up to walk over to a walnut tree that cast its mottled shade on the ground beneath.

"It gets harder and harder to hold on to the little you have," she stated, as we sat down beside her. "Too many leopards running about," she added, waving expansively towards the forested slopes beyond the valley, "they've stolen two of my goats. That's about a thousand rupees at least, now stewing in the leopards' bellies."

Her voice rose a pitch. "The district officer says that the government must save tigers and leopards," she said, fixing her gaze on me, "but I ask you, who is going to save us?"

I was mildly startled soon after my arrival in Dehra Dun to find that wildlife protection was a topic of heated debate in local newspapers. Reports on the depredations of leopards – one of which was stated to be a man-eater – resulted in a flood of letters to the editors offering a wide range of suggestions and advice on how the problem could be solved.[1] Stories of rogue wild elephants marauding nearby villages spawned articles on their foraging and mating habits and migratory routes.[2] Wild boar were reported to be destroying sugarcane fields near forest areas in the sub-Himalayan tracts; erudite farmers discussed possible ways of controlling the menace to their crops. For a while it appeared as though Dehra Dun was besieged by wildlife.

The Dehra Dun valley is known in India for its elite schools, its *basmati* rice, the Indian Military Academy, and other venerable government institutions such as the Survey of India and the Forest Research Institute. It is also a haven for retired officers of the Indian armed services, and a refuge for erstwhile rulers of small principalities whose days of glory have gradually faded since the sun set on the British Raj. The gentlefolk maintain a deep attachment to the mountains and to ways of life that they regard as distinctive of the Dun valley. Many of them are deeply distressed by the growth of the town, of the people and boxlike housing that threaten to engulf their bungalows, orchards, and carefully nurtured gardens. Some withdraw into their private worlds, lamenting the slow death of nature, dignity, and gentility in the world surrounding them. Among them are others who valiantly refuse to be overwhelmed: novelists, columnists for local and national newspapers, gentlemen farmers, wildlife photographers, and keen naturalists. They form citizens' groups for protecting the valley environment in all possible ways: fighting against limestone quarrying, planting trees, encouraging nature walks in schools, and protecting wildlife.

A month or so after my arrival, I received an invitation to dinner at the home of an erstwhile *raja*. His home bore all the markings of a family steeped in the traditions of *shikar*, big-game hunting Indian-style. Tiger trophies sprawled the walls of the graciously proportioned rooms, welcoming guests with a glassy-eyed leer. Fading photographs of men resplendent in hunting gear and posing casually beside their trophies graced the walls, lovingly sheathed in frames.

I sat next to a gentleman farmer who, as it turned out, was not only a keen hunter but also passionately interested in wildlife preservation. He kept the conversation alive at the dinner table with tales of his past hunting exploits; soon enough, others joined in with their own. Since wildlife is now protected by Indian law, the stories recalled the heydays of *shikar*, when hunting was orchestrated through a veritable army of elephant-keepers, beaters, drummers, gun-bearers, skinners, and taxidermists labouring together to transform a living tiger or leopard into a snarling, yet utterly dead, trophy for posterity. My thoughts drifted in the pleasant hum of conversation until I heard his voice boom out with passion.

"Too many damned people these days, if you ask me, that's what's the problem! Just creep up from everywhere before you can blink an eye. No hope for wildlife in this area, absolutely none!"

He looked across the room at a trophy that festooned the wall, but his gaze seemed to carry him back to memories of the glorious days when history was made by men of his ilk. He returned from his reverie with a quick, sad smile and mused, "Those were the days . . ."

Almost every person I chatted to that evening was eager to assure me that everything – forests, wildlife, the ambience of life in the Himalayas – had been so much better in the past; there hadn't been so many people, so much deforestation, there was plenty of game, and hill stations weren't infested by the sorts of crass commercialism aimed primarily at tourists with cheap taste. People had led simple lives, and nature had been bountiful and relatively undisturbed. But now life had become corrupted, that natural, uncomplicated past lost forever. I was fascinated by the repeated use of the evocative phrase, "the good old days". Could I perhaps locate in time the good old days when the Himalayas were pristine and simple?

It was an exercise that proved both fascinating and frustrating. It took me farther and farther back in time as I systematically began exploring a variety of narratives. The primary narrators of the Chipko story had differing views regarding the exact moment when irreversible decline began to occur. Bhatt seemed to think that life was pretty decent in the Himalayas until the 1970s and 1980s.[3] Dogra went back a decade earlier, marking the end of the Indo-Chinese conflict of 1962 as the moment when Himalayan nature and life faced destruction.[4] Bahuguna, Shiva, and Guha went farther back, locating the demise of Himalayan nature and culture with the advent of the British in Garhwal in the early nineteenth century.[5]

Perhaps the period before colonial rule was an era of ecological balance and social harmony. Investigating the region's precolonial history proved more difficult due to the paucity of published material. Yet from the few historical accounts and travelogues available, it appeared that Garhwal had been conquered by rulers of the neighbouring kingdom of Nepal and held for nearly twenty-five years before they were defeated in a battle by the British East India Company's troops in 1815. The economy and social life of Garhwal had evidently suffered under Nepalese rule. As Moorcroft and Trebeck travelled through various Himalayan kingdoms on their way to Central Asia, they noted that

> Garhwal was conquered by the Gurkhas in 1804, and the capital about the same time was visited by the natural calamities of an earthquake and an inundation. It had not recovered from these disasters at the time of our visit, and more than half the [capital] city was in ruins.[6]

During this period, large numbers of people had apparently fled to neighbouring states to avoid the crushing exaction of taxes; nearly 200,000 people had been sold by Gurkha rulers as bonded servants to raise revenues; terraced slopes were abandoned, fallow lands were succeeded by jungle and secondary growth, and a disastrous famine in 1794 and 1795 further devastated the countryside.[7]

Maybe the times before Gurkha conquest had been good. But all

I could learn about the pre-Gurkha times was that there had been nearly a century of bitter rivalries between neighbouring kingdoms, mainly with Kumaon, but also with Tibet, Bushahr, and Sikh principalities for gaining greater control over the trans-Himalayan trade routes. Farther back, between the fifteenth and the seventeenth centuries, the rulers of Garhwal had maintained relations of tribute with the Mughal empire, routinely warding off invasions by rulers from the plains, and wild incursions by robbers and brigands.[8] In short, there was little in the precolonial history of Garhwal that went to show that life in the good, old days had been one of harmony between wild nature and humans, social peace, and isolation from the rest of the world.

I scoured the geological literature on the Himalayas, curious to find out whether the physical landscape showed signs of stability or serenity in the past, whether the inundations and landslides that Moorcroft and Trebeck had observed during their journey through Garhwal were an exceptional moment in the region's geological history. It is common knowledge that the Himalayas are an earthquake zone; geological studies pronounced that

> [m]ass wastings such as slides, avalanches, and creep are common in the Garhwal Himalaya. Their accumulations cause blockades of the river systems, formation of transient reservoirs, and subsequent flood pulsations . . . Mass wastings occur mainly along fracture zones, which may be due to faulting, shearing and jointing, or due to irregular deposition of quarternary sediments over areas of uneven topography. The crushed and pulverised rocks along such zones may add to slope failures in wet seasons. It appears that the reactivation of fault zones and dislocations along fold axes may be largely responsible for sliding.[9]

Pilgrims travelling to the source of the Ganges in the Inner Himalayan ranges (close to the Indo-Tibetan border) come to hear the legend of the river, a parallel explanation of geological processes in Garhwal through a different kind of lens. It tells the story of a river's extreme indignation on being commanded by Shiva to flow down to earth from the heavens at the supplication of his devotee. Enraged, Ganga angrily resolved to flow with great force and destroy the earth. She gushed forth from the mountains, smashing everything in her way. It took the effort of several gods, hermits, and sages to tame her arrogance and pacify her as she coursed her way to the plains, but she continues to resent having to descend to earth. The legend appears wholly convincing to pilgrims who trudge along a narrow footpath that clings to highly eroded, towering, sand-like slopes, approaching the river's source at the Gangotrí glacier, nearly 13,000 feet above sea level. The Ganges rushes out with extraordinary energy from beneath the glacier at Gómukh,[10] bringing down boulders and huge shards of melting ice, pulverising every living and inanimate object along its path, and leaving behind stark, eroded landscapes that echo its rage with deafening clarity. Standing precariously near the water's swirling edge at Gómukh, the senses freezing and crumbling under the onslaught of the river's force, I found it hard to conjure an image of the Himalayas as "the eternal silence of vast snowfields and icebound peaks".[11]

The good old days in the Himalayas remained elusive. Indeed, many would have assured me, had they known of my search, that it was bound to be fruitless. From whose perspective was it good? – they would have asked. Which aspects of the past did these people consider good? The exercise nevertheless proved useful in other ways. It allowed me to see that Garhwal's social and political history was inextricably woven with neighbouring regions, and that its features and boundaries were dynamic, constantly changing and reforming in complex ways. How could a region so relentlessly transformed by geological processes and human activity offer the pleasant vision of an ecosystem isolated, stable, and in serene harmony?

THE IDEAL HIMALAYAS

The Himalayan landscape is – to a very large proportion of Indians – a single, homogenous symbol of spiritual nature. The sentiment is best expressed in the words of a contemporary Indian philosopher:

Existentialism says that potentiality is more important than actuality. This is true: the Himalayas of the *rishis* and *yogis* [sages and hermits] is more important as an ideal to us than are the actual rocks and miserable huts of the people there.[12]

Garhwal bears an additional aura of spirituality because it is seen as *déva bhúmi*, the land of the gods. The Ganges and its major tributary, the Yamuna both originate in the region and flow down to the densely populated plains of northern India. Several important Hindu and Sikh shrines are located at the foot of majestic peaks and glaciers; thousands of pilgrims make their way up the mountains between May and October each year to worship at these shrines and perform rituals commemorating their ancestors.

The Himalayas have also been a perennial font of romantic inspiration for the Indian bourgeoisie and western travellers. British travellers and explorers of the Victorian and Edwardian eras found a reading public spread across the Empire that eagerly devoured every account of their exploits in the region. The Royal Geographical Society followed their travels carefully, honouring them with gold medals if they returned alive to tell their tales.[13] The landscape was described in awe-inspiring prose by European travellers who found their way across some part of this great mountain chain. Whether it was Bhutan or Sikkim in the eastern Himalayas, Nepal, Kumaon, Garhwal, Tibet, Kashmir, Gilgit, or Ladakh, each part of the Himalayas was, for them, unparallelled in grandeur; each one claimed that he had discovered the most fantastic, dramatic, vivid, or exquisite landscape in the world. Officers of the British Raj were seen as discharging their "national duty" as they attempted to scale Mount Everest and other "unconquered" peaks.[14] The task of furnishing such descriptions has now been taken over by photojournalists and nature-seekers – Indian and non-Indian – who trek or hike in the Himalayas, and by mountaineering expeditions that set out to scale peaks such as Kamet, Kanchenjunga, K2, and Everest, faithfully extending the colonial experience to the ludic level.

Nineteenth-century readers also found their curiosity whetted by thrilling prose hinting that secrecies and intrigues enveloped the region. No European trader, explorer, or missionary could venture into the Himalayas without being subjected to political considerations that dictated the pace and direction of their travels in these mountains. British officers travelled in a shroud of secrecy through the region, while unofficial adventurers bore enormous tribulations as they wandered through the arduous, never ending maze of mountains beset by capricious weather. Constant surveillance and checks along trade routes and mountain passes by wary officials of the Tibetan government, hill kingdoms, Central Asian *khanates*, and the Chinese empire made travel in the region as formidable as the mountains themselves. Many explorers died or were killed in the Himalayas; as the circumstances of individual journeys became increasingly obscure, the atmosphere of Himalayan travel and exploration was charged ever more with adventure and intrigue.[15]

These are the ideal Himalayas, the ambiguous landscape that straddles the imagined boundary between human domain and wild, untrammelled nature. The Himalayan landscape of the past and present is the realm of wild grandeur, the land of spiritual revelation, of mystery; it is nature's monumental artifice expressly created, as it were, for the play of human imagination and test of human will.

Separation and observation – both are implied in the construction of a landscape.[16] The idealised Himalayan landscape emerges from the active visions of those privileged souls who are able to separate humans from nature; they see Himalayan nature existing by itself, untouched and unspoilt, in remote spaces, lonely heights, a refuge for wild animals, dense forests, untamed wilderness, and the terrain of exotic adventure.

The viewer's perspective also defines how human beings are incorporated within this idealised landscape. Inhabitants of the Himalayas may appear to share the baser characteristics of humans elsewhere, who, as opposed to nature, are unpredictable, selfish, competitive, and capable of wanton destruction; or they may be seen as an essential part of the landscape, imbued with or shaped by its features, as simple, rugged, hardy folk living in isolation from the rest of the world and in harmony with their surroundings. Or, as the Indian philosopher quoted above suggests, their presence can be dismissed as irrelevant.

The idealised Himalayan landscape can thus yield a variety of images which incorporate or exclude its inhabitants. Its rugged and remote terrain may be seen as limiting, deterring, or satisfying the conditions and means of their existence. They may be seen as primitive people that live off the land, lacking the ability to transform it into a productive landscape, or they may be seen as simple peasants with limited wants, producing whatever is necessary for basic subsistence, or, lacking means of communication (or content on their own and not desiring communication) with the world beyond, they may be seen as uninterested in commerce or incapable of engaging in profit-orientated production. The inhabitants may be seen as primitive and tribal – communal or egalitarian – collectivities or as simple associations that function as "village republics" without any hierarchical forms of social organisation.

But all this faced the threat of extinction. As my genteel acquaintances sought to assure me, the good old days were lost, life in the Himalayas had been irrevocably altered. Nature had been destroyed, and the Himalayan ecosystem was a shambles.

How did this happen? Who was to blame? How could the past be restored?

CAUSES OF THE HIMALAYAN CRISIS AND EFFECTS

I cannot possibly discuss at length the vast literature on ecological change, deforestation, and environmental crises in the Himalayas. I propose, however, to focus on three modes of explanation that are commonly offered on this subject. All three begin with the assumption that the region was, by and large, a self-sustaining ecosystem in equilibrium until one key factor or independent variable caused a whole chain of processes and behaviours that inevitably resulted in environmental degradation.

The first, which is generally found in documents written by government planners and policy-makers, follows a Malthusian line of reasoning and regards natural increase in population as the main cause of environmental problems in the Garhwal Himalaya. It argues that the mountainous topography, along with the extreme variations in climate and soil quality, constrains the availability of cultivable land. Population growth increases pressure on available natural resources and rapidly exceeds the "carrying capacity" of the ecosystem. Under conditions of growing scarcity, peasants struggle to meet their subsistence needs by encroaching on nearby forests to bring more land under cultivation; they are ignorant or unaware of the natural constraints inherent to the ecosystem. Their encroachment reduces the lands available for grazing and fuelwood collection and consequently increases the pressure on remaining forests and pastures. The relentless pressure on limited natural resources results in deforestation and erosion of mountain slopes. Heavy downpours during the monsoons cause enormous landslides and destruction of terraced slopes, and transport vast quantities of silt and fertile soils downstream; this in turn causes floods in major rivers and destroys the stability of lowland cultivation. Such natural and ecological disasters further erode the subsistence economy, forcing young and able men from peasant households to migrate to the plains and cities in search of employment. Agricultural land becomes more unproductive because the people left behind – the women, children, and the aged – lack the necessary skills and strength to engage in cultivation and repair of the damaged ecosystem. This results in a further deterioration of the ecosystem and perpetuates the conditions of poverty in the region.[17]

The second mode of explanation regards economic growth-orientated policies of the Indian government as the main cause of environmental and social crises. It argues that the Garhwal Himalaya was a delicately balanced ecosystem which existed for millennia without any disturbance because it was remote and inaccessible. Its inhabitants were mainly simple peasant communities who had maintained the ecosystem through their cultural traditions. The modernising agenda of the Indian government destabilises the equilibrium of this ecosystem through the expansion of transportation and communication networks which incorporates the region into the larger national economy. Businessmen and traders from other regions of the country gain easy access to forests and other natural resources which they ruthlessly exploit for their own profit. Silvicultural practices promoted by the government, catering primarily to industrial and urban demand, lead to extensive commercial extraction of timber and other forest resources and cause rapid deterioration of the regional ecosystem. Annual monsoons batter deforested mountain slopes, causing landslides, destroying cultivated terraces and carrying vast amounts of fertile soil downstream. Peasant households are affected in two ways: one, since they can no longer meet their basic needs they are forced to participate in the cash economy, with young men migrating to other regions in search of employment; two, those who remain behind – women, children, and the aged – spend more time and effort on obtaining the few necessities for survival; extensive deforestation forces peasant women and children to walk longer distances from their villages to obtain drinking water, fuelwood, and fodder.[18]

The third mode of explanation is a variation of the foregoing version. Here the causal factor is not merely the modernising Indian state, but more importantly, the colonial state, which originally established the foundations for an economy orientated towards ruthless exploitation of forests and other natural resources. Being geographically isolated from other regions of India, the peasant societies of precolonial Garhwal were largely homogenous, without hierarchies or class divisions. They managed natural resources such as timber, fodder, minerals, fish, and game through traditional systems of communal management for meeting their basic needs. The advent of colonial rule, however, resulted in the imposition of state ownership over natural resources and institution of scientific management systems to maximise resource exploitation for revenue and profit, which then led to the deterioration of the ecosystem. The postcolonial state continues to employ these colonial systems of natural-resource exploitation and management, further aggravating the rapid deterioration of Garhwal's ecological and social conditions.[19]

To sum up, these three modes of explanation identify particular "external" or "natural" processes as causes for ecological and social decline in Garhwal. The first links natural increase in population with environmental degradation and blames peasants for contributing to the region's decline. The second mode, employed largely by environmentalists and activists, views the actions of the modernising Indian state as the cause of environmental degradation in Garhwal; and the third mode of explanation, largely offered by environmental and social historians, regards colonial institutions and their systems of resource management as the cause of environmental crises in the region. All three modes are based on the assumption that the Garhwal Himalaya forms a clearly bounded ecosystem, that it was relatively isolated and stable until external forces disturbed its steady state and caused irrevocable damage to its health and composition.

(I often wonder whether the woman I met in the village would find that these modes of explanation helped her to cope with the situation she found herself in; probably not. She was there, the leopards were there, her goats were gone, her source of potential income had travelled through the digestive system of some leopard instead of some relatively well-off human being in Dehra Dun or New Delhi. Nature's way? Divine justice? Perhaps, but not much compensation for someone eking out a marginal living.)

Are there alternative modes of explanation that are not based on the notion of a clearly bounded, stable Himalayan ecosystem? Explanations that recognise the Himalayas as a region where geology, ecology, society, economy, and politics are not only mutually interactive but also dynamically linked to other regions and constantly changing? Before attempting to answer this question, I shall explore how the idea of a clearly bounded, self-regulating ecosystem functioning in equilibrium has prevailed among those who study the processes of environmental change.

ECOSYSTEM MODELS AND
HIMALAYAN APPLICATIONS

Ecosystem models, like myths, are abstractions of reality in that they attempt to link cause and effect, form and function, in the most economical and elegant manner possible. They employ the language and methods of science to explain bio-geochemical processes and changes in interactions between and behaviours of non-human species by abstracting "from the available assortment of data . . .

which in their very nature generalise so as to bring order to the incessantly fluctuating flow of messages in and messages out that constitutes human consciousness."[20]

Ecosystem models are self-validating narratives. Their assumptions are based on the telos they wish to achieve; together, they shape the models, their constituent forms, their functions and interactions through tropes that imbue the models' narratives with significance and authority. They are similar to myth, in that they contain a paradoxical relationship between abstraction and reality. In so far as they function at the level of abstraction, ecosystem models do not, indeed cannot, adequately represent real processes and actual experiences; conversely, if they strive to incorporate existing realities, their explanations are unlikely to resemble or even support the abstracted models. Despite the problems ensuing from this inherent paradox, ecosystem models are widely used for explaining environmental change, developing technologies, or formulating public policies that reshape social behaviour in relation to the environment.

What is an ecosystem? An ecosystem is generally recognised as a fundamental organisational unit in ecology and an important structural unit of the biosphere, but its properties are less amenable to precise definition. The boundaries of ecosystems are often ambiguous, as is the time scale for studying their functions or processes of ecological change. The fundamental ambiguities in ecosystems, as O'Neill and his colleagues point out, stem from the fact that it is difficult for ecological scientists to define temporal and spatial scales across the board for ecosystems; generalised explanations of ecological change are always conditioned by very specific spatial and time scales.[21]

Any study of ecosystems requires careful examination and understanding of the infinitely complex web of relationships connecting nearly all living things in particular places and moments. Ideally, this would mean that nearly every known physical and biological science, as well as most disciplines connected with the study of humans, such as anthropology, history, economics, sociology, and politics, are integrated within the mode of inquiry. While such an endeavour is extremely daunting to begin with, it is made even more difficult by the fact that each living thing may require a different boundary, time and spatial scale for analysis. If these are clearly established (but they usually are not), then another set of questions relating to human perception emerge. Should the ecosystem be viewed as networks of interacting populations, the *population-community* approach?[22] Or should it be viewed as a "system composed of physical-chemical-biological processes active within a space-time unit", generally referred to as the *process-functional* approach?[23]

Determining the spatial and temporal boundaries and the approach for observing ecosystem change is not enough. It becomes necessary to have some notion of change itself. Some changes in ecosystems may be seen as short-term fluctuations and disturbances and described as abnormal contingencies;[24] from another perspective, change in ecosystems may be seen as occurring in successive phases progressing along a known direction towards a state of stability or climax. Yet another view can describe ecological change as part of the internal self-regulating mechanism of an ecosystem which controls the growth of populations and their behaviours so as to maintain a state of equilibrium or minimum entropy.[25]

The *process-functional* approach, for instance, employs a "mechanical view of nature" for explaining the processes, direction, and character of ecosystem change.[26] This approach rests on two premises: first, that it is possible to identify an ecosystem as an isolate for study, and that the unit represents an abstraction *from* nature; that is to say, if nature, of which the chosen ecosystem is a unit, operates like a mechanical system functioning through its constituent parts in predictable ways, then it is possible to understand and explain ecosystems using general laws and principles of nature expressed in the language of mathematics and physics. The second premise is that nature *as mechanism* exists in a stable state unless disturbed (a body is at rest until it is set in motion); it returns to its constant state when disturbances or the source of disturbances are removed. When left alone, it exists as a self-contained, self-regulating mechanism.[27]

The idea of self-regulation, which is based on the second law of thermodynamics, implies that systems when disturbed always return to a state of low entropy, a near-equilibrium condition characterised by stability.[28] Disturbances in the ecosystem result in periods of high entropy and disequilibrium, but their removal gradually allows various species to increase to a constant maximum population; the ecosystem is restored to a state of low entropy through self-regulatory processes. In short, to borrow a metaphor popular among neoclassical economists, the invisible hand of nature guides the ecosystem back to equilibrium and stability.

While this form of reasoning offers a coherent and persuasive narrative, it is exceedingly difficult to corroborate through accepted methods of scientific validation. Ecologists inevitably return to the observation that "actually the systems we isolate are not only included as parts of larger ones, but they also overlap, interlock, and interact with one another".[29] There is little evidence to support the assumption − given the continuous changes occurring through geological, climatic, and human disturbances in the ecosystem − that nature, when left alone, always returns to its primordial, stable state. There is no way of confirming a general law of self-regulating ecosystems that holds true across all time and spatial scales.[30]

The *population-community* approach, on the other hand, focuses on particular species and their networks of interactions within an ecosystem. It is informed by theories of natural selection, and explains ecosystem changes as the result of changes in predation, competition, population growth, changing relations between categories of producers, consumers, and decomposers.[31] Apart from the obvious problems of boundary definition, the approach depends on the ecologist's perception of important and unimportant species, and thus cannot be used to generalise the changes in population behaviour across all species in all ecosystems. Entities that do not fit the species or population concept would be considered as 'external' to, or subsumed as part of the environment within which the species interact. The models that emerge from such an approach thus tend to reduce the complex modes of interactions between species and between functional components into a few simple observable relationships.[32]

The fundamental problem faced by the approaches described is that neither can form a complete theoretical foundation for explaining ecosystem processes, behaviour, or ecological change. The process–functional approach is far too general to be applicable to all spatial contexts, while the population-community approach is far too specific for making general claims regarding ecological change that are applicable across the board for different spatial and temporal scales.

Explanations of environmental crises in the Himalayas have routinely confronted these problems. Thompson and Warburton describe these as *cis-science* problems, which is to say that they emerge *within* the context of disciplinary conventions of 'normal' scientific practice. Conducting an exhaustive survey of the literature on ecological crisis and degradation in the Himalayas, Thompson and Warburton point to numerous problems faced by scientific models of explanation:

> Analysis in terms of physical facts, the appropriate method [for "normal science"], has first to identify all the components of the Himalayan system and all the connections between these components. The result is a qualitative model made up of numerous boxes that represent the components of the system, connected together by a web of labelled arrows representing the dynamical processes that *in toto*, sustain or transform the system. Before you can tell whether the system is being sustained or transformed (and, if the latter, the direction of transformation) you need to know the relative rates of all these processes. At the very least, you will need to know the rates of those that can clearly be seen to be the key variables of the system. Uncertainty can enter into this analysis at several points. You may not have identified all the components of your complex system, you may not have identified all the dynamic processes that link those components, you may not have identified the key variables correctly and, lastly, you may not have achieved a sufficiently accurate measurement of the rates of these key variables. The Himalaya notch up impressively high scores on all these possible sources of uncertainty.[33]

Thus despite utilising and generating vast amounts of data, the various causal models of ecological change in the Himalayas have limited explanatory power because of the high levels of uncertainty that form part of the key variables identified within the ecosystem. For example, a commonly drawn conclusion that links human population growth in the mountains to increased soil erosion and flooding in the Indo-Gangetic plains is a weak explanation, because these outcomes may result from increased seismic activity and mass-wasting which are 'normal' geological processes in the Himalayan region. Take another case: the key variables used to estimate the rate of deforestation in the Himalayas are the annual per capita rate of firewood consumption, and the annual sustainable yield of timber from forests. Both these variables are useful for predicting deforestation by local populations only if they can clearly establish that: (1) local populations are the sole users of forests and dependent only on the resources within their immediate locality for subsistence; or (2) forests are uniformly distributed and uniformly perceived and utilised as a renewable resource by all populations in the entire Himalayan region. It is impossible to establish the first condition, because historical and empirical evidence indicates that a large proportion of communities living in higher and middle valleys have always inter-acted with regions beyond their immediate localities, and, more often than not, organised their livelihood activities around trade and seasonal wage labour through migration rather than depending solely on subsistence agriculture.[34] The second condition is also not met, because it is impossible to find either uniform distribution and use, or uniform perception of forests as renewable resources across time and space among communities within the Himalayan region.[35] Similarly, the cause–effect relationship between environmental degrada-tion and the out-migration of young males from the Himalayas is problematic against historical evidence which indicates that migration and trade have been a traditional part of household economic activity in most parts of the region over many centuries.[36]

Why, despite these inherent problems, are scientific models rou-tinely invoked and asserted as valid explanations of ecological change in the Himalayan region? Thompson and Warburton argue that the debates centred on ecological change in the Himalayas stem not only from cis-science problems, but also from *trans-science* problems.[37] While ecosystem models may struggle to overcome problems associ-ated with spatio-temporal boundaries or uncertainty through various means available within scientific practice,[38] their explanatory abilities are further challenged by the complexity of human perceptions, changing social and economic interactions, and politics. But the need to employ scientific arguments stems from the fact that 'normal' scientific discourse occupies a privileged and authoritative position in the contemporary world of policy-making. Scientific models are self-contained narratives that both authenticate and derive their authenticity from a 'normal' mode of scientific discourse; and as Thomas Kuhn notes, normal scientific practice "does not aim at novelties of fact and theory, and, when successful, finds none".[39] It is therefore not surprising to find policy-makers, theorists, or activists adopting discursive strategies that invoke scientific models for establishing the legitimacy of their arguments which, in essence, are reflections of their conscious political choices and claims. Concluding their discussion of degradation in the Himalayas, Thompson and Warburton observe:

> The uncertainty around the key variables in the Himalayan ecosystem is not inherent in the biophysical properties of the system (although they are not irrelevant to it), nor is it a product created by accident, or for its own sake. It is generated by institutions for institutions. The survival of an institution rests ultimately upon the credibility it can muster for its idea of how the world is, for its definition of the problem, for its claim that its version of the real is self-evident.[40]

Different scientific models of ecological crises in the Himalayas can be seen as competing myths that are used by various institutions and actors to authorise and authenticate their political claims in public discourse and policy formulation.[41] For example, government planners and policy-makers facing fiscal constraints may use a particular scientific mode of explanation to argue for environmental policies that require minimal institutional reorganisation and financial expenditure. Environmental activists or nature conservationists may use other scientific modes of explanation that valorise and reshape policies to reflect their ideas of Himalayan nature. Resource-based industries may articulate their claims through yet another set of scientific models to ensure that environmental policies continue to provide them with cheap and reliable access to natural resources. In each instance, particular ecosystem models are selected and consciously deployed in their discursive strategies for authorising and asserting political claims, material privileges, and social authority.

Is it possible to develop other modes of analysis that overcome the cis- and trans-science problems identified by Thompson and Warburton? Ecologists have attempted to address cis-science problems (such as the specification of spatial and temporal boundaries of ecosystems) through alternative analytical approaches such as the pattern-process hypothesis,[42] surprise and opportunistic adaptation,[43] non-equilibrium thermodynamics, ecological integrity,[44] stress-response and clinical ecology.[45] Human ecologists have attempted to incorporate human population interactions and behaviours within ecosystems through approaches such as progressive contextualisation,[46] socio-cultural adaptation,[47] opportunity structure,[48] and place relations.[49] Even so, Thompson and Warburton's trans-science problems, or what Allen and Gould call "wicked" problems[50] – the realm of human politics, of conflicts in meaning, and unequal distribution of social power – persist. An alternative approach that seeks to address these problems in the analysis of ecological and social change is political ecology.

POLITICAL ECOLOGY

Political ecology has emerged as an analytical approach over the past decade or so in the context of an ever-expanding discourse on environmental change.[51] Two of its earliest proponents, Piers Blaikie and Harold Brookfield, describe it as an approach that "combines the concerns of ecology and a broadly defined political economy. Together this encompasses the constantly shifting dialectic between society and land-based resources, and also within classes and groups within society itself." The approach, they add, is regional in scope, because "it is necessary to take account of environmental variability and spatial variations in resilience and sensitivity of the land, as different demands are put on the land through time. The word 'regional' also implies the incorporation of environmental considerations into theories of regional growth and decline."[52]

Blaikie and Brookfield attempt to explain the ways in which poverty and environmental degradation can become mutually reinforcing in distinctive ways. Inequalities within society, which create conditions of marginality for some groups more than others, impose a variety of constraints on land managers (peasants/farmers) which, in turn, increase the pressure on their productive capacities. The wide variation in perception regarding both social and ecological problems adds to the pressures faced by land managers who may be left with no choice but to increase production by intensive or extensive use of resources. The authors illustrate how various chains of causes and effects may lead to conjunctural outcomes which mutually reinforce the link between poverty and environmental degradation.

Although Blaikie and Brookfield offer a more spatially contextualised and historicised explanation of ecological and social change, others hold the view that their approach is not "a theory which allows for . . . and identifies complexity",[53] but an "*ad hoc* and frequently voluntarist view of degradation".[54] Peet and Watts argue that "if political ecology reflects a confluence between ecologically rooted social science and the principles of political economy, its theoretical coherence nonetheless remains in question . . . political ecology seems grounded less in a coherent theory as such than in similar areas of inquiry".[55] For Peet and Watts, the lack of theoretical coherence in political ecology results in the approach being "radically pluralist and largely without politics or an explicit sensitivity to class interest and social struggle".[56]

Much of Peet and Watts's general criticisms about political ecology are valid; the literature produced under this broad appellation is indeed fairly diverse and does not fit within any coherent theory.[57] I would, however, counter their criticisms by arguing that political ecology as an analytical approach has far greater theoretical coherence than existing methods (including political economy) for explaining *how* processes of environmental and social change occur within dynamic spatial and political configurations. The diversity within the political ecology literature is not a consequence of the lack of a coherent theory, but because this diversity is fundamental to its theoretical coherence. The theoretical coherence of political ecology has so far been implicitly understood by its practitioners. The task, therefore, is to make its theoretical coherence explicit.

Let me set forward a broad definition. Political ecology is an analytical approach that explains the biogeographical outcomes of social relations in the context of particular spatial and political configurations. What are the theoretical premises underlying this definition?

1. It regards the non-human environment (the biotic and abiotic surroundings) as a dynamic context (as opposed to a static backdrop) for the evolution of human life.
2. It regards human populations and their social actions as part of the spatio-temporal unit chosen for studying change (as opposed to viewing humans and their interactions as 'alienated' from or 'external' to nature).
3. It recognises that the ambiguities of spatial boundaries are produced from social perceptions of place and hierarchies of geographic scale, as well as from the complexity of interactions occurring within and between recognisable ecosystems.
4. It views spatial boundaries as dynamic, constantly changing in relation to shifting cultural values, networks of social and material practices, and political configurations.
5. It is based on the fundamental recognition that human and non-human life are linked through dynamic processes and constantly transforming relationships which may yield unpredictable or unknowable outcomes within and across networks of political and spatial configurations.

Almost all of these premises would appear obvious and common-sensical to any development geographer or geographical historian (many of whom are engaged in the most interesting and challenging research in political ecology to date).[58] Political ecology adopts a distinctive epistemological perspective towards temporal change, that is to say, the 'nature' of history. It views history not as a teleological process marching up the ladder of evolution towards a climactic state of equilibrium, but as a process that is continually shaped by contingency and uncertainty. It is premised on the recognition that, to borrow Stephen Jay Gould's words,

> Life's history is massively contingent – crucially dependent upon odd particulars of history, quite unpredictable and unrepeatable themselves, that divert futures into new channels, shallow and adjacent to old pathways at first, but deepening and diverging with the passage of time. We can explain the actual pathways after they unroll, but we could not have predicted their course. And if we could play the game of life again, history would roll down another set of utterly different but equally explainable channels. In this crucial sense, life's history does not work like the stereotype of a high-school physics experiment. Irreducible history is folded into the products of time.[59]

Political ecology, therefore, recognises the openness and inherent unpredictability of social and ecological processes as well as the dynamism of spatial and political configurations. It directs its inquiry towards understanding dynamic processes rather than relationships between fixed things or idealised concepts such as "nature", "culture", "place", or "society". It offers a clearer focus on *how* rather than *why* ecological change occurs over time, and *how* rather than *why* ecological change varies between various spatial and political configurations.

The analytical approach focuses on five distinctive, yet interactive, processes that shape the ways in which ecological and social change occurs within and between different levels or networks of spatial and political configurations over time. They are listed below in logical order.

First, it focuses on *social discourse* by examining various perspectives regarding the relationships between humans and the life spaces they inhabit.

Second, it examines the forms of *production, consumption,* and *accumulation* (economic growth) that involve the use or extraction of biotic or abiotic resources within and between spatial and political configurations.

Third, it seeks to understand the *linkages between various sectors of economic activity*, such as agriculture, natural resource extraction, industrial manufacturing, tourism, and other service-based activities occurring within localities and regions, each of which may contract or expand in scale or scope over time and space.

Fourth, it examines the varied ways in which *institutional control is exercised* over biotic and abiotic resources through social practices that are regarded as customary, legal, or extra-legal, which shape the ways in which human labour and technologies are organised and employed in various economic activities.

Fifth, it examines the various ways in which institutional control and prevailing social relations are contested by different social groups, and how the outcomes of such contestation reshape biogeography, social discourse, economic activity, and institutional practices, as well as the networks and boundaries of spatial and political configurations.

In sum, political ecology is an analytical framework that provides an understanding of how social and ecological processes occur, as well as a comparative perspective of how these processes give rise to distinctive regional landscapes over time. It offers an historicised understanding of human interactions and activities – accumulation, social differentiation, regulation, and contestation – in relation to other biotic and abiotic interactions and processes – species variation, soil formation, climatic shifts, and variations in precipitation – within and between changing political and spatial configurations.

The theoretical coherence of political ecology lies in its ability to recognise the dynamism of ecological processes and social life from a geographical-historical perspective. It is by far the most useful and comprehensive analytical approach that exists at the moment for understanding the processes of ecological and social change through the shifting patterns of human values, economic activity and natural-resource use, related institutional practices and their contestation, and the ensuing distributional outcomes for populations, places, and regions. It is the approach I have adopted in writing this book.

FOUR

HIMALAYAN
BACKWARDNESS

The fan creaked and swayed, swirling warm air and flies above our heads. The files and papers on the table fluttered eagerly in response, seeking to escape the weights that held them down.

"It is a mountainous region," said the district officer, thwarting a fly's attempt to land on his face with a wave of his hand, "that's why it is poor and backward."

"You mean, like Switzerland or Austria?" I volunteered helpfully. His glance flickered with ill-concealed annoyance.

"They're in Europe," he pronounced in a stern tone that warned against further flashes of flippancy, "and they are *not* backward."

His chair squawked in protest as he leaned back, linking his hands behind his head and resting one foot on his knee. "In *our* country," he continued, "mountain and forest regions are *usually* backward and marginal."

The word 'backward' possesses a remarkable power not shared by many others of its kind; it has the ability to seize upon an entity, a place, a social group, and transfix its entire character into a frozen moment of history. Like Medusa's gaze, the word can sap the very life out of any living thing and turn it into immutable stone. The countryside, the city, all the spaces that form vibrant theatres of activity, the turmoil of changing experiences, the fires of hope that are carefully guarded and nurtured by people, none of these can breathe life into something that is bestowed the title of 'backward'. A backward region has no markings of industry on its terrain, not

Garhwal and Kumaon Himalaya

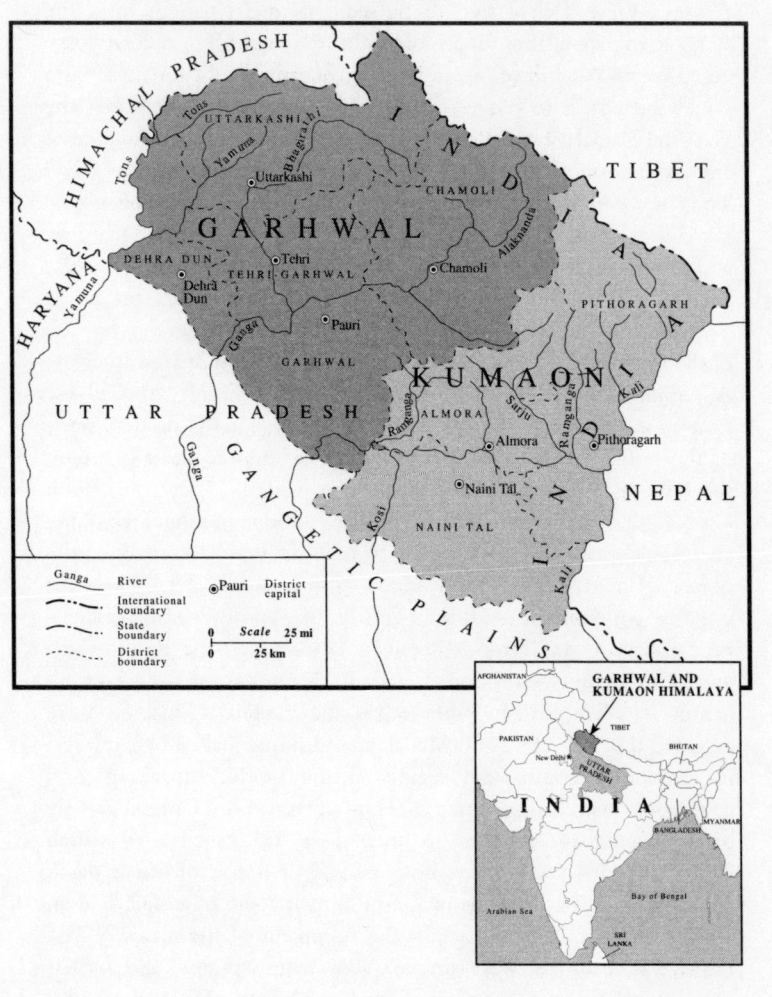

even a crumbling edifice to indicate the merest flutter of time's passage. Were such a sign to be seen, it might benefit from the sympathetic appellation of an 'old industrial region', or receive some attention as a victim of 'economic restructuring'. But for those who wield the power to judge regions as 'backward' or 'advanced', the Garhwal Himalaya stands as the immutable sentinel of backwardness along the northern horizon of the Indian subcontinent. As they travel along the entrails that wind their way through the maze of mountains, their vision ossifies the landscape, distances it to the margins, and transforms it into a state of backwardness. People, events, history, even time, leave but the barest whisper of scratches on its surface.

'Backward' was not an adjective easily found in earlier descriptions of the Garhwal Himalaya; nor was it considered marginal in any way. A region along the periphery, the frontier defining the Chinese Empire to the north, perhaps, but never *marginal* in the modern sense of the term. To the contrary, for nearly a hundred years or more, the Himalayas, and more specifically the western Himalayan region – a complex physiography of six different mountain ranges, covering an area 600 miles in length and 300 miles in width – remained the object of avid interest for intrepid businessmen, adventurers, the imperial governments of Britain and Russia, and every major scientific institution in Europe. Between 1831, when the Royal Geographical Society was founded, and the beginning of the twentieth century, twelve British 'pioneers' in the western Himalayas were awarded the Society's Gold Medal, a record unequalled by explorers in any other comparable region in the world.[1] Speaking as a geographer who had explored these mountains, Lord Curzon gravely pronounced that "frontiers are indeed the razor's edge on which hang suspended the modern issues of war or peace, of life or death to nations ... The holders of the mountains", he observed, had an "immense advantage ... against the occupants of the plains."[2] The Himalayan frontiers were unlike those that explorers and settlers were occupying in other parts of the New World. These mountains were populated territories, and different kingdoms and empires extended their political and institutional control over the diverse communities in the region. John Keay describes European travellers to the western Himalayas encountering a complex and hybrid frontier of intermingling cultures:

> Interlocking with, rather than confronting one another, the worlds of Mongol, Aryan, and Turanian here coalesce. This ethnic jigsaw had its religious counterpart with Buddhist, Hindu, and Islamic adherents occupying neighbouring valleys. Polygamy is the rule in one place, polyandry in another. Here the wildlife is sacred, there it is hounded unmercifully. For the boundary maker this ethnological confusion only compounded the geographical problems. It is a measure of the complexity of the human and physical geography that the boundaries of the Western Himalayas are still today in dispute. No less than five countries, Pakistan, Afghanistan, Russia, China and India, now have a toe-hold in the mountains.[3]

What made the Himalayas such an object of attraction and conflict for kingdoms and empires? There clearly was little wealth to be gained from agriculture or industry. The primary advantage lay in gaining control of the mountain passes so as to profit from the commerce that moved through two interlocking circuits of trade, one between the Himalayan region and Tibet and Central Asia, the other between the Himalayan region and the Indo-Gangetic plains.

Between the sixteenth and early nineteenth centuries, the kingdoms of Garhwal and Kumaon competed to establish a monopoly over the gate-keeping of transit trade. It was extremely difficult to gain effective control over vast stretches of this mountainous region.[4] Large armies needed to be maintained to defend territories against incursions from neighbouring kingdoms and to safeguarde trade routes against robbers and brigands. Rulers attempted to solve the problem of rounding up large armies by placing fertile lands along trade routes under the control of *faujdars*, or military deputies, who collected revenues from villages to maintain troops that could be quickly mobilised in times of need.[5]

Sustaining a regional economy that primarily depended on transit trade remained a difficult balancing act for the rulers of these Himalayan kingdoms, faced as they were with the constant threat of political instability caused by war with each other, as well as occasional challenges from their own ambitious military deputies.

On the one hand, cultivators could not be taxed at higher rates for fear of desertion to other areas where taxation was less burdensome; loss of this revenue was usually accompanied by a parallel dwindling of troops and army recruits. On the other hand, a substantial increase in transit duties and levies on trans-Himalayan trade would inevitably lead traders to follow alternative routes through neighbouring kingdoms where taxation was more lenient.

GARHWAL'S ECONOMY PRIOR TO 1815

The regional economy of Garhwal emerged from the articulation of three dominant sectors of activity: transit trade and related services, resource extraction, and agriculture. Trans-Himalayan trade was, in the language of development economists, the 'propulsive' sector that sustained the regional economy, with agriculture and natural-resource extraction functioning as important subsidiaries. The fortunes of agriculture and natural-resource extraction were closely tied to that of transit trade; they prospered as it grew, and dwindled when it declined.

Successive kings of Garhwal exercised the power of eminent domain over their territories. Nearly *half* of the kingdom's total revenue was obtained from transit duties, customs, and levies, which were fixed at the turn of the nineteenth century at approximately 6 percent of the value of merchandise carried by traders through the mountain passes; the right to collect these duties was usually farmed out to the king's courtiers or high-ranking military officers.[6] He also derived revenue by controlling the exploitation of mineral resources such as gold, copper, iron, and lead. Individuals engaged in panning gold from rivers paid a fixed amount every year to the king irrespective of the quantity collected. Lead mining was directly controlled by the king, who hired wage labourers for production and also granted them small plots of land for cultivation, free from taxation, to sustain themselves through the four to six months when mines were snowbound every year.[7] Iron mines were freely open to extraction, while half of the copper ore mined was claimed by the king.[8] Forest resources such as timber, bamboos, and *catechu* were charged a royalty, or proprietary duty, payable by exporters.[9] House-holds owning cattle and livestock were also subjected to a grazing tax.[10]

All in all, the duties, taxes, and direct income from mining and natural-resource extraction comprised between 15 and 20 percent of the total revenue. The king exercised nominal control over natural resources when commercial demand was low, or relatively stable; growth in commercial demand for particular commodities (such as lead and copper) led him to exercise more direct forms of control over production and trade of these natural resources. The ruler also levied taxes during the pilgrimage season (between May and October) on non-religious service establishments and shops located along main routes; the pilgrim economy contributed an additional 10 to 15 percent of the ruler's revenues.[11]

The kings of Garhwal generally granted taxation, ownership, and usufruct rights in three ways. Military deputies, courtiers, and religious establishments were granted the right to collect revenue from a group of villages. Important pilgrimage shrines such as Badrinath and Kedarnath were each endowed with a large number of villages which yielded revenues for the upkeep of shrines, pilgrim shelters (ashrams), and subsidiary establishments. Grants that conveyed property in the soil were given as awards for service in war or to compensate the heirs of those slain in battle, but on the condition that the *thatván* (landlord) did not expel the cultivators already settled within the allocated lands. *Khaikars* (cultivators) were required to pay an annual tax for retaining their rights to cultivate land and consume (or dispose of) its produce. If landlords cultivated their lands themselves, they were permitted to settle new families on their lands as tenants and also retain some households with the status of temporary or attached labour.[12]

Because of marked variations in soil quality and availability of irrigation, lands held by households were assessed on the basis of the quantity of seed sown on plots, and varied from one-half of the value of produce from fertile lands, to about one-third of the produce from unirrigated and poorer lands.[13] Soil or land taxes were paid partly in kind and partly in monies. Lighter assessments on agriculture were supplemented by a house tax, taxes levied on households retaining low-caste families as attached labour, a tax on the number of looms maintained by households, a pasturage tax, and a tax on offerings made during annual festivals held in different parts of the ruler's domain. In regions where cultivation was sparse, taxation rates were based on the estimated profits from trade carried on by households, and amounted to a sort of poll tax.[14] All in all, less than a third of the total revenue was obtained from agriculture and was mainly spent in the upkeep of the king's armies.[15]

Mr G.W. Traill, the first Settlement Officer to be appointed to Garhwal by the East India Company in 1815, observed that it was common for many households, "possessed of a small capital, either singly or jointly with others", to trade in commercially valuable natural resources:

> With an investment composed of iron, copper, ginger, turmeric, hill roots and drugs, the adventurer proceeds to the nearest mart in the plains and there receives in exchange for his merchandise, coarse chintz, cotton cloth, *gur* [unrefined sugar], tobacco, coloured glass beads and hardware, which in return, after supplying the wants of himself and friends, is disposed of at the villages in the midland and northern *pergunnas* [districts] or is reserved for sale till a fair occurs in the neighbourhood. Those again, whose credit or resources are more considerable enter eagerly into the Tartar [Tibet] trade.[16]

Garhwali households carried on their trade with Bhotia communities which, in turn, traded with their Tibetan counterparts. Hill produce and merchandise from the plains were exchanged for cash as well as Bhotia and Tibetan products. Bhotia traders sold musk pods, woollen blankets, frankincense, wax, and other drugs and herbs collected from alpine tracts, while the Tibetans' products were mainly borax, salt, gold dust, and yak tails.[17]

During a brief reign of peace in the seventeenth century, the king of Garhwal was said to have commanded great respect from the Mughal emperor at Delhi because of his vast wealth and army of 80,000 men in both cavalry and infantry. By the late eighteenth century, however, constant warring against invaders from the plains and neighbouring kingdoms led to a steady decline of both cultivators and traders within the region. When the Gurkha rulers of Nepal embarked on their ambitious attempt to consolidate the entire stretch of the Himalayas under their control, the Garhwali army had dwindled to no more than 5,000 infantrymen who were swiftly disposed of in battle.[18] As the Gurkha rulers entered Garhwal, the regional economy was already weakened by loss of trade, and consequently, cultivation and resource extraction also suffered.

The Gurkha kings ruled over Garhwal from 1804 until 1815. Extending control over the Himalayas had exacted a heavy toll on the Nepalese treasury. In their attempt to recover the expenses of war, Gurkha administrators imposed heavy taxes on both trade and agriculture,[19] which further resulted in large-scale desertion of cultivators and the dwindling of trade in Garhwal. Households that could not meet their annual payments of produce or cash were sold as slaves and bonded servants, and it is estimated that nearly 200,000 people were sold at markets in the plains so as to meet the revenues demanded by the Nepalese rulers.[20] Gurkha rule over Garhwal was thus essentially concerned with deriving as much revenue within as short a period as possible, even if it meant stripping the region of every asset that could be exploited. Given that the region's economy was already weakened by the loss of trade to neighbouring kingdoms, the attempts of Gurkha rulers to extract as much revenue as they could wiped out any possibility of economic restoration. Villages remained abandoned;[21] forest and wildlife reclaimed uncultivated lands until the British East India Company brought the region under its control in 1815.

Despite the ravages of Gurkha rule, the region was viewed favourably by the British East India Company, for various reasons. The prospect of gaining entry into the famous trading cities of Bokhara, Yarkand, Samarkand, and Lhasa along the old Silk Route was immensely alluring. Garhwal, with the neighbouring region of Kumaon to the east, contained several passes used by trans-Himalayan traders. By controlling Garhwal and Kumaon, the Company aimed to gradually secure access to the trans-Himalayan trade in *pashm* (Cashmere wool), gold, borax, and salt.

The Company's officers also saw immense geopolitical advantages in controlling this part of the western Himalayas. Garhwal and Kumaon provided a strategic location for monitoring transactions between Imperial Russia, Tibet, and the kingdoms lying in the western reaches of the Chinese Empire. Moorcroft and Trebeck, both employees of the Company, travelled through most of the hill kingdoms in the western Himalayas on various exploratory missions; Moorcroft apparently died under mysterious circumstances during these travels. His first expedition in 1812 saw him travel to Tibet through the Mana Pass in Garhwal and then on to Ladakh to procure superior breeds of *pashm* goats and Central Asian stallions for the Company stables (he was the Company's veterinary officer).[22] His memoirs and missives to the Company repeatedly warned of the impending threat of military and commercial competition from the eastward-expanding Russian Empire.[23]

At one level, then, the British East India Company's control over the region was similar in intent to that of previous rulers of Garhwal and Kumaon; it was driven by a desire to profit from trans-Himalayan trade. But there was an important difference between them. The East India Company was not a relatively independent ruler or satrap paying occasional tribute to the Mughal emperor, but a commercial institution whose functions and activities were sanctioned by a Royal Charter of the British Crown and regulated by its accountability to investors in Britain. The Company's activities in Garhwal and the Indo-Gangetic plains were inextricably linked to its expanding economic role in the rest of the subcontinent, as well as to the changing economic motivations, social developments, and political alignments occurring within Britain and among its European competitors in ocean-going trade.

FACETS OF THE COLONIAL STATE

British rule in India has been the inexhaustible font of material for powerful narratives that find triumphant, regretful, or tragic ends. It is the stuff of high drama, the monolithic object against which the colonised relentlessly engaged in a Manichean struggle. It serves as the pivot around which oppositions are articulated: precolonial harmony against colonial discord, tradition against modernity, the 'periphery' against the 'core', a hallowed and distant paradise transformed into a wasteland by colonial marauders and capitalists.[24] Despite their compelling rhetoric, such narratives are remarkably opaque regarding the character of British rule in India. They usually imply that colonial power was monolithic, autonomous, uniform, and unchanging in purpose. These kinds of narratives give rise to two common-held assumptions about colonialism: first, that colonial rule was based on a remarkably coherent and tightly orchestrated set of policies that remained unaltered by the forces of necessity or contingency; second, that colonial rulers were endowed with the sorts of abilities which would normally fall within the realm of demonic power or divine omnipotence. However much they may appeal to nationalist sentiments, such characterisations of colonial rule in India are extremely unhelpful for an understanding of the processes of regional change in the subcontinent. These narratives tend to view the relationship between colonialism and colonised regions as clashes between two entities, rather than as a set of processes emerging from the exercise of political control that reshape social interactions and practices so as to produce differential economic and geographical outcomes.

What I wish to emphasise here is that there is little to be gained from attempting to explore the 'character' of 'the state', be it precolonial, colonial, or postcolonial. 'The state' is shaped by what it *does*.[25] As many scholars have argued, the political entities that we call 'states' have attempted, through varying combinations of formal practices, to foster the accumulation of wealth and related social benefits for particular groups within their territories.[26] It is far more relevant, from an analytical perspective, to examine state actions, to look at *how* 'official' control is exercised over territories through the processes of jurisdictional demarcation and definition of what constitutes acceptable (legitimate) and unacceptable (illegitimate) social practice within these formal boundaries.[27] The ensemble of 'official' institutions that we call 'the state' employs a wide range of administrative and juridical practices to create and sustain regional differentiation.

Thus the character of the state is, in itself, fairly ambiguous, but becomes clearer when analysis is directed towards the modes of governing, or what Foucault calls 'governmentality', that occur within different jurisdictional boundaries.[28] Over more than nine centuries, kingdoms, empires, city- and nation-states have all performed a variety of actions in their attempts to forge links across the world for the purposes of wealth accumulation.[29] Their actions have been, and continue to be, shaped within the context of changing conditions and relationships occurring through these linkages in the process of accumulating wealth. The aspirations and strategies adopted by states in response to prevailing constraints and conditions – which I call *dominant policy phases* – have been routinely problematised and altered when confronted by new conjunctures and events emerging from interactions with other political entities, as well as from the unforeseeable outcomes of earlier policy phases.[30]

It is necessary, therefore, to recognise two facts about states, past and present: *first*, states have never been completely autonomous, independent of the structures of everyday life, nor have they been mere adjuncts to market processes; and second, their policies and modes of exercising control, or 'governmentality', have been constantly reshaped by social practices and processes both within and beyond their formal jurisdictions. State actions can thus be comprehended and distinguished in terms of their dominant policy phases, and can change whenever they are faced with conjunctures and events emerging from within and beyond their control.

When seen from this analytical perspective, the colonial encounter between British and Indian rulers becomes a complex and variegated experience, rather than a singular cataclysmic event. It enables us to see that although the East India Company was established in 1600 to serve the interests of both British merchants and the British state, the Company did not continue to function with the same intent or purpose through the eighteenth and nineteenth centuries. As the Company expanded its economic and political control over large parts of the Indian subcontinent, its own policies and imperatives often clashed with those of the government and the dominant interests of the newly emerging bourgeoisie in Britain. Throughout these two centuries, the Company constantly contested and evaded attempts by the British Parliament to limit its powers, challenged its critics, and altered its motivations as new economic opportunities appeared, and in the process, forged new institutional roles, linkages, and relations between different regions in the subcontinent. For over one hundred years, beginning in 1757, the East India Company mutated from a mercantile, trade-based institution into a powerful Anglo-Indian monarch ruling over most of the subcontinent. Direct control of India by the British Crown was achieved only in 1858, and after nearly a hundred years of protracted debate and political contention between the British Parliament and the Company.[31]

The following sections of this chapter outline the dominant policy phases that emerged as the British East India Company expanded its political and economic control over the Indian subcontinent. It explores the ways in which these policy phases translated into various schemes and projects in the Himalayan regions of Garhwal and Kumaon, and reveals the contradictory manifestations of intended actions and unintended outcomes on these regions.

DOMINANT POLICY PHASES OF THE BRITISH EAST INDIA COMPANY

The British East India Company was a product of the 'mercantile system', which arose from the political and economic relationships between rulers and merchants forged during the sixteenth and seventeenth centuries, when the present-day forms of modern European governments were also shaped. These were times when

> [k]ings wanted money, which only merchants could supply, in order to expand their regal activities. Businessmen wanted public order, the freedom of operation within a large territory, which only a well-financed royal administration could assure them. But soon they went beyond this basic aim and sought the positive help of the royal power in altering the supply conditions of labour in their favour and above

all in securing advantages over their competitors in international commerce. 'Mercantilism' thus implies that the economic unit is the state, that governments are in business, and that merchants are necessarily in politics.[32]

Economic historians classify European mercantilist policies under three broad headings: staple, protection, and provision. The policy of *staple* was designed "to secure a bigger share of the profits of international commerce for one's own citizens"; the policy of *protection* was inspired by fear of both overproduction at home and a shortage of bullion reserves, and consequently sought to reduce imports and increase exports. The policy of *provision* aimed at securing the flow of imports, and in particular the 'essential supplies' required for production in the home country.[33] Each of these policy phases not only reflected changes in economic motivations over time, but

> [can] also be arranged, roughly but significantly, in order of historical succession, staple being dominant in the pre-industrial era, protection in the early industrial period, and provision towards the end of the nineteenth century. And to each of these policies there corresponds a characteristic mode of imperialism [or exercise of control].[34]

Established by a Royal Charter of the Crown in 1600, the East India Company held the monopoly of trade in India. It was a mercantilist institution carrying out an ambiguous mixture of commercial and political functions. Its identity and role, however, grew more complex as it began expanding its control over territories in the Indian subcontinent. In 1757, after the Mughal emperor awarded the Company the formal right and titular authority to collect revenues and administer civil justice in Bengal,[35] it took on a new *seigneurial* role with a fair degree of confusion. It was, on the one hand, a commercial institution, accountable to its investors and the state in Britain, while on the other, it had become a tributary state of the Mughal empire. As the ruler of its newly awarded territory in Bengal, the Company bore responsibility for ensuring the appropriate conditions and policies for the prosperity and well-being of the region and its inhabitants. This responsibility, among others, implied that it needed to maintain a treasury with healthy reserves of bullion and ensure that revenues remained greater than expenditures on administration, and that earnings from exports exceeded the monies spent on imports. But as a mercantile institution in competition with similar institutions promoted by other European states, the Company needed to follow the policy of 'staple', which meant that its main concern was to ensure that profits accrued to the Company's investors in Britain, regardless of whether the region benefited from the movement of goods between places.[36]

The dominant policy phases of European mercantilism identified by economic historians serve as a useful point of departure for understanding the strategies adopted by the East India Company as it grappled with the outcomes of new political alignments in Britain and competed with other European mercantilist institutions in the subcontinent. These phases provide a framework for analysing the ways in which the Company performed its peculiar, hybridised institutional role as Anglo-Indian merchant–monarch in the subcontinent, and also serve as analytical markers for understanding why the Company embarked on particular economic ventures at particular times in the areas under its control in Garhwal and Kumaon Himalaya.

Three conjunctural moments mark the era of the East India Company's rule in the Indian subcontinent. The first, in 1813, came about because of the growing pressure exerted by proponents of free trade, which resulted in Parliament's denying the Company a renewal of its charter and ended the its monopoly over the East India trade.[37] The second moment occurred in 1833, when free-trade lobbyists in Britain were, again, successful in forcing Parliament to limit the "unfair" trading advantages held by the Company. This was the year when the Company's commercial operations in India were formally abolished and the East India trade was opened to 'free' competition. From then onwards, the Company functioned in a purely administrative capacity in India. The third conjunctural moment came in 1858, one year after the suppression of the Indian Mutiny, when the Company government in India was criticised in Britain for its ineptitude and mismanagement. The Company was formally abolished, and its Indian territories were brought directly under the rule of the British Crown.

These three moments can be seen as marking the shifts in dominant policy phases during British rule in the Indian subcontinent: the policy of staple between 1813 and 1833, the policy of protection between 1833 and 1858, and the policy of provision between 1858 and 1914 (the start of the First World War). The first two of these phases are discussed below, and I turn to the third chapter 5. The last three decades of British rule, between 1918 and 1947 (discussed in chapter 6), mark a different phase which, while reflecting some aspects of the mercantilist policy of protection, indicate a distinctive shift towards industrial development in the subcontinent.

THE STAPLE POLICY PHASE
IN GARHWAL, 1815–33

Until its commercial functions were officially abolished by the British Parliament in 1833, the Company's administrators in India broadly followed the policy of staple, deriving a large proportion of income from trade and commerce. Garhwal came under Company rule in 1815, two years after it failed to have its Charter renewed. Northern Garhwal – comprising the present-day districts of Tehri and Uttarkashi – was returned to the *Rajah* of Tehri, and the remaining areas were retained under British control. The Company's officers confidently viewed its territorial expansion as evidence of its superior military power and continuing prosperity in the subcontinent.[38] As new areas came under its control they could be coordinated to enhance the Company's revenues from trade, thereby compensating for the losses incurred from being stripped of its commercial monopoly. Linked to the vision of a vast mercantile empire was the promise of overland access to central Asia through Garhwal and Kumaon so that trade could be established with Tibet and Turkestan.[39]

Between 1815 and 1833, the Company's officers encouraged cultivators in the region to return to villages that had been abandoned during Gurkha rule. They were keen, as previous rulers of Garhwal had been, to provide favourable conditions for the revival of trade through the region and to ensure political stability by settling cultivators along the trade routes. For the first three years transit duties continued to be collected at the passes between Garhwal and Tibet, and between the hills and plains. But in 1818, when efforts to restore cultivation and commerce in the region had yielded paltry results, the Company's Settlement Officer abolished all transit duties on trade, hoping all the while that these actions would provide the necessary economic incentive for trans-Himalayan traders to carry their merchandise through Garhwal, and gradually enable the Company to gain access to the central Asian trade.

Given the prevailing scarcity of cultivators and cultivable land in Garhwal and Kumaon, the administrators offered land with relatively light revenue assessments, encouraging the cultivatation of food crops or commodity crops such as hemp. The Company "procured a portion of its annual investment from the Garhwal and Kumauon hills in the shape of hemp", which meant that it advanced cash payments to headmen of villages and principal cultivators for growing, harvesting, and supplying the Company with hemp fibre.[40] Hemp cultivation was seen as a potentially lucrative activity, since the plant could be cultivated for its fibre, for manufacturing rope, sacks, and hempen cloth, and for its oilseeds and resin (*charas*), all of which found ready markets in the plains.[41] During the first two decades of Company rule, cultivation slowly expanded, as did revenues from land and petty commodity production. The volume of trans-Himalayan traffic also increased as taxes on trade and transit duties were abolished.[42]

THE PROTECTIONIST PHASE
IN GARHWAL, 1833–58

Parliament's refusal to renew its commercial charter in 1813 had little or no effect on reducing the Company's overarching control of the East India trade. Its critics in Britain realised that it had successfully retained its leverage over Indian commerce by controlling the access to markets and land within its jurisdictions. Hence, British merchants who eagerly made the ocean voyage to India found themselves in a quandary. The Company did not accord them the right to own land. It charged them a licencing fee for setting foot on Company territory. When they finally gained entry, independent British merchants confronted a bewildering array of customs, duties, and tariffs designed to benefit the Company, its allies, and intermediaries. These strategies, not surprisingly, provoked enormous criticism of the Company in Britain. Twenty years later, the Company's critics succeeded in persuading Parliament to take a further step in 1833 and pass legislation that put an end to its commercial functions. British traders then gained the right to purchase land in India for establishing businesses and other profitable economic ventures. The legislation also managed, to some extent, to undo the complicated *mélange* of custom duties and internal restrictions on trade created by the Company's administrators in the subcontinent.

Yet, even as the free-trade lobby came to dominate British economic policy and forced Parliament to curtail the Company's commercial activities, one important feature of its institutional identity remained unchanged. The East India Company was still a functioning business enterprise, a commercial corporation governed by a Court of Directors based at India House in London. Its Court of Directors were firmly committed to ensuring that the Company's activities and ventures were profitable to its investors and shareholders. It was not surprising, therefore, that the Company set out to restructure its economic policies with profitability in mind as Parliament furiously debated and then passed the legislation that abolished its commercial functions. Between 1813 and 1833, the Company, apparently anticipating future losses from the East India trade, reorganised its activities to ensure that more profits were generated by internal revenues collected from its Indian territories than from international commerce.[43]

From 1833 onwards, having been restricted to the administration of its Indian territories, the Company's identity mutated from its cloven identity as British merchant–Indian ruler into a hybrid Anglo-Indian administration with a strong mercantilist pedigree. The policies emerging from this new hybrid identity were largely protectionist in nature, but different from the sort of protectionism displayed by Britain in the early industrial period when it sought to safeguard and promote the interests of its textile industry. (As I mentioned above, the mercantilist approach to protection emphasised conservation of bullion by reducing imports, and increasing exports; it focused on production rather than consumption, sale rather than purchase.)[44]

Between 1833 and 1858, the Company implemented its economic policies in two ways: first, it made investments in infrastructure to increase production of exportable commodities, so that profits generated from their sale could be used for the purchase of essential imports, and for paying dividends to shareholders in Britain; second, the Company provided incentives for particular economic ventures that would help reduce expenditure of bullion for importing expensive commodities such as tea from China. These strategies complemented the Company's continued monopoly of the opium trade. It expanded opium production in India and skilfully blended the rhetoric of free trade with imperial force to persuade the Chinese government to remove barriers against the sale of opium and other commodities by British merchants at Chinese ports.[45]

The policy of protection led to the promotion of new economic ventures and projects in the Garhwal and Kumaon Himalayas. For the first time, perhaps, in the region's history, the dominant policy emphasis was on export-orientated production rather than on revenue generated from customs and duties on transit trade. Trans-Himalayan trade continued to be encouraged, but was now regarded as an activity that complemented commodity production. Three major projects were launched in the region: tea cultivation, commercial production of wheat and sugarcane, and the construction of the Ganges Canal. I will briefly outline these in the following sections.

TEA CULTIVATION IN GARHWAL

The East India Company had, as far back as 1788, regularly speculated in tea cultivation in India. But apart from launching a few small-scale experiments for propagating Chinese tea plants at the newly established Botanical Gardens in Saháranpur, a small town located at the southern end of the Dehra Dun valley, the venture was not vigorously pursued. However, when faced with the prospective loss of commercial revenues and the high cost of importing tea from China, the Company administrators considered the tea-cultivation venture with a new sense of urgency. The discovery of indigenous species in Assam and Kumaon gave additional impetus to the hope that bullion could be saved by extensively promoting tea cultivation in the Himalayas.

The first major proposal was put forward in 1827 by Dr Royle, the Superintendent in charge of the East India Company Garden at Saháranpur. Soon after, a Tea Committee was formed to consider the possible regions where tea cultivation could be promoted. In 1834, Dr Royle pronounced that

> there is, perhaps, no part of the Company's territories in India which supplies all the conditions of tea districts in China in respect of climate; but there are situations which approach it so nearly as strongly to bear out the conclusion that tea may be so successfully produced in this country as to be an object of high commercial importance . . . In the Himalaya mountains . . . all the conditions of the temperate climate are found, and here, above all parts of India, we may look for successful cultivation of tea.[46]

Kumaon was chosen as the first site to launch the experiment. Between 1835 and 1842, several nurseries were established in the region for propagating tea seeds and seedlings imported from China. As the plants began to thrive, artisans were brought over from China to establish factories for processing tea. Small quantities of tea were made from the leaves harvested during the year, and were shipped for sampling to tea-brokers in Britain. On tasting the tea from the region, Messrs. Ewart, Maccaughly, and Delafosse, an English firm involved in the tea trade pronounced its judgement:

> [T]he tea brought by Dr. Falconer as a specimen of the growth of the China plant in the Himalaya mountains resembles most nearly the description occasionally imported from China under the name of

Oolong . . . It is not so high flavoured as the fine *Oolong* tea, with which we have compared it, and it has been too highly burnt in the preparation, but it is of a delicate, fine flavour, and would command a ready sale here.[47]

Soon after, between 1844 and 1858, nine tea plantations[48] were established under the Company's direct ownership in Garhwal and Kumaon, expanding the area under this crop from 700 to 10,937 acres. As tea production increased, Dr Jameson, the new Superintendent in charge of the Botanical Gardens at Saháranpur, advised the Company government to further expand the area under tea cultivation in the region, noting that

> a vast field for enterprise will be opened up, whether Government considered it worthy of their own attention, or it be brought about by private capital. Water carriage will soon it is hoped . . . also be a strong inducement, in addition to the above, to make capitalists invest their capital in this channel, and thus we trust ere long to see the hill provinces, which at present yield but a trifling sum to the revenues of the State, become as important, in an economical point of view, as any of those in the plains of Hindustan.[49]

Although tea plantations in the northeastern Himalayas and Assam had already begun shipping substantial quantities of the commodity from Calcutta to England, tea production in the Garhwal and Kumaon Himalayas was aimed towards neighbouring overland markets across the mountains in Tibet and central Asia. In 1847, Dr Jameson observed the vigorous purchase of *Pouchong* (black) tea by native merchants with undisguised pleasure, noting that the coarse *Bohea* tea produced in British Garhwal and Kumaon was sold to Bhotias for export to Tibet where it successfully competed against the tea imported from China. In his official reports on the foreign trade of the Company's territory of the Northwestern Provinces and Oudh, the administrative officer for the region, Mr J.B. Fuller, remarked that

> [s]o far as the commercial interests of these provinces are concerned, the most interesting point in the traffic they transact with Tibet is the opening it might afford for the inferior classes of Kumaon tea, *which*

will not bear the cost of carriage to the sea board. At present the markets of
Tibet are closed by the united influence of the Chinese government
and the Tibetan Lamas, who, having the monopoly of the wholesale
and retail tea supply of the country, are naturally averse to the
competition of a traffic in Indian tea, which might be more difficult
to engross ... Yet the Tibetans on our frontier are compelled to
purchase tea of atrocious quality, the price of which has been swelled
by a long and difficult transport from the eastern extremity of the
country; *while immediately across the frontier there are tea gardens whence
they could be supplied with a better article, at a cheaper price, and with profit
to the Kumaun tea planters as well as to the itinerant traders (Bhotias) through
whose hands it would pass* ... So heavily is Kumaun tea handicapped
by the expense of transport to Calcutta that the most profitable
portion of the trade even now is that transacted in green teas with
merchants from Central Asia who purchase the tea at the factory and
carry it away themselves, saving the planters the expense and trouble
of packing.[50]

GENTLEMEN FARMERS IN GARHWAL

As tea cultivation expanded in the region, the Company administration launched a second economic venture that attempted to
promote the Garhwal Himalayas as a "seat of European colonisa-
tion".[51] The strategy took shape around the time when Europeans
were legally permitted to own land in the Company's territories.
The Company saw its own officers and administrators as potential
entrepreneurs who might engage in the production of agricultural
commodities for export, and thereby strengthen its protectionist
policies. It began encouraging its officers and European merchants to
purchase land grants at reduced prices for cultivating wheat, sugarcane, and opium. Lands along the sub-Himalayan tracts which had
been officially classified as "uncultivated wastes" (either abandoned
fallows or lands with scattered shrubs and bushy vegetation not used
by native cultivators) were demarcated for sale.

The site selected for this venture was the Dehra Dun valley,
ensconced between the Shiwalik hills and the Garhwal Himalaya.
Although Gurkha rule had left the valley in disrepair and bereft of

population as in the rest of Garhwal, the Company's military corps of engineers who were stationed in the area had begun reconstructing the ravaged canals that had once irrigated most cultivated areas in the valley. By 1837, the canals in Dehra Dun had been rebuilt and extended further to irrigate large tracts of previously uncultivated wastes. In 1838, nine land grants were given to European officers and merchants in the Dehra Dun valley, on the condition that land would be rent-free for the first three years, following which rent was to be charged at gradually rising rates until they reached the maximum rate at the tenth year. The lands thus purchased were to be held at this maximum rent for fifty years, after which they were to be open for resettlement.

In Dehra Dun, six grantees joined together to form a joint-stock agricultural company under the name of Maxwell, MacGregor, and Company, consisting of forty shares with a paid-up capital of £20,000. The joint-stock company then proceeded to acquire additional land in Saháranpur.[52] Within the first three years of obtaining land grants, European entrepreneurs supervised the rapid clearing of uncultivated wastes and planted them with Mauritius and Otahite sugarcane, cotton, wheat, and rice, looking forward eagerly to the substantial profits that would be derived from the sale of these commodities. Land prices rose rapidly as British merchants and officers eagerly rushed in to buy remote tracts in the Company's territories, creating a land mania fanned by wild speculation and mysterious stories of windfall profits.[53]

CONSTRUCTION OF THE GANGES CANAL

As I mentioned above, the Company's policy of protection and flow of profits relied crucially on the stability of agricultural production and increased output of commodity crops. Most of its commercial crop production in northern India occurred in the Indo-Gangetic plains, particularly in the lands between the Ganges river and its major tributary, the Yamuna. This region, called the Doáb, despite being remarkably fertile and productive during good monsoon years, suffered immensely during years of drought. Between 1837 and 1838, famines affected the population across the entire stretch of the Indo-Gangetic plains controlled by the Company. As famine-relief operations proceeded in the Doáb, the Company's administrators resolved to reduce uncertainties in agricultural production by constructing a large canal system which would draw its waters from the Ganges for irrigation. The Court of Directors noted that

> apart from the consideration of financial results, which we are far from contemplating with indifference, there are few measures connected with our revenue administration in India more calculated to the general improvement of the country, the amelioration of the condition of the people, and to raise the character of the Government, than those of the nature now under our consideration . . . Two years . . . have scarcely passed since the very country through which the proposed canal will be excavated was laid waste by famine, which cost the lives of thousands, and presented a scene of suffering still fresh in the recollection of all classes; to such another visitation the canal will afford a palliation, if not a remedy.[54]

The construction of the Ganges Canal began in 1841, originating in Haridwar, a pilgrimage site located in the foothills of Garhwal, and gradually extended over the following twelve years across the Upper and Lower Doáb. The pace of construction was affected by various wars fought by the Company against the rulers of Afghanistan, the Mahratta rulers in western and central India, and the Sikh rulers of the Punjab.[55] By 1854, most of the canal was constructed and, according to the Canal Committee's estimates, was expected to yield an annual revenue assessed at nearly 1.5 million rupees.[56] In little over twenty years the Ganges Canal – which, at the time, was the largest canal system in the world – comprised a network of 5,600 miles of aqueducts and distribution channels constructed at the cost of nearly £4.5 million. By 1877–78, the Canal irrigated nearly 1.5 million acres in the western districts of the United Provinces that formed the Upper and Lower Doáb. The expansion in irrigation brought about an increase in acreage under commodity crops, such as sugarcane, indigo, cotton, and opium, as well as wheat, which became an important export crop from the mid-1870s.[57]

The effects of these ventures on the regional economy and

landscape were immense. Tea plantations and agricultural commodity production had already increased the demand for labour for clearing lands, cultivation, tea-picking, and processing. The construction of the Ganges Canal added to this demand by requiring labour for digging, lime-burning, and brick-moulding. Even though the Company's engineers routinely bemoaned the frequent strikes and work stoppages by labourers, they continued to draw their labour from a large area spanning the Upper Doáb, the sub-Himalayan tracts, and lower elevations of Garhwal. The Chief Engineer's estimates for the labour required in constructing the Solani aqueduct in the Upper Doáb, not far from the commencement of works at Haridwar, gives a sense of the vast numbers of labourers involved in the works:

In brickmaking, inclusive of wood-cutting, 3,143,333 labourers; in building masonry and laying floor, 781,946 ditto; in pounding *soorkee* [brick powder], 641,632 ditto; in undersinking the blocks, 311,040 ditto; in the earthwork of the aqueduct (exclusive of draught cattle), 1,972,750 ditto.[58]

Although there is no information regarding the geographical locations that supplied this vast army of labourers, it is very likely that the demand for labour in canal construction had an enormous impact on the economies of surrounding regions. There may have been temporary and permanent migrations of wage labour from other parts of the Indo-Gangetic plains as well as from the lower elevations of the Himalayan tracts. Large numbers of households may have been involved in subsidiary activities, such as providing a variety of support services for those involved in canal construction. The scale of activity described in the preceding quotation and other details from the Chief Engineer's report also suggest the extent to which the canal project may have intensified demand for other resources such as timber, clay, and charcoal. The greatest demand would, in all likelihood, have been for wood, vast quantities of which were used for constructing the formwork for the canal, for buildings, for roads, for making charcoal for brick kilns (and for tea-curing in the plantations). Large numbers of households would have been involved in timber extraction spreading outwards from the submontane tracts and upwards into the lower ranges of the Garhwal and Kumaon Himalayas.

The cumulative effect of these ventures was reflected in the restructuring of trade and employment in the region. A profitable trade in timber – which, in the past, had been largely for local markets – emerged in the region as wealthier households involved in the trans-Himalayan and transit trade redirected their investments towards timber extraction from forests in higher elevations for sale to charcoal producers and markets in the plains (the Company's earlier policy of abolishing taxes and duties on transit trade worked to their advantage). Households without such access to capital continued to participate in the trans-Himalayan trade, or sold smaller quantities of fuelwood and fodder at hill resorts and military cantonments. They also found seasonal employment in plantations, farm estates, and public-works projects in the region.[59]

All in all, the Company's dominant policy phase of protection resulted in the rapid transformation of the region through increased timber extraction and expansion of commodity agriculture in Garhwal and Kumaon. However, the expansion of economic activity in the region, was, as it turned out, short-lived. Both tea cultivation and agricultural commodity production in Garhwal and Kumaon were struck by a series of misfortunes resulting from unforeseen problems and unexpected outcomes of other policies adopted by the Company.

The Collapse of Agricultural Commodity Production and Tea Cultivation in Garhwal

Routine attempts by the British Parliament to weaken the economic and political power of the East India Company often took the form of decrees that attempted either to undermine or to subvert its economic ventures in the Indian subcontinent. In 1841, Parliament banned civilian administrators, employees, and military officers of the Company from engaging in private enterprise. The ban was received with outrage by the Company's officers who, not unreasonably, pointed out that they could not abandon the ventures they had undertaken with the encouragement and incentives provided by the government. Despite the hue and cry against the decree, Parliament remained firm, and the Company's employee-entrepreneurs were forced to accept the ruling.

The wild speculation in land grants and farming estates in the sub-Himalayan tracts collapsed almost immediately, resulting in distress sales by British landowners. Recounting the ignominious demise of several joint-stock agricultural companies in Dehra Dun, G.R.C. Williams observed that the speculators had "rather freely indulged in what the *Sudder* Board of Revenue styled, with happy felicity of expression, an 'anticipative incubation of profits'".[60] Although the parliamentary decree was amended in 1845 to allow examination of ownership rights of civilian and military officers, and monetary compensation on a case-by-case basis, production of agricultural commodities on land grants and farming estates was irrevocably damaged. Machinery imported for milling sugarcane lay idle as cultivation was abandoned. Given the prevailing hostility of Parliament towards the Company, most landowners and grantees expected little or no financial compensation for the losses they had incurred. As a result, most of them stripped their lands of all valuable assets, including timber, to recover as much money as they could before selling their property to Indian merchants and landlords.[61]

Yet, despite the misfortunes heaped on the Company's employee-entrepreneurs by the parliamentary decree, Williams found little evidence to indicate that agricultural commodity production in the region would have proved financially profitable for the aspiring gentlemen farmers. He observed that soon after the 1837–39 famine most native labourers who migrated from their villages to find employment on these farms returned home as soon as conditions improved. People from neighbouring communities were unwilling to engage in the demanding and labour-intensive work of clearing jungle and cultivating crops such as sugarcane or rice on daily or weekly wages. The process of reclaiming jungle and uncultivable wastes gave rise to innumerable illnesses and diseases which diminished the availability of labour. Grantees bitterly complained to the

District Officer (Williams himself) of the lack of government assistance in supplying labour, pointing out that nearly 2,000 cultivators
had either deserted or perished from fever. Water supply was erratic
despite the repair and extension of irrigation channels in the Dehra
Dun valley.[62] Elsewhere along the sub-Himalayan tracts bordering
Kumaon and Nepal, lessees of forest and land grants also abandoned
their efforts for want of additional capital investment, or when they
realised that returns on their investments were unlikely to materialise
in the near future. The Company's administrators had already begun
doubting the practicality of any scheme that involved agricultural
production by "English gentlemen, allured by the exquisite beauty
of the Oudh wilderness".[63] Thus, according to Williams, the parliamentary decree only served to expedite the reassessment of agricultural policies by the Company administration.

Tea cultivation, on the other hand, faced a different set of
problems, arising not from the interference of Parliament, but from
the growing political tensions between Britain and China. Although
the treaty signed in the aftermath of the Opium War of 1842
favoured the Company's opium monopoly as well as British merchants who wished to enter the trade along the eastern seaboard of
China, it had the opposite effect on tea-planters in Garhwal and
Kumaon who were struggling to gain access to central Asian markets.
When the Company's Boundary Commission approached its Chinese counterpart in 1847 to establish formal boundaries dividing their
territories, they also requested permission to set up trading posts in
central Asia and Tibet. The Chinese authorities politely declined
both requests. The Chinese government's refusal to allow British
merchants access into Tibet and central Asia arose from the fact that
the treaty following the Opium Wars required it to allow British
merchants free access to five ports on the eastern seaboard of China
and pay compensation of 21 million dollars to Britain as part of the
settlement.[64] The Chinese responded to the Boundary Commission
by stating that boundaries between both countries were already well
established by tradition and did not require formal demarcation; it
also pointed out that British authorities and traders had already gained
access to five trading ports and could not, therefore, gain access to

any more.[65] Thus the Company's tea-planters and traders in Garhwal and Kumaon found it nearly impossible to gain entry into western China. Nor could they attempt entry into central Asia through the far western frontiers of the Himalayas. There, the Russian Empire, which had gained control over most of the Central Asian *khanates*, was hostile towards Britain and the presence of British traders. Tea planters in Garhwal and Kumaon struggled well into the 1870s, steadily reducing labour and production on their estates and yet unable to turn in any profits. Atkinson noted:

> Trade with Central Asia, which at one time gave great hopes of proving remunerative, has been practically closed by the action of our Russian friends in putting a prohibitive duty on all articles imported from India. The planters also complain that the reduction in duty on Chinese teas has also affected them injuriously.[66]

Trans-Himalayan trade in other commodities also suffered as cheap imports of American borax became available, and as sea-salt production increased in other parts of the subcontinent. *Pashm* (cashmere wool) was the only valuable commodity that survived competition, but the trans-Himalayan wool trade, too, had been substantially transformed. With the establishment of a woollen textile factory in Cawnpore (Kanpur) and rising prices for cashmere, Tibetan traders sought to maximise their profits by directly selling their produce to factories and markets in the Indo-Gangetic plains, thus bypassing the Bhotia and Garhwali traders who had earlier served as their trading partners.[67]

The collapse of agricultural commodity production and dwindling trans-Himalayan trade weakened the regional economies of Garhwal and Kumaon. The only sector of economic activity that grew rapidly was the trade in timber and forest products, which had not been directly promoted by the Company, but had nevertheless emerged in response to the demands generated by expanded commodity production and infrastructure development in the region. Households and traders redeployed their resources from trans-Himalayan trade into the timber trade, either directly engaging in forest extraction, transport, and marketing in the plains with the help of hired labour, or by controlling the tax-farming leases (which were auctioned by the revenue administration) on forest products. Poorer households extracted fuelwood and fodder from forests which they then sold in nearby cantonments and hill resorts that had been established by the Company for its officers and their families.

By the time the Company's territories in India came under Crown rule in 1858, forest-based extraction had emerged as the dominant economic activity in the region, providing a growing share of the income earned by households in the region. Incomes from forest-based extraction had become so integral to households that, some forty years later, the district officers of the colonial administration were astute enough to question the discrepancies between the occupations reported in the Census and those actually pursued by households. The District Commissioner of Garhwal, Mr H.G. Walton, commented on the results of the published Census:

> The forests according to the census returns afford employment to 1,172, but this must be well below the real number. It is fairly obvious that, as practically every man in Garhwal is a *zamindar* [landowner], he has declared himself an agriculturist, ignoring his miscellaneous occupations which are often of much more importance.[68]

The foregoing historical analysis of the British East India Company's dominant policy phases of staple and protection raises a critical question in the context of regional change in the Garhwal and Kumaon Himalayas: did these policies necessarily signal the region's move towards economic backwardness and marginality? There is no unequivocal answer. We can see that the Company's administration began its control over the region by largely following what earlier rulers had done: ensure that the regional economy sustained trans-Himalayan trade which, in turn, stimulated agriculture and resource extraction and sustained them at modest levels. The policy phase of staple provided opportunities for households belonging to various social groups and classes to participate in the region's transit trade. With the shift towards the policy phase of protection, both Garhwal and Kumaon received substantial capital investment through the ventures promoted by the Company. There were increased opportunities for household engagement in wage labour in tea plantations, commodity agriculture, and infrastructure projects. Timber extraction expanded alongside commercial agriculture and infrastructure development, providing new income-earning opportunities for households in the lower mountain ranges. Alterations to social networks and material practices continued to sustain and be sustained by regional interactions between central Asia and the Indo-Gangetic plains through the trans-Himalayan trade. The collapse of commodity agriculture and the tea trade with central Asia and the weakening of particular segments of the trans-Himalayan trade were not caused by the Company's policies for the region, but rather by contingent events and unexpected outcomes of its actions in other spheres of economic and political interaction.

There is also no reason to assume that the misfortunes suffered by tea-planters and gentlemen farmers would have automatically pushed the region into the realms of economic backwardness and marginality. The decline of both commodity agriculture and the tea trade was more than offset by the growth of the forestry sector. Indeed, it is possible to envisage a scenario where the growth in timber extraction could have led to different kinds of linkages with agricultural production, perhaps given rise to the development of new forest-based industries and related services, and resulted in new and expanded patterns of trans-Himalayan trade between the region and other parts of the subcontinent. But this did not happen.

As forestry became the most important economic activity in Garhwal and Kumaon, its role in the region's economy was reshaped by the policies devised under the colonial authority of the British Crown. The colonial administration in Garhwal and Kumaon saw the need to exercise control over forest extraction, given that it had become the most lucrative source of income for both local traders and British merchants in the region. In so doing, the administration acted in a manner that was in no way different from that of previous administrations of the region. It began controlling forest-based extraction, first, by imposing a royalty on timber, the most commercially valuable of forest commodities. This was followed by other revenue-enhancing strategies such as auctioning tax-farming leases for harvesting other kinds of commercially valuable forest produce. None of these actions was markedly different from those of the Company or the preceding kings. The major difference between the administrative strategies of the colonial government and those of its predecessors was the fact that this lucrative sector of the region's economy came to be controlled by a newly created state institution called the Imperial Forest Service. And it is to this state agency and its activities that the next chapter turns.

FIVE

BIOGEOGRAPHY
OF CONTROL

Saar Singh was, by all accounts, a man of stature in the village of Konain. He owned about 1.5 hectares of land in the village and was also employed as a peon by the Forest Department. Saar Singh's job in the Chakrata Forest Division required him to serve as messenger, valet, and occasionally cook for the Range Officer; he was his personal odd-job man.[1] Most residents of Konain considered him a lucky man: a *sarkari* (government) job offered the prospect of economic stability, access to better schools in the district headquarters for his children, better health care, and the benefit of a modest pension at retirement.

Saar Singh was the oldest of three brothers and, ever since his father's death, regarded as the head of the household. The three brothers jointly held about 1.5 hectares of land. One was a *jawan* (soldier) who had recently been recruited to serve in the Garhwal Regiment. The second brother stayed mostly in the village, managing the land and livestock with the help of their wives and children, occasionally working as a casual wage labourer for projects implemented by the Public Works Department or the Forest Department in nearby areas. A migrant sharecropper from the western districts of Nepal, along with his wife, cultivated a piece of their land which lay at the edge of the village adjoining the Reserved Forest.[2]

Saar Singh and I were on our way from Konain to a neighbouring village when we passed by the sharecropper's hut. Both husband and wife were at home and offered us a cup of tea. As we sat outside the hut drinking, Saar Singh noticed a chicken pecking around the yard.

"Your bird looks healthy," he exclaimed, "how did you manage to save it?"

A mysterious epidemic had apparently killed off most of the chicken population in the village, but the sharecropper's bird had fortuitously survived since his hut was nearly a mile away from the main settlement.

Saar Singh paused for a moment and said, "Madam *Sahib* is a very important official from Dehra Dun. You should give us the chicken so that we can celebrate her visit to our village. Don't worry," he added in the same breath, "she'll pay you for it."

It was a clever ploy that placed the sharecropper in an awkward position; were he to refuse outright, it would have been construed as an insult towards me, the supposed village guest, as well as a challenge to the social authority vested in our presence.

The sharecropper hesitated.

"*Sahib*," he said respectfully, "the bird is being raised for sacrifice to the Goddess, and it is her power that has saved the creature from disease. I can't invoke her wrath by giving it to you."

Saar Singh persisted in nagging the hapless man until I decided to join his protest with the hope of ending an argument that might well have continued on through the afternoon.

"Saar Singh," I intervened firmly, "it is wrong to take the Goddess's sacrifice. The next time I visit, I'll give you some money to buy a few chicken in the town market so that you can have a feast in the village."

The sharecropper and his wife looked obviously relieved as Saar Singh accepted my offer. We rose to leave, thanking them for their hospitality. As we walked away from the hut, he turned to me and said cheerfully, "He's a good man, he is; I wouldn't have anyone other than a Gurkhali [the generic term for anyone from Nepal] on my land."

"His hut looks terribly run down," I remarked. "Can't he get some timber from the Forest Department for repairing it?"

Saar Singh looked amused. "No, *Sahib*, he'll never get any timber from the Forest Department."

"Why not?" I asked. "Doesn't the Forest Department allocate

some quantity of timber to villages for repair and construction of houses?"

"Yes, it does," he said, "but this man has no rights at all. We village people have rights and concessions with the Forest Department; he doesn't belong to the village, you see, so he doesn't have any. Besides," he added, "poor fellow, he can't help it, but he's a Gurkhali."

I was bewildered. "What do you mean, he's a Gurkhali? What does anything have to do with his being a Gurkhali?"

"That's the way it is with Gurkhalis around here," he replied, "*Gurkhali kháli háth áta hai, aur kháli háth játa hai.*" (He emphasised the word *kháli*, which means 'empty' in Hindi; he meant that the Gurkhali sharecropper arrived empty-handed and left empty-handed.)

Access, control, property, authority: these are crucial terms that determine how land is used and who prospers in Garhwal, as in any other part of the world. The terms 'control' and 'access', in particular, have special relevance for households in this region, because nearly 70 percent of the geographical area is under the control of national and state government agencies. More than two-thirds of this state-controlled area is classified as 'forest' and falls under the authority of the Uttar Pradesh State Forest Department. It is, in effect, the largest landlord in Garhwal.[3]

The forests of Garhwal are generally described according to their vegetational characteristics which are seen to vary by altitude, climate, and levels of rainfall. A forest type is defined as a "unit of vegetation which possesses (broad) characteristics in physiognomy and structure sufficiently pronounced to permit its differentiation from other units".[4] Following this method of classification, subtropical forests in Garhwal range between 500 and 1,500 metres, containing commercially valuable tree species such as bamboo, *sal*, *sheesham*, and *khair* (*Dendrocalamus strictus*, *Shorea robusta*, *Dalbergia sissoo*, and *Acacia catechu*); montane or temperate forests range between 1,500 and 3,500 metres, containing, among others, species such as *banj*, *chir*, *kail*, *deodar*, *moru*, *kharsu*, ash, walnut, rhododendron, fir, spruce, and cypress (*Quercus incana, Pinus roxburghii, Pinus wallichiana, Cedrus deodara, Quercus semicarpifolia, Quercus himalayana, Fraxinus xanthoxyloides, Juglans regia, Rhododendron arboreum, Abies pindrow, Picea smithiana,* and *Cupressus torulosa*); subalpine and alpine forests, which extend from 3,000 metres to the snowline on the southern face of the Inner Himalayas and contain species such as alder, birch, rhododendron, and juniper, (*Alnus nitida, Betula utilis, Rhododendron campanulatum, Juniperus communis,* and *Juniperus wallichiana*), as well as moist alpine grasses and dry alpine shrub.[5]

But this mode of classification is overlaid by other patterns and marked differences in the density of tree cover and quality of vegetation. These variations become apparent at the scale of a watershed or an administrative division: in some places, densely forested slopes abruptly end at ridges beyond which there is no vegetation; sometimes they adjoin tracts where trees appear heavily lopped and stunted. In other places, areas officially categorised as 'forest' are latticed by well-worn cattle tracks, interspersed with a few stunted trees and shrubs. Such sharp contrasts in vegetational density and quality within localities are not an outcome of micro-level ecological adaptation within forest types, but rather a reflection of the variations in institutional relations governing access to and control over forest resources.

Although cultural and symbolic meanings attributed to forests do, indeed, vary substantially from one locality to another in the region,[6] households and communities in Garhwal identify their surrounding forested landscapes according to institutional categories such as civil, reserved, protected, or village forests. These official distinctions between different forest categories are crucial for several reasons. First, each forest category is defined according to the authority exercised by particular state agencies or locally governing institutions. Second, even though the UP Forest Department functions as the biggest landlord in the region, its administrative authority over the forests within its jurisdiction is exercised in varying ways; that is to say, the Forest Department does not adopt a standardised form of management or control over its forest resources. Third, each forest category carries distinct rules of access to various vegetational resources for purposes ranging from household and communal use to commercial extraction. Rules defining the rights of access or concessions to forest produce – known as *haq-haqooq* – are extremely important for households whose livelihood opportunities beyond subsistence cultivation and forest-based extraction are severely limited. Finally, real power is invested in groups that have the ability to negotiate with government institutions and gain access to various forest categories to extract resources. Thus the forested landscapes of Garhwal are, in effect, palimpsests upon which a complex and fascinating history of the biogeography of control is repeatedly inscribed and incompletely erased by social actions and material practices.

Current data on land use in Garhwal indicate that approximately 15 percent of the total geographical area is used for agricultural purposes (under private or state ownership, including fallows), 3 percent is for urban use, 15 percent comprise wastelands (cultivable and uncultivable under state ownership), and the remaining 67 percent contain forests. This broad distribution in land use has not undergone any dramatic shifts over the past century. Although exact data are not available for comparison, I have calculated that around 1893, the land-use distribution in colonial Garhwal was as follows: 19 percent under agriculture, 1 percent for town and urban settlements, 15 percent under wastelands, and 65 percent under forests.[7] Over the past hundred years, therefore, land under agricultural use has been reduced by 4 percent, while land under forests and for urban use have each increased by 2 percent.

The changes in land use based on available data appear to contradict the ongoing debates about deforestation in the Garhwal Himalayas. If anything, the calculations indicate that the forested area in this region has increased rather than decreased over the past hundred years. Why, then, is there a continuing argument about the deforestation crisis in this part of the Himalayas?

Clearly, the debate on deforestation is not only about the scientific accuracy of measurements pertaining to the rates of depletion of forest cover or changes in vegetational composition and quality. It is also about identifying those social agents that can be held culpable for these changes. Arguments over the scientific accuracy of data are about reallocating blame among particular social agents and their actions in relation to decline in forest cover or quality; they produce narratives that link each of these agents to a particular set of formal properties or characteristics which are seen to cause such outcomes. It is not surprising, therefore, that debates over deforestation inevitably centre on 'property', or rather, the properties of formally instituted categories of social relations that appear to define or represent the actions of these agents. Most narratives about deforestation either begin or end with a discussion of the virtues or weaknesses of particular forms of property or social 'ownership' of forest resources – private, public, corporate, state, or common – and usually offer solutions that involve the transfer of forests from one formal category of ownership to another.[8]

The idea that the problem of deforestation can be resolved by transferring forests from one ownership category to another stems, in part, from the assumption that formally instituted or legal rights to property automatically determine the ways in which forest resources are used or managed. Such an assumption is problematic for at least three reasons. First, and most obvious, is that regardless of whether forests are legally defined as private, common, or state-owned, the use and management of forest resources are shaped by a variety of changing economic, ecological, and political processes occurring both within and beyond particular territorial boundaries. Second, it is necessary to distinguish *de jure* rights of property from *de facto* modes of access to, and use of, forests; the two do not always correspond. Third, there is a difference between legal rights of ownership and actual exercise of authority over forests, i.e. between *property* and *control*. Juridical rights of property, in fact, play a very minor role in explaining the vegetational quality or extent of forest cover in regions. In contrast, one can gain a far more accurate understanding of biogeographical processes – changes in vegetational density, quality, species composition and diversity – by examining how social relations and material practices have shaped *modes of access* to and *exercise of control* over regional forest resources.

The need to distinguish between juridical rights of property, modes of access, and exercise of control becomes apparent when examining the actions of state agencies such as the Imperial Forest Service. The following section elaborates on the theoretical distinctions between these concepts so as to establish an analytical framework for understanding the role of the Forest Service in the Garhwal and Kumaon Himalayas.

PROPERTY, ACCESS, AND CONTROL[9]

Property is usually defined as the exclusive right to possession, use, or disposal of something. As a right, property is imbued with the social privilege of excluding others from the use of or from deriving a benefit from a particular resource, be it soil, trees, water, money, or something else. Access, on the other hand, as Ribot points out, refers to the "freedom or ability to obtain or make use of" any of these resources. The two terms, while being closely related, are distinguished from each other by the fact that the definition of property hinges on *right*, implying "an acknowledged claim that society supports (whether through law, custom, or convention)", while access centres on *ability*, which is a broader concept than right. Ability, as Ribot notes, refers to the actual demonstration of social actions irrespective of whether they have received socially articulated approval. Property is, therefore, a prescriptive concept; it is *de jure*. Access is a descriptive term that includes the *de jure* and *de facto*, legal and extra-legal.[10]

Property as a prescriptive concept also needs to be distinguished from control, a term that refers to checking and directing social action, the function or power of directing and regulating free action. The term 'control' refers to an exercise of social power, a social act or a process through which access to things and resources are regulated in varying degrees; control, like access, hinges on ability, the ability to regulate social actions and access. Thus control, like access, encompasses both *de jure* and *de facto* exercise of social power.[11]

Access and control are, therefore, descriptive terms that become operative for analysing the patterns and processes of resource use. Property rights are only a part of the whole array of mechanisms contained within the concept of access and shaped by the exercise of control. Possession, as the common saying goes, is nine-tenths of the law, but as Ribot succinctly observes, "law may be only a fraction of access".[12] Individuals or agencies may, regardless of legally prescribed rights, exercise control over access to particular resources in ways that lead to *de facto* possession or proprietorship.

Ever since Garrett Hardin propounded the virtues of private property as a means of preventing "the tragedy of the commons", theoretical discussions about the use of natural resources have been forced towards arguments specifying or defining forms of ownership that fall within the opposing category of public, or non-private property. The term *common property* is interpreted in widely differing ways. For Hardin, common property means open-to-all, *res nullius*, open access, and therefore open to misuse and overexploitation.[13] Bromley challenges Hardin's definition of common property by counterposing its meaning as 'private property for a group', *res communis*.[14] He clarifies his definition by noting that individuals of the group share rights and duties in the maintenance and use of resources held in common, adding that "the management group (the owners) has a right to exclude nonmembers, and nonmembers have a duty to abide by exclusion".[15] Macpherson, on the other hand, asserts that common property "is created by the guarantee to each individual that he will not be excluded from the use or benefit of something".[16] McGranahan offers a more accommodating definition, noting that private and common property represent two extremes of a broader class of property regimes, and that the term "common property" refers to any property regime which ensures that more than one user has non-exclusive access to the same resource.[17]

Although Bromley successfully challenges the negative connotation of common property, it seems that his definition merely transposes the notion of 'corporate' (which is an extension of individual private property) on to the definition of common property; his distinction between private and common property seems to rest mainly in the size of membership. Macpherson's definition is also problematic because it can easily be interpreted as being "the property of all individuals" and hence, by logical extension, as *res nullius*, the property of none. McGranahan's definition is a basic statement of non-individual ownership without excessive specification of the distinctive characteristics of common property.

State property is also interpreted in widely differing ways. Macpherson argues that "it is not common property as we have defined it: state property is not an individual right not to be excluded. It is a corporate right to exclude. As a corporate right to exclude others it fits the definition of (corporate) private property".[18] Bromley and Cernea, on the other hand, describe state property as a regime where "ownership and control over use rests in the hands of the state. Individuals and groups may be able to make use of the resources, but only at the forbearance of the state."[19] The definitions imply, on the one hand, that state property exists as private/corporate property (according to Macpherson), or, on the other, as corporate/common property (according to Bromley and Cernea). But herein lies an interesting question: if, according to these scholars, something called 'state property' assumes differing formal characteristics of proprietorship, then what has led to these differences in form? Clearly, the character of whatever is deemed 'state property' clearly depends on the actions employed by state agencies for controlling access to the resources in question.

For example, state property may constitute all things and resources not privately or corporately owned within its jurisdiction (eminent domain). The state's possession of such things and resources does not provide it with the right of exclusive access, but accords it the legal or formal power of controlling their use. The state can, by exercising its legitimate powers of governance and control, regulate access to or check the use of resources within its possession in ways that may, in certain cases or circumstances, ultimately result in arrogating the right of corporate/private property (fitting with Macpherson's definition). Under different political and economic conditions, the very same state may reduce, weaken, or even abdicate control over some of its possessions. If this process leads to the assertion of the individual right not to be excluded from the resource, then it fits Macpherson's definition of common property. But if the process results in control being exercised by a group or by individuals, then it conforms with

Bromley's definition of common/corporate property. Or, if ensuing processes result in complete abdication of state control over particular resources under its possession, i.e. nominal ownership, then Hardin's definition of *res nullius* prevails. In each of these instances, the actual character of what is broadly termed state property depends on the ways by which control over access is exercised by the state.

The analytical distinctions between property, access, and control offer the means for refocusing attention on the socially defined parameters within regional and historical contexts that directly shape the actions and practices of state agencies involved in conserving forests or managing natural resources. The key factors that require detailed analysis are: (1) broader political and economic processes that create pressures or increase demands on forest resources; (2) competing perspectives and concerns regarding forests and their resources which shape the forms of state intervention; (3) legal, ecological, and production parameters for resource extraction and conservation within the jurisdictions of state agencies; (4) instruments (such as capital, labour exchange, rights of entitlement or concessions) used for controlling access to resource extraction; and (5) conflicts, disputes, and negotiations that reshape the instruments and regimes of access, and redefine the forms of control exercised by state agencies over forest resources. The variations in the vegetational density and quality of forests are, in effect, reflections of different resource access and management regimes which are continually shaped and altered by the interplay of these factors. The following sections of this chapter focus on these factors to describe the historical evolution of the role played by the Forest Service in the Indian subcontinent and in the Garhwal and Kumaon Himalayas.

BROADER PROCESSES SHAPING THE DEVELOPMENT OF FORESTRY IN THE INDIAN SUBCONTINENT

Historians generally begin their accounts of forestry management in India in 1805, when the British Royal Navy requested the East India Company to provide a permanent supply of teak from the Malabar region for ship-building in England. The Company responded by appointing a Forest Committee,

charged with a very comprehensive programme of enquiry regarding not merely the forests but the status of the proprietary rights in them. The reports submitted showed that the capacity of the forests in mature timber had been over-rated, that the nearer forests had been almost cut out, and that it would entail the construction of costly roads to exploit the more distant parts; but that protection would result in the gradual formation of a valuable property. The immediate result was a general proclamation, declaring that the royalty right in Teak trees claimed by former Governments was vested in the Company, and prohibiting all further unauthorised felling of such trees.[20]

In 1806, the Company appointed a police officer by the name of Captain Watson as Conservator of Forests. Watson apparently had little idea of what was expected of him and therefore chose to assume substantial powers which, according to Ribbentrop, he used, "with great energy and less discretion. Within a couple of years he had succeeded in establishing a timber monopoly throughout Malabar-Travancore, and practically annihilated more or less all private rights in the forests by assuming their non-existence."[21] Although Captain Watson's rough-and-ready enthusiasm provided plentiful and cheap supplies of timber, the proprietors of forests and timber-traders were not particularly enamoured of his methods. They launched a vigorous campaign against him and succeeded in forcing the Company to abolish the Conservatorship in 1823.

Charged with the duty of exploring practical means of procuring timber, some district administrators suggested that rather than creating an independent authority such as the Conservatorship, the Company's revenue officers could take steps to prevent cutting of small timber and undersized trees. The Court of Directors, on the other hand, proposed that current supplies of timber were to be ensured by arranging contracts with timber firms, and that future supplies of timber could be safeguarded by establishing plantations. Their suggestions were based on an investigation of the timber revenues derived through the contract systems established by Burmese rulers in the forested province of Tenasserim.[22]

Despite these preliminary attempts to ensure steady supplies of timber for infrastructure projects, the Company's administrators, in Ribbentrop's view, displayed a shockingly cavalier attitude towards forest conservation.

> No apprehension was felt that the supply of forest produce would ever fall short of demand, and forests were considered an obstruction to agriculture rather than otherwise, and consequently a bar to the prosperity of the Empire. It was the watchword of the time to bring everywhere more extensive areas into cultivation, and the whole policy tended in that direction ... forest conservancy hardly rose above the level of a revenue administration. As a matter of fact hardly anybody believed in the possibility of a conservative treatment of State forest property through a State department ever being remunerative.[23]

After its first war with Burma, in 1826, the Company took control of Tenasserim and immediately sent Dr Wallich, then Superintendent of the Botanical Gardens in Calcutta, "to enquire into the resources of the country in regard both to botanical science as well as military and commercial objects".[24] On completing his investigation, Dr Wallich observed that the Company government was wrong in assuming that the existing contract system in Tenasserim would remain indefinitely successful. He warned that although timber extraction in the province was vigorous due to the existence of largely unexploited forest tracts, the stock would rapidly disappear with increased demand. Dr Wallich urged the government to establish a formal system of management and conservation:

> Unless the principle be acted upon from the very outset, I will venture to predict that private enterprise will very soon render fruitless all endeavours to perpetuate the supplies for public services, and one of the principal and most certain sources of revenue of this Province will thus be irrevocably lost.[25]

The Court of Directors of the Company, however, favoured the existing system of timber exploitation and consequently chose to disregard Dr Wallich's advice. The forests of Tenasserim were "thrown open to speculators in 1829, who paid an *ad valorem* duty on the timber extracted. They were not otherwise interfered with, and fire-protection was not introduced ... A further period of inaction followed on the part of the authorities, but not on that of private exploiters."[26] As a result, within a few years, the Company government was forced to regulate timber extraction. It proposed that all old contracts and leases be cancelled and substituted by new agreements that would ensure suitable conditions for safeguarding the future of forests in Burma.

The need for regulating forest extraction, therefore, arose during the first quarter of the nineteenth century when the Company reorganised its economic policies in India. The reorientation from the policy of staple towards the policy of protection meant that it was involved to a greater degree in promoting production of commodities within its territories so as to reduce expenditure of bullion for costly imports. The rapid deforestation that accompanied public works and plantation schemes vigorously promoted by the Company was, by and large, unforeseen by its administrators. Their enthusiasm was dampened by the prospect of imminent timber scarcity which, they realised, would not only undermine the construction of public works, but also subvert the Company's aim to conserve bullion because timber would need to be imported at greater expense from other countries.

THE QUESTION OF OWNERSHIP

The need for establishing state ownership over forests began to emerge as a persistent theme alongside these concerns. Regardless of particular views held by various officers of the Company, there was general agreement that "Government should claim and exercise the proprietary rights to all such forests as could not be clearly proved to be private property, a stricter conservative control, and above all an immediate restriction of shifting cultivation in the hills".[27]

But there was considerable disagreement over the issue of how exactly the government was to exercise its proprietary rights over forests. In many ways, the controversy over forests was similar to the debates that occurred between 1760 and 1793, when the Company's administrators in India attempted to devise laws for establishing property rights in land and revenue assessment.[28] The Permanent Settlement of 1793 in Bengal had been debated by three distinctive lobbies in Britain and India, the free-traders, physiocrats, and mercantilists. Despite their disagreement over who should benefit from settlement of property rights, all three groups shared the view that the institution of private property was necessary for establishing a sound revenue administration and for promoting economic prosperity in India. The mercantilists saw secure property rights as the means by which trade and commerce could flourish and thereby strengthen Indian society. The physiocrats regarded private property as a stimulus to agricultural production among the peasantry. The proponents of free trade envisaged private property as the most effective method for creating a new class of improving landlords as well as a market for agricultural land, both of which, they argued, would act as engines of economic growth.[29]

The institution of private property in land had not gone unopposed. The Governor-Generals of the Madras and Bombay Presidencies such as Sir Thomas Munro and Lord Mountstuart Elphinstone argued that it was inappropriate to introduce English laws and concepts of property which were alien to natives.[30] Administrators from other provinces cautiously admitted the need for establishing general principles regarding revenue settlements, but proposed that "the application of them must be directed by circumstances of time and situation".[31] Although the Permanent Settlement was implemented in Bengal with the creation of the *zamindári* or landlord system proposed by Lord Cornwallis, property settlements in the Madras and Bombay Presidencies followed the *raiyatwári* or peasant system advocated by Elphinstone, Shore, Metcalfe, Munro, and Malcolm. The views of the latter group gained strength as the *zamindári* system gave rise to absentee landlords and rack-renting and led to worsening conditions in agriculture in Bengal.[32] As the Company gained control of other territories in the subcontinent during the first half of the nineteenth century, property settlements and revenue assessment either followed the *raiyatwári* system or readapted preexisting systems of rights and customary ownership.[33]

This institutional experience informed later debates over forest ownership. But there was also an important difference between the two debates. Unlike agricultural land, where private ownership was seen as the necessary incentive for increasing production, state ownership was generally advocated for forests. Administrators argued that it was necessary to continue local traditions by adopting systems of forest ownership previously established by native rulers. Examples were drawn primarily from Burma, where the Alompra dynasty had claimed teak forests as royal property and derived substantial revenue from timber exports. The following observation by Ribbentrop regarding the form of ownership exercised by previous rulers provides an indication of how state ownership of forests was conceived and argued for:

> The despot preceding the British Government allowed every one to take what he required, but reserved to himself full power to do, at any moment, with his property whatever he liked without let or hindrance . . . But though the Oriental Governments, from which the British Government inherited its forest property, never recognised a prescriptive right, it had to be admitted that, under the system originally in vogue, and which had remained entirely unchecked for some time after British occupation, rights of user had in some instances been acquired by the legal process of prescription, in consequence of the substitution, or at least intermixture, of Western laws and ideas, in cases where it had been exercised neither by force nor secretly, but fully, openly, and unchecked, for sixty-two years.[34]

In 1852, following the second war against Burma, the Company annexed the province of Pegu and promptly declared forests to be government property. The proclamation, however, had little effect on the rate of timber extraction. Within two years of annexation, the forests of Pegu were threatened by "spoilation and development . . . by merchants sharing in the scramble and profits . . . along much the same lines as had been witnessed in Southern India and Tenasserim".[35] The Superintendent of Forests in Pegu argued that it was necessary to augment government ownership with a more comprehensive set of regulations that would limit timber extraction by private traders. The Company finally responded in 1855 by outlining a policy for forest administration in its Burmese provinces.[36]

COMPETING PERSPECTIVES REGARDING FOREST CONSERVATION

The demand for forest conservation and management also emerged from "the medical service in India in its increasingly determined efforts to elicit government control on deforestation as part of their wider programme of public health reforms".[37] Medical officers stationed in different parts of the Company's territories debated the writings of naturalists such as von Humboldt, Boussingault, and Bonpland, which pointed to the influence of forests on the climatic conditions of countries and on local precipitation;[38] others challenged these views by invoking Oskar Peschel's studies which argued that the amount of annual rainfall over continents would continue to be the same even if there were no forests at all.[39]

As arguments between medical and administrative officers grew more heated and vehement, the Company's Court of Directors ordered a committee to be appointed in 1847 to inquire into "the effect of trees in the climate and productiveness of a country or district as the result of extensive clearance of timber" in its administrations across the subcontinent. Dr Cleghorn, who later served as the Conservator of Forests for the Madras Presidency, cautiously tread the middle ground in his report, presented to the Committee in 1850:

The question as between the maintenance and removal of forests appears to us to be a question of compensation. Whenever the progress of population requires that every portion of the soil be made to yield its quota of human food, then the destruction of forests is to be desired, and the disadvantages to which want of wood for social and general purposes may lead, must be compensated for, as they will doubtless be, by the ingenuity which is borne of necessity. But there are localities in nearly all countries to which the tide of population can never flow, but where the forest can flourish, and where it ought to be maintained. In tropical countries the preservation of the springs which feed the rivers, on which the fertility of land and the prosperity of the people are so essentially dependent, is of the greatest importance. These springs arise in the mountain regions where forests prevail, and it is to such regions that a protective agency should be extended, for there can be but little doubt that the entire removal of wood leads to the diminution of water. In a single sentence, we would say that where human exigencies, whether for subsistence or for health, require the destruction of forests, let them be destroyed; but where neither life nor health is concerned, then let a wise system of preservation be introduced and acted upon.[40]

Other reports were more emphatic in their demand for forest conservation, offering numerous examples of deforestation and its negative effect on regional climatic conditions and soil quality. The Committee ultimately responded to the Company administration in India and the Court of Directors in England:

> In the course of the researches instituted in the Department, the effect of trees upon the climate and productiveness of a country and the results of extensive clearances of timber have been brought under notice . . . that an abundance of wood increases moisture and that a deficiency promotes aridity are conclusions which seem clearly deducible from the researches and observations which have been made on the subject.[41]

In sum, the demands for state intervention in forestry reflected four distinctive perspectives and competing concerns: (1) the need to ensure steady supplies of timber for public works and building infrastructure; (2) managing forests for a sustained yield of commercially valuable resources to meet the demands of a growing internal economy; (3) increasing revenues by taxing a lucrative and burgeoning sector of economic activity and (4) ensuring stability of regional climatic conditions, water supply, and soil fertility for the public health and social and economic welfare of subjects within the Company's territories.[42]

Although the Company's role in forest administration came to an end in 1858, following its abolition by the British Parliament, the new colonial government pursued earlier policies aimed at developing formal systems of forest management. The Imperial Forest Service was established in 1862;[43] three years later, the colonial government passed the Indian Forest Act. The Forest Act 1865 represented the government's efforts to mediate between competing claims to forest exploitation made by government departments, merchants, landlords, and peasants. It attempted to alleviate these tensions by distributing the responsibility of forest management among different government agencies and defining their powers of authority through the following forest classifications:

- *Reserved forests* were lands under the exclusive control of the newly formed Imperial Forest Service for the managed commercial extraction of forest resources. Rules and regulations for extraction from these forests were to be defined by the Forest Service.
- *Protected forests* were areas controlled by the Revenue Department for purposes of maintaining watersheds and preventing soil erosion. These forests were to remain inaccessible for extraction and use, and could be subject to reclassification only under extraordinary circumstances.
- *Civil forests* also came under the control of the Revenue Department, but were areas where limited extraction of forest resources was permitted; households belonging to nearby villages were accorded free rights of access to collect fuelwood, fodder, and timber for everyday needs. The Revenue Department held the right to alter land uses within civil forests, but could only do so after ensuring that all prior rights enjoyed by local communities remained intact.
- *Village forests* were to be maintained by village institutions to serve local consumption needs. Villages were accorded full proprietary rights over such forests; commercial extraction of forest resources was to be allowed only after obtaining permission from the Forest Service.
- *Private forests* owned by landlords were subject to transit taxes and levies imposed by the Revenue Department only on commercially valuable forest resources exported to other areas.

- *Bénap, or unmeasured lands,*[44] commonly referred to as wastelands, were unsurveyed areas not claimed as private property. These uncultivated scrublands came under the eminent domain of the colonial government. Resource extraction and use of these lands was controlled mainly by the Revenue Department.[45]

The forest classifications outlined by the Indian Forest Act 1865 not only represented different views regarding the need for forest conservation and management, but also reflected the relative power wielded by various government departments and the intense rivalries between them. The fact that the Forest Service controlled the most extensive and valuable forest tracts across the country made it a coveted entity. During the first two decades after its establishment, the Forest Service was shuffled between various government departments. It was placed under the control of the Secretary of Public Works in 1862 and the Department of Revenue and Agriculture in 1871. In 1879, it was moved to the Home Department, and transferred again, in 1886, to the newly created Agriculture Department. Each department attempted to reshape the Forest Service to suit its dominant aims and objectives.[46]

LEGAL, ECOLOGICAL, AND PRODUCTION PARAMETERS DEFINING STATE CONTROL

The division of forests into different classes meant that resource extraction and management varied according to the forms of control exercised by different state agencies. The Forest Service was legally forbidden to convert its forests to other land uses (given that it was established for the sole purpose of conserving and managing forests). It was required to organise extraction and management in ways that maintained forest stock, ensured a steady supply of forest resources for other economic activities, and yielded healthy revenues for the government.

The Forest Service, therefore, faced a set of problems associated with making forestry a profitable activity without undermining its productive base, problems which are similar to, but also different from those faced in agriculture.[47] The growing time for commercially valuable timber species can be extraordinarily long; substantial investment of labour in maintenance and management is needed before trees can be extracted and sold in markets. For example, valuable timber species such as deodar, *sal*, and teak require anywhere between 80 and 120 years to mature, and their quality (or rather, their value as timber) depends on the systematic application of labour-intensive activities such as thinning, clearing, and fire-lining. In addition, some commercially valuable tree or plant species may not successfully regenerate through plantation forestry.[48] These, in effect, are the ecological parameters that shape the ways in which forest management and production are carried out. Thus, if forestry is to be made a profitable activity – that is to say, if production is to occur without treating forests as non-renewable resources (as is the case in mining), and without converting them to other uses (such as agriculture or real estate) – it requires forms of production that involve a diverse mix of labour and contract regimes, and which vary according to the characteristics of plant or tree species bearing commercial or use value.[49]

The Revenue Department, on the other hand, was subject to fewer restrictions. It retained the privilege of converting its forested areas, if necessary, to other land uses, except in areas set aside for watershed protection. The Revenue Department rarely concerned itself with afforestation or conservation activities since it was not legally bound to do so, and hence adopted a relatively lax attitude towards forest extraction. As far as it was concerned, forests were generally a hindrance to the advancement of agriculture and rural prosperity, and hence an impediment to securing more stable and long-term sources of revenue. Forest tracts, if cleared or depleted of resources, were distributed as freeholds to cultivators.[50]

INSTRUMENTS CONTROLLING RESOURCE EXTRACTION FROM FORESTS

The instruments used by the two state agencies for controlling resource extraction within their forests varied according to these legal, ecological, and production parameters. The Revenue Department thus allowed petty (small-scale) commercial extraction to occur in its forests. Transactions between petty extractors and the Revenue Department amounted to a single royalty paid according to the quantity of extracted forest resources, which could be sold with relative ease in local markets. Fuelwood, timber, and fodder for household consumption were also assured in its forests – through rights and entitlements bestowed on villages – without any demands for labour exchange towards conservation and maintenance.

The Forest Service, on the other hand, organised production within Reserved forests by controlling access to commercial extraction of particular resources (such as timber, resin, fodder/grazing, collection of medicinal and edible produce) through auctions, levies, rents, and tax-farming leases. Forest conservation and maintenance, being labour-intensive activities (tree-planting, thinning, fencing for natural regeneration, fire-lining), were largely carried out through corveé arrangements with local villages.[51] Usufructary rights and concessions for the extraction of fuelwood, fodder, and timber from Reserved forests for household consumption (i.e. non-commercial purposes) were accorded to villages in exchange for labour contributions towards conservation and maintenance of forest stock.[52]

The mix of controls used by the Forest Service gave rise to socially differentiated access to resource extraction. Since access to commercial extraction could only be gained through auctions, contracts, and tax-farming leases, it was necessary for individuals or firms engaging in these activities to have access also to substantial amounts of capital.[53] For example, individuals or firms had to attend annual auctions held by the Forest Service and bid for demarcated trees and tracts in Reserved forests.[54] The buyer then required sufficient finances to settle an 'honour' fee – ranging from 10 to 20 percent of the final quotation, depending on the volume of transactions – with the agency, hire skilled labour for felling the timber, incur the costs of transporting logs to sawmills or regional markets, complete remaining payments to the Forest Service,[55] and absorb a variety of unforeseen expenses (such as damage and loss of timber). The whole process might stretch over two or more years before profits could be

FOREST CATEGORIES AND ACCESS REGIMES

	Reserved Forests	Protected Forests	Civil Forests	Wastelands	Village Forests
Controlling Agency	Forest Service	Revenue Department	Revenue Department	Revenue Department	Village panchayat
Function	Sustained yield production	Watershed protection	Small-scale extraction, local and household consumption	Small-scale extraction, agriculture, potentially open for other uses	Household consumption and other village uses
Potential for land use conversion	No	No	Yes	Yes	No

Table comparing access and extraction regimes:

Instruments for controlling access	**Commercial extraction:** auctions, tax-farming leases, production contracts, rents **Non-commercial extraction:** labour contributions in exchange for village rights & concessions for household needs	No access allowed for resource extraction	**Commercial extraction:** royalties levied on the basis of volume and market value of resources **Non-commercial extraction:** for meeting household consumption	Similar to Civil forests established by village *panchayats*; commercial extraction not allowed Commercial extraction not allowed Non-commercial extraction
Regulations				
Relative ease of access			Relative ease of access, ranging between common and corporate regimes	Tending towards open access regime
Form status of access regime	Tending towards private/corporate property	Highly regulated/non-usable status		Tending towards corporate/common property

realised. Thus if individuals or firms were to be successful in the business of forest extraction, they needed to possess extensive finances or have access to sources of credit. They also needed to find secure buyers and maintain close access to wholesale and retail markets for timber and other forest commodities.[56]

Despite both being agencies of the state, the Forest Service and the Revenue Department exercised control over their forests in different ways. The social relations of extraction organised by the Forest Service led it to function as the *de facto* private/corporate owner of Reserved forests. The proprietary role of the Revenue Department, on the other hand, ranged from corporate/common ownership of Civil forests to nominal control/open access vis-à-vis wastelands (see the adjacent figure comparing different forest categories and access regimes based on the Indian Forest Act 1865).

EVOLUTION OF FOREST MANAGEMENT IN GARHWAL AND KUMAON

The central factor affecting the classification of forests in Garhwal and Kumaon was the system of ownership and usufructuary rights that had existed prior to the 1865 Forest Act. It served as the basis for distributing authority over forests among different government agencies and establishing the parameters for controlling access to and management of forest resources.

Following 1815, when most of Garhwal and Kumaon were brought under the direct control of the East India Company, district settlement officers adopted the broad policies of taxation established by previous rulers. The Company's initial attempt to revive trans-Himalayan trade by abolishing customs and duties on exports offered greater opportunities for local households to extract commercially valuable forest resources for sale outside the region. Later, as the Company began promoting agricultural commodity production in Garhwal, its administrators reimposed taxes on timber, bamboo, and *catechu* extracted from sub-montane tracts. Between 1818 and 1828, revenue collection from the *káth*, *báns*, and *kathá mahals* (tracts containing timber, bamboo, and *catechu*) was leased by auction to tax farmers. As timber extraction steadily increased in the submontane tracts, district administrators attempted to regulate it by preventing *thaplá* (terraced areas and tracts at higher altitudes) from being exploited by leases.[57] Further intervention occurred in the form of leases that allowed traders to extract timber from limited segments of the forests with their own hired labour. This system of forest extraction existed until 1858, after which forests came under the direct management of the district administration (i.e. the regional office of the Revenue Department).

The ruler of the neighbouring principality of Tehri Garhwal adopted similar systems for controlling resource extraction from forests. In an attempt to increase state revenues, the Rajah of Tehri leased his forests to an English businessman by the name of Mr Wilson in 1844, granting him the right to extract products such as musk, game hides, and timber for a period of twenty years. Wilson's exploitation of forests in Tehri Garhwal was remarkably exhaustive during this period. He adapted German and Swiss methods of transporting timber from higher elevations to the plains by floating large logs of deodar down the tributaries of the Ganges during high water months, a practice that was later adopted by the Forest Service in mountainous districts. Wilson's zestful approach to resource extraction in Tehri forests became legendary among foresters and villagers. As Richard Tucker notes, "later forestry reports refer to Wilson with ambivalence, admiring his entrepreneurial drive but appalled by the impression that in little more than a decade he managed to decimate the major stands of *deodar* in Tehri."[58]

By the time Mr Wilson's forest leases ended in 1864, the Rajah of Tehri Garhwal opted to lease his forests to the newly established Imperial Forest Service which had assumed control over Reserved forests in British Garhwal and Kumaon. In the following two decades, the income from forests increased from 50 percent to nearly two-thirds of the total revenues of his kingdom.[59] This proved a sufficiently strong motive for the Rajah to establish a Forest Department for his own territories. Revenue from forest production continued to increase under the management of the Tehri Forest Department; by the turn of the century, the Rajah's revenues from forestry were more than twice the receipts from land revenue.[60]

FOREST DISPUTES IN
GARHWAL AND KUMAON

Forest classifications and regulations outlined by the Forest Act 1865 were challenged in almost every region of British India, and were subsequently modified by numerous local and regional rules. For example, in the very year of its legislation, the Act was amended to include a separate set of rules for British Burma, Central Provinces, and Rawalpindi (western Punjab, now part of Pakistan); in 1866, the North-West Provinces and Oudh Rules were added to the list. In 1871, the Act incorporated special rules for Berar, Bengal, and Coorg, and in 1873, the Act was repealed in Burma and replaced by the Burma Timber Act. In some cases, regional governments opted for selected forms of state control over forests. The Madras Presidency overruled the Forest Act in 1878 – even after seven amendments had been made – as it acquiesced to the protests of timber merchants and landlords who claimed that the humble peasant would suffer most under the regulations imposed by the Act.[61]

The Forest Act was amended at least five times between 1865 and 1950 in the Garhwal and Kumaon Himalayas. According to the rules laid out by the Act, nearly 60 percent of the forests in British Garhwal and Kumaon were classified as Reserves and therefore came under the authority of the Forest Service; this included large tracts in the inner and middle Himalayan ranges which were not yet accessible for exploitation. The Revenue Department controlled approximately 28 percent of the forested area classified as Protected and Civil forests and wastelands; the remaining 12 percent of forests came under the category of Village and Private forests.[62] The fact that the Forest Service exercised control over such a large area was, in itself, a point of extreme irritation for the Revenue Department, as well as for local and regional elites who found their access to resource extraction from forests severely constrained by new laws and regulations.

One of the first recorded disputes occurred in 1893, soon after a cadastral survey and assessment of wastelands was completed in the region. The Forest Service appealed to the colonial government to reclassify substantial portions of these areas as Reserved forests. But since the Forest Service already controlled two-thirds of all forested areas in Garhwal and Kumaon, its proposal faced vehement opposition from the Revenue Department and regional elites.[63]

Most of the tensions between the Forest Service and the Revenue Department centred on the issue of forest conservation and management. Forest Service officers complained that lack of conservation and management in Civil forests led to deforestation and ecological degradation, and, in turn, increased the pressures of resource extraction in adjacent Reserved forests. They argued that these areas could be managed more effectively for the government and for the needs of local populations if they were transferred to the authority of the Forest Service. The Revenue Department vehemently objected to any change in the classification of wastelands on the grounds that a large proportion of the present and future revenue base would be reduced; wastelands, it argued, could potentially be converted to agricultural use to meet the needs of a growing rural population, and serve as the basis for increasing rural prosperity.

Petty extractors and traders belonging to local communities also opposed reclassification on the grounds that the Forest Service's regulations would substantially restrict their ability to engage in resource extraction. They took advantage of the prevailing animosity between the two agencies and allied with the Revenue Department in its protests against further expansion of the Forest Service's control;[64] village leaders pointed to the numerous rules and controls imposed by the Forest Service and argued that the agency was bound to apply these cumbersome regulations to all new areas brought under its authority. They criticised the boundary demarcation procedures followed by the Forest Service, and complained about the limited entitlements given to communities for timber and grazing, the prohibition of cultivation, and the restrictions on extraction of minor forest products from Reserved forests.[65]

The colonial government attempted to settle the controversy by instructing the Revenue Department to reclassify its wastelands and forests. Two new categories emerged as a result: *Closed Civil* and *Open Civil* forests. Closed Civil forests were defined with the aim of slowing the rate of extraction by limiting the amounts of timber and other forest commodities that could be harvested. Open Civil forests, on the other hand, were freely accessible to village communities to meet fuelwood, fodder, and grazing needs.[66] But the exercise in reclassification did not necessarily alter the Revenue Department's attitude towards forests; no effort was made to introduce management systems involving artificial or natural regeneration of forest stock.

Reclassification, however, altered the prevailing forms of access for resource extraction in the region. While wealthier merchants and timber contractors continued to extract resources from Reserved forests according to the conditions and guidelines set by the Forest Service, petty extractors, for their part, could still obtain the necessary permits from the Revenue Department for extracting timber and other resources from Closed Civil forests. In contrast, poorer households in surrounding areas found their access restricted to Open Civil and Village forests to meet their needs for timber, fuelwood, and fodder. Thus, between 1893 and 1910, it was the Open Civil and Village forests that suffered most from extraction. Closed Civil forests went through a similar, but slower, process of resource depletion.[67]

The pressures of extraction spilled into Reserved forests in the decade following reclassification. In 1911, the Forest Service again urged the colonial government to transfer Closed and Open Civil forests in Garhwal and Kumaon to its authority. The Revenue Department refused again to give up its control, but was nevertheless ordered by the government to reclassify its forests. Three new categories emerged from this round of reclassification: *Class A, B,* and *C* forests. Class A forests allowed limited extraction of timber and other forest produce following royalty payments to the Revenue Department; Class B forests were demarcated solely for the extraction of fuelwood and fodder, while Class C forests remained freely accessible for village communities to exercise their rights to obtain timber, fuel, and fodder for everyday needs.[68] The new classifications allowed the Forest Service a limited role in the management and conservation of Class A and B forests, but ensured that these categories remained under the authority of the Revenue Department.

The second round of reclassification did little to ease the pressures on Reserved forests, since the onset of the First World War added to the prevailing demand for timber. Thus, in 1916, the Forest Service appealed, once again, for the reclassification of Class A, B, and C forests as *New Reserves*.[69] This time, local elites and petty commercial extractors in Garhwal and Kumaon (with ample support from the Revenue Department) were at the forefront of opposition to the proposal. Numerous petitions were filed in local courts. Leaders of the growing nationalist movement in India charged the Forest Service with displaying callous indifference towards the plight of humble Himalayan peasants.[70] Local protests also erupted in various forms, ranging from litigation to arson and poaching in Reserved forests.[71]

The colonial government appointed a Forest Grievances Committee in 1921 to resolve the disputes in Garhwal and Kumaon. Local elites and political representatives, in turn, formed the Kumaon Association, and submitted a report to the Forest Grievances Committee demanding that forests in Kumaon and Garhwal receive special status, and exemption from forest laws and regulations that applied to the rest of the United Provinces.[72] The report advised the government to: (1) revoke all restrictions on extraction of minor forest produce from Reserved and Civil forests contiguous to villages; (2) reclassify New Reserves as Village or Civil forests; (3) give village *panchayats* and local representatives the power to regulate extraction from forests; and (4) exempt local communities from forest laws that banned ownership of firearms, so that households could protect their crops and livestock from wild animals straying from nearby forests.[73]

The Kumaon Association advised the Forest Grievances Committee to reclassify Civil forests and New Reserves into two categories: *Class I* and *Class II* forests. Class I forests were to be controlled by the Revenue Department, but could no longer be converted to agricultural use; limited extraction of forest commodities needed for local artisans and industry was to be allowed through permits issued by the District Administration. The management of Class II forests

was to be given to the Forest Service, but on condition that free
access be maintained for meeting the fuelwood, timber, and grazing
needs of local communities. The Kumaon Association also recommended that the Forest Service assume responsibility for soil conservation, watershed protection, and reforestation in all forest
categories.[74]

The government's acceptance of the Kumaon Association's recommendations without any major alterations indicated a changing
balance of power in colonial India. Village leaders and regional elites
were gradually being drawn into the nationalist movement for
independence from Britain, and were, in the process, discovering
new ways of challenging the colonial administration. The final
recommendations of the Forest Grievances Committee burdened the
Forest Service with additional responsibilities for maintaining forests
in the region but gave it no scope for generating revenues that would
compensate for increased management costs. Soil conservation, reforestation, and forest protection were labour-intensive activities that
were expensive if carried out entirely by wage labour. When forest
officers sought labour contributions from local communities, or
attempted to redefine access rights and concessions in Class II forests
through labour *corvées*, village leaders drew on the support of nationalist leaders to demand that all forms of unpaid labour services be
abolished by the government.[75]

Faced with severe fiscal constraints arising from the escalating costs
of forest conservation, austerity measures imposed during the
Depression years, and the loss of revenues due to the collapse of
timber prices, the Forest Service set aside large tracts of Reserved
and Class II forests for natural regeneration, fencing them off to
prevent extraction and grazing. This strategy, too, met with protests
in the region.[76] In 1938, the colonial government set up yet another
commission of inquiry – formed this time by three district committees consisting of government officials and local elites – to
examine the rights and concessions held by villages in Class II and
Reserved forests. The committees recommended building additional
roads into forest areas, new demarcations of forest boundaries,
settlement of lower-caste households on forest lands, provision of

arms licences for village households, and the expansion of resin extraction in Garhwal.[77] Legislation in 1941 further relaxed controls in Class II and Reserved forests by ruling that village communities in Garhwal and Kumaon could freely extract fuelwood and fodder and fell all unprotected species of timber for household needs.[78]

The growth of towns in the foothills of the Garhwal Himalaya led to increases in population and demand for construction timber and fuelwood. Private forests were steadily depleted as owners sought to profit from the spiralling demand generated by the growth in railway construction and industrial and urban energy consumption outside the region.[79] The Second World War increased the pressure on Reserved forests as timber was extracted to meet the targets set by the War and Munitions Board; routine forest management and silvicultural plans were temporarily set aside due to labour scarcity.[80] Local elites and petty commercial extractors profited from exploiting wartime shortages because the internal demand for fuelwood, charcoal, and construction timber remained relatively inelastic. By the time India gained independence from Britain in 1947, all categories of forests in Garhwal and Kumaon had undergone rapid depletion due to the cumulative effect of wartime and civilian demand.

THE STATUS OF FOREST MANAGEMENT FOLLOWING THE END OF BRITISH RULE

In the years following independence from Britain, the national and state governments debated proposals for land reform to improve agricultural productivity and revive an Indian economy which had stagnated during the war and suffered the exhausting effects of Partition. The National Planning Commission advised state governments to implement agrarian reform policies by redistributing lands appropriated from large landowners to marginal peasant households. But since agriculture was declared a "state subject" by the Indian Constitution (which meant that state governments could decide, without direct intervention by the national government, how policies were to be pursued within their jurisdictions), each state in the Indian Union adopted a different approach towards agrarian reform.

In Uttar Pradesh (UP), large landowners exercised considerable political clout in the state legislature and consequently subverted any proposal for ceilings on land ownership or redistribution of landed estates as freeholds to peasant cultivators. Land reform in UP was, as a result, fairly minimal in scope. The state government urged landowners to voluntarily give up some portions of their lands to poor and needy peasants; it reclassified forests controlled by the Revenue Department as Civil-*Soyam* (the term *soyam* can be roughly translated as semi-arid, cultivable waste) so that some of these areas, after being cleared, could be made available for peasant cultivation. The UP Private Forests Act 1948 was introduced to demonstrate the state government's commitment to managing natural resources for the welfare of its populace; owners of Private forests were to be given due compensation for the loss of property, and areas thus acquired were to be transferred under the control of the UP Forest Department as *Vested* forests. These actions were largely successful in containing opposition and averting public criticism. In Garhwal and Kumaon (now part of UP), the area under Private forests was negligible and largely degraded; by the time the Forest Service gained control over Vested forests, these had been stripped by their previous owners of almost all resources bearing any commercial value.[81] Civil forests and wastelands, which had earlier been the object of contention between the Forest Service, the local elites, and the Revenue Department, remained under the Department's control and were rendered more accessible to resource extraction and conversion to agriculture and other land uses.

Thus, over the course of a century of forest management in Garhwal, the institutional control exercised by the Forest Service expanded over nearly 75 percent of state-owned forests in the region (see the adjacent figure showing forest reclassifications between 1865 and 1975). Village forests remained relatively unchanged at about 5 percent, and the Revenue Department's control over forests was limited to the remaining areas classified as Civil-*Soyam* and wasteland.[82]

The history of forest management in the Garhwal and Kumaon Himalayas illustrates that shifts in the exercise of control were not

FOREST RECLASSIFICATIONS IN
GARHWAL AND KUMAON: 1865–1975

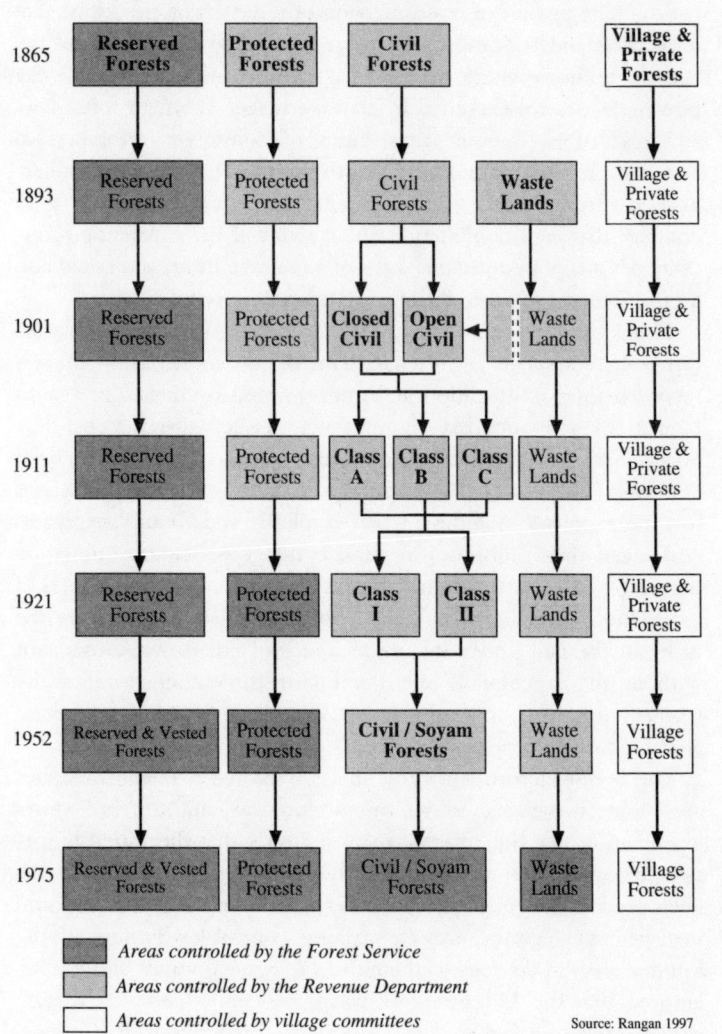

driven by some unchanging logic of colonial scientific forestry, nor did they relentlessly override the needs of local communities in the region. The process of reclassification of forest categories shows that local elites and regional leaders were able to take advantage of the internal tensions within the colonial administration to redefine the powers of control exercised by state agencies. Although forest laws and regulations imposed new kinds of constraints on access to resources, regional elites found that the colonial government's adherence to "rule by law" opened possibilities for challenging it in courts,[83] that legal contestation could result in their retaining economic advantage in profitable areas of extractive trade, and could also be manipulated to subordinate rivals or social groups.

Thus, contrary to Ramachandra Guha's argument that colonial foresters functioned as scientific managers, most forest officers recorded their exasperation at being besieged by litigations against regulations and boundary disputes within their jurisdictions. The Forest Service's attempt to coordinate the preparation of Forest Working Plans and ensure implementation along scientific principles became exercises in futility when landlords and timber merchants challenged their legitimacy in civil courts.[84] Ribbentrop observed that forest officers often found themselves yielding to the pressures of local elites; "deviations from the provisions of such plans were the order of the day, and were, more frequently than not, carried out without the sanction of the Local Government or even of the Conservator, who under the Forest Department Code is permitted to sanction such changes".[85]

The Forest Department's role in Garhwal and Kumaon may thus appear at first glance to be monolithic and uniform, but closer examination (see the adjacent map) indicates that the varied biogeography and quality of vegetational landscape within its forests has been produced through diversified ensembles of resource access and management regimes. Despite gaining control over most of the forested areas in the region, the historical legacy of forest disputes has ensured that the UP Forest Department cannot completely erase earlier rights of access and concessions to forest resources; Garhwal and Kumaon remain to this day the exceptions, the *only* regions in

DISTRIBUTION OF VEGETATION WITHIN
RESOURCE CONTROL REGIMES

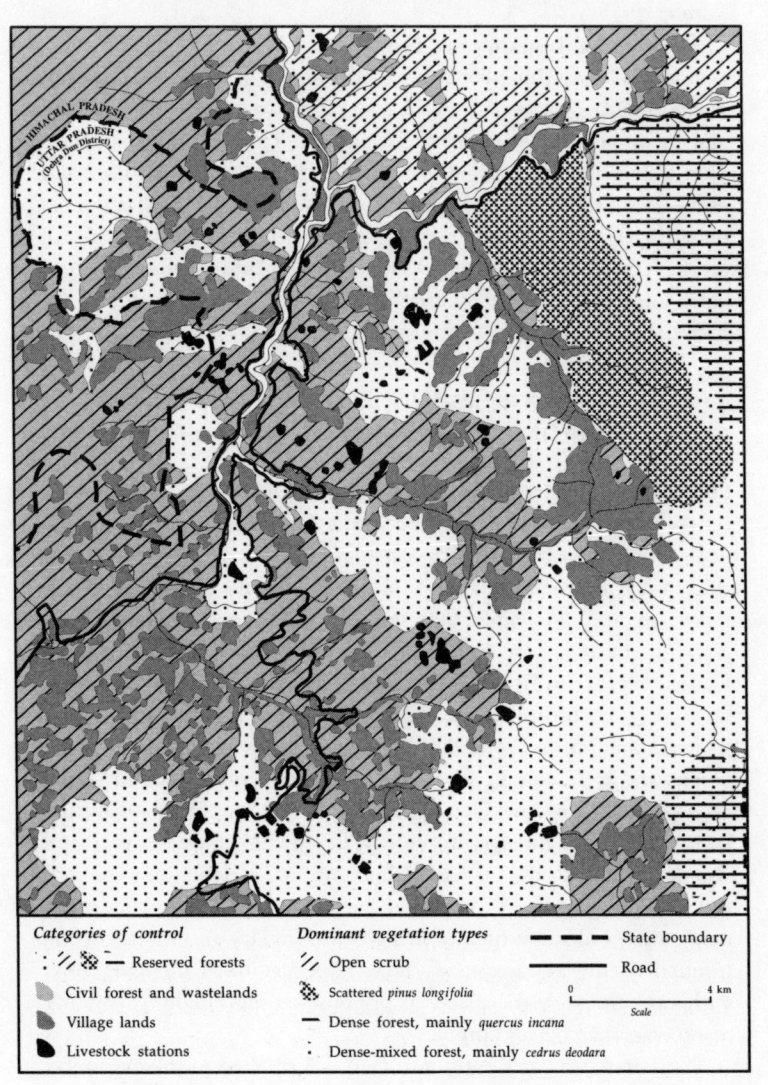

Categories of control	Dominant vegetation types	
Reserved forests	Open scrub	State boundary
Civil forest and wastelands	Scattered *pinus longifolia*	Road
Village lands	Dense forest, mainly *quercus incana*	0 4 km
Livestock stations	Dense-mixed forest, mainly *cedrus deodara*	Scale

the state of Uttar Pradesh where the category of Civil forests continues to exist alongside Reserved, Protected, and Village Forests.[86]

The forested landscapes of Garhwal and Kumaon are, as I mentioned above, palimpsests upon which patterns of resource access and management regimes and their contestation are repeatedly inscribed and incompletely erased by social actions. Their changing patterns over time reflect the varied ways in which control is exercised and reshaped by the complex interplay of ecological and social processes occurring in localities and regions, and at national and international levels. The variations in vegetational quality and density are, in a sense, muted narratives through which the political ecology of regional transformation is expressed in the region's landscape.

CONTESTED LANDSCAPES AND REGIONAL TRANSFORMATIONS

How do the contested forest landscapes of Garhwal and Kumaon reflect the changes that occurred in the localities and in household economies between the 1850s and 1940s (the end of British colonial rule)? Clearly, the appearance of the Forest Service in the region was linked to shifts in dominant economic policies of, first, Company government and, later, the colonial and postcolonial state in India. But its presence in British Garhwal and Kumaon was also due to the sectoral restructuring of the regional economy as trans-Himalayan trade declined from the mid-nineteenth century onwards. Tea plantations and agricultural commodity production of wheat and sugarcane promoted by the Company in Garhwal had collapsed by the last quarter of the nineteenth century; hemp cultivation in the region also declined with the growth of jute and sisal production in eastern India.[87] The growth of towns and the construction of public irrigation works and infrastructure in the sub-Himalayan tracts also contributed to the extraction of forest resources from montane areas with easy access to the plains in response to the rapidly expanding market for charcoal and timber.

The Forest Service's entry into Garhwal resulted in the expansion of the scale of production and market-deepening in the forestry sector. As each commercially valuable resource was regulated by taxes, leases, levies, or auctions, access to resource extraction in Reserved forests became increasingly contingent on access to capital. Wealthier households redirected their capital towards extraction and trade of forest resources; some retained their competitive edge in this business by moving to cities in the Himalayan foothills so as to maintain close links with credit networks and gain greater profits from participating in wholesale and retail trade in timber and charcoal.

Market-deepening within the forestry sector led poorer households to reorganise their internal division of labour and diversify their livelihood strategies. As taxes, levies, and auctions became mediating instruments for regulating extraction of commercially valuable natural resources from Reserved forests (such as medicinal and edible plants, fodder, and resins), their access was limited to small-scale or petty commodity extraction of firewood from Civil forests and wastelands which they sold in regional towns, hill stations, and military cantonments. In cases where household earnings were used to obtain leases for extracting particular forest resources, male members were more likely to function as intermediaries for selling produce collected by women and children in regional market towns and cities;[88] earnings from such sales were generally controlled by male heads of households and reinvested in land or livestock holdings.[89]

The livelihood strategies of households diversified in a number of ways, often in varying combinations of activities carried out by members: some worked seasonally as wage labourers for timber contractors and the Forest Department; some gained access to small plots of land within Reserved forests through increased labour contributions to the Forest Department for cultivating potatoes (the only commodity crop permitted for cultivation within Reserved forests by the agency); others invested in larger livestock holdings and gained access to increased grazing rights in Reserved forests in exchange for additional labour contributions.[90] Colonial forest officers observed that ownership of livestock multiplied rapidly "on account of the security afforded under a settled Government, and in consequence of the higher prices that could be realised for cattle",[91] little realising that the regulatory activities of the Forest Service in the region had been far more significant in contributing to this shift.

Extremely poor or marginalised households, particularly women and children within them, were often those that were unable to diversify their livelihood strategies within the region;[92] they were, as a result, further pressed into poverty, reduced to depending on subsistence cultivation and compelled to extract the only "free" resources – fuelwood and fodder – prescribed by forest laws. Migration became an increasingly common strategy for such households. Some, encouraged by the Revenue Department, moved to *terai-bhabhar* areas (sub-Himalayan tracts) to clear swamplands and jungle for settlement and cultivation. In other cases, male members of households sought work as wage labourers in plantations, construction, and other service trades in towns and cities outside the region. Military service became an occupation eagerly sought by young men, particularly with the establishment of the Garhwal Rifles in 1879, and the colonial government's military campaigns in Burma, Afghanistan, and Tibet.[93] Women, the elderly, and children belonging to these households stayed on in their villages, cultivating food crops in small tracts by themselves or with the help of sharecroppers, tending a few sheep and goats (either raised for sale, or maintained as insurance against inflation and for emergency cash requirements), but increasingly depending on cash remittances for their subsistence.[94] By the 1920s, most households in Garhwal depended on incomes earned from activities other than cultivation or sale of agricultural produce.[95]

The increased out-migration of Garhwali men brought, in turn, a new class of in-migrants to the region. Men from towns and villages in Afghanistan and the North-west Frontier Provinces moved in to work as small-scale contractors in building and road construction for the Forest and Public Works departments. Impoverished families from western Nepal came to work as sharecroppers, cultivating subsistence crops for landowning households whose members had either migrated, or were increasingly employed in non-agricultural activities; some worked in labour gangs organised by 'mates' who supervised the felling and floatation of timber down to wholesale merchants in the plains.[96] Most of them, as Saar Singh pointed out to me, had little or no rights of access to extract resources for household consumption from Village or Reserved forests because they were regarded as migrants or 'outsiders'.

By the 1950s, Garhwal's regional economy approached the condition that most policy-makers have come to describe as backward or marginal. Reorientation of trade and market-deepening in the forestry sector had combined to reshape the livelihood strategies of households, which, in turn, led to new forms of social and spatial differentiation within the region. The possibility of sustaining livelihoods became an increasingly tenuous and elusive goal. Postcolonial India's "tryst with destiny" through development and democracy offered the only glimmer of hope.

SIX

DEVELOPMENT IN
THE MARGINS

"I'm not surprised," commented Balbir Singh, staring at the political pamphlet I'd picked up at the market in Chakrata. "People around here have been saying this again and again for so many years, and I've said it too. How much longer do we have to wait for development to occur in our region?"

The frenzy of canvassing for national and state elections that possessed most cities and towns in Uttar Pradesh had found its way to the quiet military cantonment in northern Dehra Dun district. The elections, scheduled for May 1991, were less than a month away. While people in cities and towns vehemently argued over the importance of Hindu nationalism, defending or opposing the inflammatory rhetoric of the Bharatiya Janata Party over the temple–mosque controversy in Ayodhya, *development*, rather than religious fundamentalism, was on the minds of most people I encountered around Chakrata.

Balbir Singh was 22 years old, a political worker for Janata Dal. The Janata Dal was a national party that had formed a coalition government following the elections in 1989. It had been in power for barely a year before internal tensions emerged within the coalition. The crisis in the Janata Dal government had begun to escalate in August 1990, when the Prime Minister, V.P. Singh, announced that the recommendations of an inquiry regarding the status of lower caste and indigenous groups (called Scheduled Castes and Tribes in the official jargon) would be implemented during his tenure in office. He declared that "reservation", which in India refers to positive discrimination in favour of social, ethnic, and religious groups that have been historically disadvantaged, would be effectively employed to increase future recruitment of lower-caste personnel in central and state government institutions. His government had been able to survive neither the wrath of upper castes, nor the jingoism of Hindu nationalism generated by the Bharatiya Janata Party. The Janata Dal later regrouped to form a coalition with the Left parties to contest the mid-term election, and Balbir Singh was canvassing for the party's candidate from the area. I found out later that although the Bharatiya Janata Party came to form the government in Uttar Pradesh following the 1991 elections, Balbir Singh's candidate took his seat in the UP legislative assembly after having won the elections in the Chakrata constituency.

I had been handed the pamphlet while walking through the market on my way back from the Revenue Collector's office to the Forest Rest House. It was a 5-mile walk from the town centre to Junglat Chowki, the local name for the cluster of residential quarters around the Divisional Forest Office and the forest toll gate at the northern edge of the military cantonment.

Balbir Singh had his own purpose in accompanying me to my destination. He was on his way to meet the Range Officer of the area who was to issue him with a permit to transport his concessional timber to a sawmill nearby.

"Are you going to sell it?" I asked him artlessly, and received a wary glance in return.

"No, madam, certainly not!" he exclaimed. "We need the wood for repairing our house in the village."

We trudged along, talking about the various issues raised by the parliamentary and state elections. By the time we approached Junglat Chowki, Balbir Singh seemed fairly relaxed in my company; perhaps he had decided that I was not going to cause him trouble with the Forest Department. As our conversation wound down to an exchange of goodbyes, he remarked nonchalantly, "I might sell the timber if I can avoid being found out by the DFO [Divisional Forest Officer]."

It took me a moment to realise that he was referring to my earlier question. "We badly need the money, you see," he added. I nodded in empathy. Then his air of casual indifference dissolved in a flash of irritation.

"What else are we expected to do?" he burst out. "How else can we earn some money living here?"

The contents of the pamphlet seemed to echo his sentiments. It bore the dramatic signature of the "People of Jaunsar-Bawar and India", and carried a message of appeal and defiance in a chaste Hindi prose that is normally used by television newsreaders and politicians.[1] It challenged the reader with a set of rhetorical questions: "Why do we suffer from the lack of development in our area? Why do we have no roads, no electricity, no schools, no employment, no industries? What is preventing us from changing the face of Uttarakhand?"

The pamphlet made me recollect a newspaper report I'd read a few months earlier about a political rally organised by the Uttarakhand Student Federation in Rishikesh, a pilgrimage town in the foothills of Garhwal. It had been a short news item bearing the caption, "Bahuguna's Statements Criticised", in *Amar Ujala*, a Hindi newspaper widely read in western Uttar Pradesh. The report described the rally and included quotes from the speech given by the representative of the student group who was critical of Sunderlal Bahuguna, the well-known leader of Chipko.

His extremist views prevent the possibility of any progress or development occurring in Uttarakhand. In the name of protecting the environment, he has promoted forest laws that prevent any local development programmes from being implemented ... He is now trying to stop the Tehri Dam from being built, which means that we will remain backward and never see the possible benefits of development in this region.

The report ended by quoting the student leader's impassioned appeal to Bahuguna, urging him not to trifle with the modest aspirations for prosperity desired by the people of Uttarakhand.[2]

I found it intriguing that so many people in Garhwal were preoccupied with *development*, given that it was being subjected to a barrage of criticism elsewhere. Many scholarly critics and activists argued that development was an old-fashioned and misguided "modernist discourse" which no longer represented the needs and desires of people living in a postmodern world characterised by economic restructuring, transnational capital accumulation, and deteriorating environmental conditions across the globe.[3] Development was, for these critics, a sinister project, a totalising and hegemonic discourse (and also, for some, male and western) that perpetuated social and economic inequalities between rich and poor regions and social groups.[4] According to one such scholar, development

> has to be seen as an invention and strategy produced by the "First World" about the "underdevelopment" of the "Third World", and not only as an instrument of economic control over the physical and social reality of much of Asia, Africa and Latin America. Development has been the primary mechanism through which these parts of the world have been produced and have produced themselves, thus marginalizing or precluding other ways of seeing and doing.
>
> To think about "alternatives to development" thus requires a theoretico-practical transformation of the notions of development, modernity and the economy. This transformation can best be achieved by building upon practices of social movements, especially those in the Third World that have emerged in response to post-World War II hegemonic social orders. These movements are essential for the creation of alternative visions of democracy, economy and society.[5]

I wondered how critics of development would react to the views of people like Balbir Singh and other regional political groups in Uttarakhand. These people were voicing the need *for* development, they were not *against* it. They did not want to celebrate their marginal status, nor did they want alternatives *to* development. They demanded to be included, made part of the developmental process that they felt had been denied them so far. Would their demands be seen by critics of development as symptomatic of the pervasive power of the global hegemonic discourse of elites? Or perhaps disregarded as marginal, unrepresentative, and reactionary? But then, many social theorists and cultural critics who questioned the idea of development also asserted that 'margins' could not be summarily dismissed or regarded as unimportant. Marginal spaces like Uttarakhand were important and needed to be celebrated; these were, according to them, places where 'difference' found expression, where multiple voices, representations, and identities emerged through alternative discourses and radical social practices![6]

Scholarly criticisms of development generally tend to follow two forms of reasoning: one that 'deconstructs' the term through a reductionist logic to reveal the underlying and unstated political motives of those in power; another that examines the aims of development against its outcomes, reveals the inadequacies of the concept, and highlights the consequent failures of translating flawed ideas into action.[7] Varying combinations of both arguments produce a wide array of critiques that range from viewing development as a sinister plot undertaken by hegemonic powers to questioning the efficacy of particular developmental strategies followed by governments.

Notwithstanding the interesting observations emerging from the development discourse, much of the criticism tends to overlook the fact that ideas about development carry complex genealogies and considerable geographical diversity in associated social practices.[8] It is only during the past six decades that the term has been linked to the formal practices undertaken by governments for the broad purpose of improving the social and economic well-being of the populace under their administrative control. Stemming from roots in the European Enlightenment, this specific notion of development as linked to modes of governance has branched out and flowered in distinctive ways in various regions of the world. Discussions about development and its efficacy need, therefore, to move beyond narrow arguments over origins or definitions of the term, and focus instead on the processes through which particular meanings associated with development have been translated, appropriated, and reshaped by practices of governance occurring within different geographical and political configurations.[9]

DIFFERENCE, NATIONALISM, DEVELOPMENT, AND DEMOCRACY

The political and geographical configuration called India is produced from difference, founded on difference, and shaped by difference. Multiple identities, plurality, hybridity, are fundamental features shaping material and social life in the subcontinent. Scholars and policy-makers in India have rarely enjoyed the intellectual luxury of assuming the existence of a homogeneous "Indian" society. It has never been possible for them, in theory or practice, to ignore difference in all its forms, be it regional, cultural, linguistic, religious, ethnic, class, caste, or gender. Difference gives rise to social and political actions that are diverse and unpredictable, from acts of immense moral courage and passionate cooperation, to acts of appalling violence and intolerance. Everyday negotiations of difference occur through the "civility of indifference",[10] and through "a million mutinies now".[11] These numerous acts, working together, produce the India that appears as a "functioning anarchy", an entity that confounds its observers, lovers, and critics by "its resilience and its survival in spite of everything".[12]

Development has equivalent translations in the various regional languages of India. In Hindi it is called *vikas*, which means 'dawn', and alludes to a process of moving towards the beginnings of a new social era. Over the past five decades since independence, this translated notion of development has borne the promise of change towards greater social equality and economic prosperity for the Indian populace. Social transformation may appear a glacial process in India, but the secular vocabulary of development combined with that of democracy has allowed lower-caste groups and poorer classes to challenge, with growing assertiveness, the structures of social and economic inequality.[13] It has been used, time and again, to challenge dominant elites and the state, to argue that the clichéd celebration of 'unity in diversity' is rhetorical eyewash that keeps disadvantaged groups 'in their place' within Indian society but continues the practice of 'divide and rule' followed by British colonial authorities in the past.[14] The process of social and economic transformation in post-independence

India occurs through numerous struggles and 'messy' politics that constantly rework the meanings, language, and practices of difference, nationalism, development, and democracy within its varied regions.

The 'messiness' of postcolonial politics in India can be seen as an outcome of the strategies adopted by nationalists in their movement for independence from British rule. As colonial administrators attempted to divide and rule, classify and control the subcontinent by defining and reifying differences, they unwittingly contributed to the imagination of a unified India in the minds of their nationalist adversaries. Leaders of the nationalist movement attempted to create a unified India by engaging in a continuous process of political accommodation and negotiation with different social groups.[15] They acknowledged the existence of differences within the subcontinent, but argued for an alternative state, an Indian Union that would be founded on recognising universality and difference. Mahatma Gandhi and his colleagues in the Indian National Congress set out their vision for a unified India by employing ideas of democracy, secularism, truth, justice, equality, and freedom in ways that simultaneously acknowledged the particularities of existing social differences and offered the possibility of transcending them.[16] Secularism was employed as a concept that not only signalled the separation of religion from governance, but also actively endorsed the freedom of people to use their distinctive religious and philosophical beliefs to act morally within private and public realms. Notions of equality and justice were consciously used to highlight social and economic differences, yet offer possibilities for overcoming them. Universal ideas were thus refashioned into tools for insurgent actions as well as for manoeuvring, positioning, and gaining political power. The strategic discourse led the Indian National Congress and other nationalist groups to forge political bargains and create spaces of alliance that provided greater representation than ever before to lower social classes and less privileged groups in the Indian subcontinent.[17] It shaped the Constitution of independent India into a testament of radical possibility and intense paradox that incorporated difference and unity, religion and freedom from bigotry, tradition and blessed release from "fetters of the past".[18]

The composite identity of an Indian nation of difference, possibility, and contradiction emerged from this new, hybrid discourse that naturalised and Indianised the idea of democracy and development. Development, seen as an enabling concept holding universal appeal, was refashioned by India's early leaders into a process committed to improving the social and economic well-being of the entire nation. Development was constitutionalised as a nation-building process, an exercise in nurturing and expanding democracy, equality, and prosperity in the second most populous country in the world.

Linking development with democracy created new paradoxes. Economic development, on the one hand, inevitably resulted in processes that benefited some sections of society more than others, some regions more than others. On the other hand, the constitutional guarantee of social development also meant that the Indian state was required to intervene and correct these imbalances. Development as nation-building ensured government a central role in the economy and a key role in political accommodation between dominant classes and other groups within civil society. The Indian state promised to act as midwife, mediator, and upholder of democratic traditions; it invoked the collective goal of national development whenever conflicts in its differentiated civil society grew violent or gave rise to secessionist demands. It created conditions of greater social fluidity that allowed less privileged groups greater access to political recognition, representation, and the benefits of economic development.[19]

Democratised development is accepted as a legitimate language, discourse, and process by India's diversified populace, but its meanings, practices, and benefits are also subjects of constant negotiation and contestation in the public realm. Political parties seeking power have found it necessary to employ this language to mobilise support within India's vast and diverse rural constituencies. In these contexts, development is used as a generic term for government-sponsored infrastructure projects, such as the construction of roads and bridges, provision of public utilities, social welfare programmes, and investment subsidies for promoting economic growth. Rural elites function as intermediaries in the development process, their status depending in large part on their ability to function in the interstices, the interlocking spaces, between and within state, market, and civil society; their status also depends on demonstrating the ability to direct the flow of developmental resources from the state to their localities.[20]

If development is the means through which political allegiance is secured by state institutions and political parties, it is also the yardstick by which the performance of local leaders is gauged by rural communities. The status or authority of local elites who fail to "bring development" is often challenged by others attempting to gain control of their local political arena. Because the discourse of development in India typically carries a broader symbolism of social justice and economic well-being, it confuses (or perhaps condenses within it) the conceptually rigid boundaries between state, market, and community. It simultaneously functions as the language, instrument, and terrain for institutional participation *and* radical protest. Social movements and protests in postcolonial India have not argued against development but have always been part of its processes.[21]

Development emerged as the subject of nationalist political discourse in India around the turn of the century, and became the dominant leitmotif during the last two decades of colonial rule. The rationale that shaped colonial policies following the demise of the East India Company in 1858, that of ensuring steady and reliable supplies of raw material for industrial development in Britain, was rendered problematic as it encountered opposition from Indian businessmen and nationalist leaders, and by the global economic depression of the 1890s. The Afghan wars, famine, and depreciation of the Indian rupee imposed enormous burdens on the Indian Treasury, forcing the government of India to renegotiate its fiscal relationship with the government in Britain. The First World War contributed to a decisive shift from the policy of provision to one that emphasised industrial development in the subcontinent. These events and processes created the context within which nationalist leaders debated the means through which state actions would establish strong foundations for greater social equality and set the nation on the path towards a self-sustaining economy.[22]

DEVELOPMENT PLANNING IN COLONIAL INDIA, 1918–47

Early efforts towards planning for industrial development emerged shortly after the end of the First World War, during the last three decades of colonial rule. As the government of India wrestled with an ongoing fiscal crisis, the British Parliament added to its woes by demanding that it contribute to the debts incurred during the First World War. In 1917, the government of India offered a £100 million contribution to the British treasury in exchange for greater fiscal autonomy and the freedom to increase tariffs on British imports and promote industrial development in India without fear of reprisal. Its negotiation of fiscal autonomy was successful for two reasons. First, the power of the Lancashire textile lobby and free-trade enthusiasts had gradually weakened in Parliament;[23] second, the colonial government had the implicit support of nationalist leaders who, alongside their demands for self-rule, campaigned for the revival of industries that had been crippled by colonial economic policies.[24]

Between 1918 and 1947, a number of state- and Indian-owned industries emerged in different regions. The expanding urban agglomeration around Calcutta contained jute factories, munition plants, locomotive works, and car factories. Coal and iron mined in the Chota Nagpur region supplied steel plants in Jamshedpur and other industries located in the metropolitan regions of Bombay and Madras. The colonial government's direct involvement in industrial development was regarded with suspicion by the nationalist movement, which accused it of devising industrial policies that favoured British-owned companies.[25] However, industrialisation proceeded at a relatively modest pace during the interwar years, and the global economic depression following the stock-market collapse of 1929 caused further slowdown in industrial production; expansion of state-sponsored industrial development was curtailed by strict limits on government expenditure, while lack of investable capital constrained the growth of Indian-owned industries.

In 1938, the Indian National Congress formed a National Planning Committee comprising representatives from trade, industry, academic institutions, provincial governments, and various political parties. The Committee's aims were directed towards preparing for the end of British rule and exploring different strategies of economic and industrial development for independent India. The planning process was beset by numerous difficulties, ranging from lack of adequate data to political and ideological differences, and was temporarily shelved with the outbreak of the Second World War.[26]

Colonial economic policies were reorientated to meet war efforts and the targets set by the War and Munitions Board. Scarcity of labour and capital constrained both agricultural and industrial development. A crisis in food production, combined with the occupation of Burma by the Japanese army and grain speculation, led to famine which resulted in more than 1.5 million deaths from starvation in eastern India.[27] In the years leading up to independence in 1947, national and provincial governments wrestled with problems emerging from populations impoverished and traumatised by the politics of partition.

DEVELOPMENT IN POST-INDEPENDENCE INDIA

The first two decades of development planning focused on overcoming these problems by establishing the necessary infrastructure for regenerating the nation's economy and industry.[28] National leaders and planners drew on a wide spectrum of ideas and experiences from India and other parts of the world, ranging from Keynesian thought, Fabian socialism, the Soviet experiment, to Mahatma Gandhi's views on *gram swarajya* (village self-rule). Even though critics of India's development policies assert that the Gandhian approach was a viable alternative to Nehru's overwhelming zeal for modernisation, it has to be said that Nehru's partiality for Fabian socialism and industrial development was tempered by the real political lessons learned from participating in the nationalist government and from Gandhi himself.[29] Since Nehru and his colleagues had made a political commitment to secularism and democracy but were also expected to deal with the problems of an impoverished economy, they chose a socialist rather than a free-market approach to social and economic development. In the years following independence, few Indian scholars, planners, or nationalists were prepared to argue for maintaining the low levels of production and consumption implicit in Gandhian economic thought. As the late Indian economist, Sukhamoy Chakravarty observed, "it may be maintained that even a more pragmatically inclined politician than Nehru could have well opted for the same set of arrangements for promoting economic development".[30]

The Indian Planning Commission was established for purposes of systematic empirical study of the country's economy, identifying sectoral priorities, and preparing a coherent set of investment policies on a recurring five-year basis to promote development. The central-ised approach to planning was seen as a means of "avoiding the unnecessary rigours of an industrial transition in so far as it affected the masses resident in India's villages".[31] During the first two plan-ning periods (1950–55, 1956–60), the focus was on state investment in heavy industries, public utilities, infrastructure, and community development for reviving the Indian economy. Agriculture was regarded as a "bargain sector" with enormous potential for growth following the necessary institutional changes, investments in infra-structure, and political mobilisation by state governments; forestry did not receive special attention in these five-year plans because it was seen as part of the agricultural sector.[32] The second five-year plan spelt out the need to promote farming cooperatives, national extension programmes, and irrigation as catalysts for promoting community and economic development in rural India. Gandhian ideas were incorporated in the plans through investment in small-scale, rurally based, artisanal 'cottage' industries and handloom cooperatives.[33]

The course laid out by planners was radically reshaped by contin-gent events in the 1960s, such as the border wars between India and its neighbours (China and Pakistan),[34] and severe drought in various parts of the country due to successive monsoon failures in 1965 and 1966. These events, combined with ongoing price inflation resulted in near-famine conditions, and led to a fiscal crisis for the govern-ment. Although famine was averted by large-scale imports of food-grain from the United States under PL 480,[35] Indian planners and policy-makers realised that their development policies had failed to assess the growing imbalance between demand and supply of food. The broad strategy of promoting regional crop specialisation had collapsed, and land reform legislation at the state level had proved largely unsuccessful in obtaining additional land for redistribution to landless peasants. Possibilities for spatial expansion of cultivation remained limited. Although industrial development proceeded at a steady pace, it was unable to absorb the growing numbers of workers seeking livelihoods in various parts of the country.[36] Indian planners were also concerned about stemming the net inflow of foreign aid during the forthcoming decades so that the nation's economy could move towards greater self-reliance.[37]

The political and fiscal crises faced during the 1960s led Indian planners to redefine national economic priorities. The emphasis of the fourth five-year plan (1969–74, which followed a series of annual plans between 1966 and 1969) shifted from the capital-goods sector – which was, by then, already producing to excess capacity – towards national security, self-sufficiency in food and industrial raw materials, and import-substitution industrialisation; a two-way flow of inputs between the agricultural and industrial sectors was seen as necessary for increasing the production of basic necessities and contributing to the growth of national income.[38] The plan thus established the formal groundwork for promoting agricultural self-sufficiency through the Green Revolution strategy; agriculture was to receive greater capital investment in the form of credit, improved seeds, and chemical fertilisers. Fiscal restraints on public spending led to a move away from large-scale irrigation works and towards financing small-scale bore-wells installed by farmers on their lands.[39] Self-reliance in raw-material production extended to the forestry sector and involved extensive plantations of fast-growing tree species for meeting the growing industrial demand for construction timber, pulpwood, and other forest resources.[40]

Development planning in India thus emerged from the necessity of addressing social problems and economic constraints faced by the nation, but was reshaped by various contingent events – wars, droughts, energy crises – and contradictory outcomes of planned interventions in the economy. India's planners set out their policies as broad guidelines within which social and economic development was to occur, reforming their strategies every five years in response to problems that were either new or unforeseen, or which stubbornly persisted despite reassessment and reformulation. Their five-year plans, when translated into specific sectoral or regional policies, were substantially reshaped by political pressures exercised by different classes and electoral constituencies. Populist programmes promoted by political parties in power produced policies that either backfired or increased government expenditure. Sectoral policies aimed at promoting agricultural and industrial growth led to widely divergent outcomes in different states and regions. Regional policies aimed at developing economically backward areas had varied impacts on labour, employment, and productivity in different sectors within and between states. Development planning in India, in short, functioned as a dynamic, state-led process, reworking and reconfiguring the roles of various actors, forcing new trajectories of change as regions, markets, and institutions of civil society contested and renegotiated its meanings.

DEVELOPMENT PROCESSES AND OUTCOMES IN GARHWAL, 1918–75

Industrial development during the interwar years found its way into Garhwal and Kumaon with the establishment of a resin-processing factory in Bareilly, a town located in the sub-Himalayan tracts.[41] The Indian Turpentine and Resin Factory was set up by the Forest Service amidst criticism by nationalist members of the state legislative assembly in the United Provinces, some of whom invoked *laissez-faire* arguments to protest against state intervention in the economy. The Forest Service, in turn, assured its critics that private entrepreneurs lacked the necessary capital for investing in large-scale industrial development, and that the factory would bring a new prosperity to village communities in Garhwal and Kumaon. By the early 1920s the plant became the sole supplier of resin products and began exporting to Europe; soon after, the Forest Service set up a bobbin factory and an industrial-scale sawmill and turnery in the sub-Himalayan tracts.[42]

Scientists at the Forest Research Institute in Dehra Dun also examined potential uses of familiar and new tree and plant species for developing other forest-based industries.[43]

Yet the growth of the forestry sector in Garhwal was modest during the interwar years. The timber market faced a collapse in the late 1920s, which was followed by the decade of the Depression, and then by the Second World War. Fiscal austerity measures adopted by the government during the Depression years resulted in a substantial reduction in the number of forest officers and in labour for silviculture. Revenues diminished as felling targets set in the Forest Working Plans failed to be met, and routine conservancy practices of clearing, thinning, marking, and lopping were carried out at very minimal levels in forest divisions. Timber extraction and transport were affected by a general shortage of labour in the region as both forest officers and men from the region left for military service.[44] Although the Forest Department's revenues remained relatively stable due to reduced expenditures, these events set aside the expansion of forest-based industries for nearly twenty years.[45]

The first and second five-year plans (1950–60) brought few changes to the regional economy. The eastern districts of Garhwal and parts of Kumaon benefited from community development projects aiming to provide basic infrastructure and promoting village-based cooperatives for artisanal production; proposals for land reform also had minimal effect on the expansion of cultivation.[46] The war between India and China over their Himalayan borders, however, had a direct impact on the region for the Indo-Tibetan border subsequently became a national security issue. Army bases and depots were rapidly established and connected by new roads to the border;[47] nearly 10 percent of Reserved forests were transferred to the Department of Defence for these purposes, which effectively meant the withdrawal of access to these areas for resource extraction.[48] Local communities, depending on their geographic location in the region, were affected in various ways. Trans-Himalayan trade, which provided most communities near the Indo-Tibetan boundary with a substantial proportion of their income, came to an abrupt halt with the closing of the border. Households that depended on this trade found it difficult to expand cultivation of commodity crops such as ginger, turmeric, amaranth, and opium, because cultivation of such crops largely depended on the extent to which profits from trade and petty extraction of natural resources were reinvested in agricultural inputs.[49] With few alternative opportunities for employment existing in their localities, most households without access to capital were reduced to subsistence cultivation, augmenting their incomes with remittances from male household members who migrated to cities and towns in northern India in search of waged work.[50]

The Green Revolution policies of the fourth five-year plan (1969–74) were aimed mainly at the grain-producing regions of the country and, consequently, had little impact on cultivators in the region.[51] Although agronomists and scientists regarded Green Revolution techniques as scale-neutral, their success crucially depended on access to both capital inputs (high-yielding varieties of seeds and fertiliser) and irrigation; cultivators faced enormous risks using capital-intensive inputs if steady and well-timed supply of irrigation was not assured. Adoption of Green Revolution techniques, therefore, required fairly specific and exacting conditions of production which were not available in the montane regions of Garhwal and Kumaon. Households that had been reduced to subsistence cultivation and remittances for survival were unable to raise the necessary capital or collateral for credit, to obtain chemical fertilisers, to invest in pumped irrigation (a high-cost investment in mountainous terrain), and to purchase high-yielding varieties of seeds.[52]

However, the fourth plan's emphasis on self-sufficiency in industrial raw materials dramatically affected the region's forestry sector. The plan directed state forest departments across the country to assume *de facto* control over all forested areas and wastelands within states for plantation of fast-growing tree species for industrial uses.[53] The UP Forest Department undertook implementation of the new forestry strategy by excluding all forms of petty extraction of resources from areas earmarked for afforestation (including lands previously controlled by the Revenue Department). Costs of competing in Forest Department auctions rose at the rate of 8 percent each year, parallelling the rising market demand for timber and other forest products.[54] Small-scale extractors were consequently marginalised because they lacked access to areas that had previously been available for resource extraction, and because most of them did not have access to credit and market networks for competing against more prosperous timber merchants and traders. Local attempts to organise labour cooperatives for extracting forest resources failed as timber traders rationalised their expenditures by recruiting migrant workers from other regions.[55]

This process of economic marginalisation was compounded by a succession of natural disasters in the region. In 1971 and 1972, heavy monsoon rains caused flooding, landslides, and extensive damage to terraced cultivation; financial aid and assistance from state and central government barely trickled through to affected populations. Village leaders assailed the UP state government for its negligence, demanding immediate compensation for flood victims and development funds for the region. The demands went largely unmet by a financially constrained and sluggish state administration.[56] Resentment against the state government escalated further in 1973 when the Forest Department denied an artisanal cooperative in eastern Garhwal (the Dasholi Gram Swarajya Mandal in Chamoli District) a concessional allotment of ash trees for making agricultural implements. Village leaders and cooperative members were incensed when they found out that their request had been rejected in favour of a contract with a sporting-goods firm based in the Indo-Gangetic plains.[57]

The Forest Department's intransigence was seen by local leaders as confirmation of the state government's apathy towards the welfare and development of communities in its Himalayan districts. They organised protests against the Department at its divisional offices and auction sites, threatening to obstruct all extractive operations in Garhwal if their demands were not addressed. During the felling seasons between 1973 and 1975, village leaders urged their communities to prevent timber merchants and contractors from extracting trees in adjoining Reserved forests.[58] A number of stand-offs proved successful. Men and women, regardless of age or caste, gathered around felling tracts, hugging trees and urging migrant labourers to return to their homes.[59] Chipko was born.

SEVEN

CHIPKO'S MOVEMENTS

"I've lived long enough to see all sorts of people," he said, "the Englishman, Nehru, his daughter, these forest officers, local leaders . . . soon I will be a hundred years old."

Kalbali Khan had reached the age of 96 in 1991. His family had migrated to the Garhwal region some time during the last two decades of the nineteenth century from a place called Chitral in the Hindu Kush mountains, near the border of Afghanistan and Pakistan. His father had owned a pack of mules and transported materials – stone, lime, and wood – for construction of rest houses for the Forest Service, and occasionally he helped build them.

"He supplied all the stone and lime for that rest house you're in," he observed. "Those Englishmen, they trusted him with the job; those forest officers depended on him."

Kalbali Khan grew up learning his father's trade, returning to it after serving as a British officer's orderly in the military campaign in Mesopotamia during the First World War. Then came the Second World War, and he joined the Indian troops sent to fight against the Japanese army in Burma and Malaya. In the postwar period and following his father's death, he began working as a small-scale timber contractor, gradually building up his modest business over twenty-five years. He married late in life, and his wife, over the years, had borne two sons and two daughters.

Kalbali Khan lived by certain values which, he said, adhered to the principles and spirit of Islam. He did not attempt to expand his business by lending money to others for profit; he had, instead, invested a fair sum of his savings in a timber wholesaling business set up in Dehra Dun by a friend and fellow contractor. The arrangement worked well because Kalbali Khan could, if necessary, obtain additional funds from his friend to compete in Forest Department auctions, and was assured a fair price and a reliable means for selling his timber in the market.

Then, one day, all his savings and investments disappeared. The state government, in response to the demands made by Chipko's leaders, had abolished the system based on forest contractors and replaced it with a newly created agency called the UP Forest Development Corporation. The new state agency was to conduct all felling operations in areas demarcated by the Forest Department and function as the wholesale supplier for timber and other commercially valuable forest products. Kalbali Khan's friend, also faced with imminent ruin, responded in panic by closing down his business, taking all the money he had access to, and using it to finance his household's passage to join his sister's family in the United States. They were, perhaps, doing well in that country.

Several senior officers and conservators in the Forest Department, who knew Kalbali Khan, had offered help, perhaps in memory of the days when they had first encountered him, in the early years of their careers as forest officers in the Chakrata Forest Division. (Many foresters told me stories of how he would appear at their door, look them straight in the eye, and tell them how to do their job, before promptly disappearing without waiting for a reply.) The Divisional Forest Officer of Chakrata had offered him employment as a forest guard at the tollgate on the northern edge of the town. Kalbali Khan had turned down the offer.

"Thank you," he'd said to him, "but I don't want government charity. I've made an honest living all these years, and by Allah's Grace, I'll continue to do so by myself."

His sons, daughters, and wife moved down to live and work in Vikasnagar, a small town to the west of Dehra Dun in the Himalayan foothills, but he didn't join them there. He said he didn't like the sort of life people led in the plains. He stayed on in his mountain village of Bhatta, 5 miles north of Junglat Chowki, the small Forest

Department complex near the forest tollgate, but visited his family regularly. Fifteen years later, still proud and erect, Kalbali Khan collected firewood from the Reserved forest every day and sold it in the market at Chakrata. It wasn't much money, he told me, but he didn't need much; he didn't want for anything. He'd had it all in his life.

Khan *Saheb*'s views on Chipko were succinct. "Neither here nor there. No benefit for the people, nothing for the Forest Department, no good for the forests, no development in the area. Just a bundle of laws around our necks."

As I listened to him, I remembered the contents of the pamphlet I'd shown Balbir Singh during my last trip to Chakrata. It had drawn the reader's attention to the injustices faced by people in the region:

> They have laws to save the environment, and what has that done? Powerful leaders of the area have created a timber mafia. A poor villager cannot even cut a tree on his own land without being harassed by the government, but who is there to control these thieves? In the name of saving the environment, these laws have put an end to development in our districts. Take control, brothers and sisters! Don't let these laws prevent development in your village!

CHIPKO: PEASANT REVOLT, NEW SOCIAL MOVEMENT, OR POSTCOLONIAL INDIAN POLITICS?

Social movements invariably arouse curiosity among observers: Why do they emerge when they do? Who is involved? What are their aims? Do they succeed? – these are the sorts of questions that from time to time and for a variety of motivations engage the interest of social scientists, historians, politicians, and bureaucrats.[1] Rural insurgencies, peasant revolts, agrarian struggles, and farmers' movements in various parts of the world have been so named by scholars seeking to understand their motivations and potential for effecting revolutionary social change.[2] These rural movements have been variably interpreted as class-based responses to political repression and structures of economic exploitation (such as feudalism, colonialism, capitalism), or to the erosion of existing privileges or the violation of moral beliefs or codes of conduct, or as resistance to religious domination.[3]

Most interpretations of social movements, urban or rural, successful or not, hinge on how the identity of the participants is characterised in the historical and political contexts of their emergence. For instance, in the scholarly debates that occurred during the 1970s and 1980s around questions of peasant revolution and resistance, the main focus of analysis was on the nature of the particular social classes in rural areas that were the principal agents of struggles for transforming economic relations and political conditions.[4] From Eric Wolf's perspective, 'middle-peasants' participated in revolts during particular moments of economic stress, social dislocation, and ensuing political crisis to resist marginalisation on all these fronts.[5] For James Scott, the peasantry – mainly precapitalist cultivators of smallholdings, sharecroppers, and tenants – rose up in revolt against their landlords and the state when the moral economy structured by patron–client relationships and mutual cooperation was severely threatened.[6] In his view, lack of mass protest did not imply that the peasantry was unaffected by change, but rather that their opposition to authority was expressed through diffused acts of "everyday forms of peasant resistance".[7] For Samuel Popkin, the segment of rural society that was severely exploited and had nothing to lose – wage labourers in capitalist or plantation agriculture – were most likely to revolt.[8] Or, as in Jeffrey Paige's view, agrarian revolutions depended not only on the characteristics and situations of the lower, cultivating classes, but equally on the extent to which the upper, non-cultivating classes were dependent on incomes from land.[9]

But what of those social movements that do not appear to centre on improving conditions of labour or altering existing relations of production? Some scholars have argued that there has been a qualitative shift in the nature of social movements with the advent of postindustrial society in the wealthier regions of the world. New social movements (called NSMs), in their view, involve mobilisation of interest groups around singular issues such as consumer rights, gender inequality, cultural identity, nuclear disarmament, or concern for the environment. Unlike older social movements, these do not attempt to seize state power but rather use a variety of tactics to achieve their particular purpose.[10] Whether or not this shift indicates the withering away of labour issues or disinterestedness in gaining an advantage over state policy-making and agenda-setting in rich countries continues to be a matter for debate.[11]

Poorer countries have also seen a remarkable rise in movements relating to gender, ethnic, and environmental issues. The literature on 'subaltern' agency asserts that marginalised and oppressed groups such as indigenous peoples, lower castes, and women in India have resisted structures of exploitation not on the basis of class solidarity, but rather through alternative expressions of nationalism, community, moral consciousness, and faith.[12] Ramachandra Guha, for instance, describes Chipko from this perspective, invoking the moral economy thesis to argue that Himalayan peasants aimed to reassert traditional community control over forests against commercial exploitation.[13] Vandana Shiva employs an ecofeminist perspective to assert that rural women in India and other parts of the Third World have persistently engaged in struggles to recover the feminine principle of nature that emphasises nurture rather than economic exploitation.[14] But such interpretations of contemporary social movements in India have, of course, not gone uncontested.[15] Tom Brass has, perhaps most virulently, argued against these perspectives, stating that new social movements in India – such as the farmers' and environmental movements – are predominantly neopopulist and middle-class in nature, seeking to maintain structures of power and privilege to their advantage rather than transforming them to benefit oppressed groups.[16] Gail Omvedt argues somewhat differently, noting that the shift away from traditional class-based movements towards those of women, lower castes, indigenous groups, and farmers in India is best understood as a process of redefining those spheres of exploitation (mainly economic) that have not been addressed by conventional Marxist analysis.[17]

All these discussions, particularly those that focus on rural struggles in rich and poor countries, have been remarkably useful in providing a richer understanding of the diversity of social movements, the conditions and contexts that contribute to their rise, and their success or failure in achieving their aims. But as is apparent in the case of every well-known social movement, the congruence between a movement's identity and the identities of its participants remains a subject of heated debate among those who study them. At first glance, these disagreements may appear to stem from differences in analytical approaches or from differences in political ideology. Indeed, they often do. I think, however, that the arguments also reflect the inherently ambiguous and malleable relationship between identities, roles, and discursive strategies.

Identity is a term that signifies the quality or condition of sameness, oneness in composition, attributes, properties, nature, substance; it implies perfect or absolute congruence. *Role* is a term used to refer to any particular set of actions performed by a person in the context of his or her sphere of life. A person within a particular social context may simultaneously perform several roles, that of mother, wife, churchgoer, gardener, waitress, weaver, and so on. Identity formation of social actors, as Manuel Castells notes, is the process through which construction of meaning occurs "on the basis of a cultural attribute, or related set of cultural attributes, that is/are given priority over other sources of meaning".[18] In other words, the construction of social identity occurs through narratives that seek to emphasise its congruency with particular attributes or roles more than others. These narratives may be self-representations, produced by others, or imposed by institutions.[19] They qualify the relationship between identity and role in particular ways to symbolise perfect congruence or, in other situations, inconsistency. A particular function chosen from the entire set of roles performed by a person can be used to establish a formal identity (form follows function); it can be seen as congruent with role (form is function); or the relationship between formal identity and the selected role can be shown as inconsistent, incongruent, or contradictory (form problematises function). In every case, the attempt to establish congruency or inconsistency between identity and role occurs through narrative or *discursive strategies*. Discursive strategies are the central means by which social movements gain particular identities. They attempt to mobilise large numbers of people who perform a variety of roles through narratives that self-consciously associate them with a particular role, thereby creating a common identity for the social movement and its partici-pants.[20] Discursive strategies combine the languages of 'legitimate' institutional action with popular rhetoric and prevailing political discourse to engage in what Antonio Gramsci would have called a 'war of position'.[21]

Chipko's participants were persons who, in the course of everyday life, performed a variety of roles within their localities and were involved to varying degrees in larger political and institutional networks. Its leading activists were part of the village elite, the *gaon ké néta* of Indian political life whom Subrata Mitra describes as

> political actors, situated at the interface of the modern state and traditional society. They use the double language of state and society, of modernity and tradition, and of individual rationality and group solidarity. They are engaged in a two-way interpretation of norms and political demands. Their methods range between acting as brokers in national, regional and local elections, lobbying and contacting the bureaucracy and higher political elites for the allocation of material resources, seeking to bolster their demands through rhetoric and occasional spells of radical protest. Their 'room for manoeuvre' is created when bureaucrats, political decision-makers, and the law of the land accept the legitimacy of multiple modes of participation from below.[22]

Chipko rose to fame through the discursive strategies employed by members of rural elites such as Sunderlal Bahuguna and Chandi Prasad Bhatt who combined the Indian government's vocabulary and rhetoric – national integrity, security, defence, development, and democracy – with symbolic acts of popular protest.[23] They gained the support of sympathisers outside their localities by drawing atten-tion to simple, yet highly dramatised, populist narratives and the actions of humble peasants pitted against both state and market.

The principal aims of Chipko centred on regaining access to small-scale extraction from forests and pressuring the state government into providing financial and developmental assistance to communities in the region. The protestors were a heterogenous group, belonging to diverse political affiliations that, in some cases, represented conflicting goals. Some demanded the abolition of large-scale extraction by non-local forest contractors; others argued that forest contractors needed to hire locally organised labour cooperatives for timber felling. Village leaders and student activists affiliated with the Communist Party of India, for example, demanded higher wages for forest labourers and a total ban on export of unprocessed raw material from the region. Gandhian organisations demanded concessions and a government-subsidised supply of forest resources for promoting locally based cottage industries. Small-scale forest contractors called on the Forest Department to privilege local entrepreneurs and forest-labour cooperatives by regulating external competition.[24]

Negotiations with the Forest Department did not realise any of these demands. Forest officers defended their stance by stating that they did not have the powers to make such policy decisions, and that they were bound to comply with the production targets established by national- and state-level plans. Demands for keeping out non-local forest contractors were similarly turned down by the Department, which argued that restricting competition would result in monopolies and in inefficient production methods, and increase the price of raw materials for industry.[25]

The impasse led Chipko activists to seek the support of alternative audiences for their cause. They resolved to bypass the UP state administration and its agencies by directing their appeals to the national government. In 1975, Sunderlal Bahuguna, a small-scale forest contractor in Tehri Garhwal, emerged as a spokesman for the movement when he urged the national government to intervene to defend the Himalayas from further ecological degradation and erosion of security.[26]

Articulating his appeal in both popular idiom and government rhetoric, Bahuguna argued that national security and defence along the Himalayan borders of India hinged on the well-being of its ecology and resident communities. Chipko, he asserted, was the groundswell of popular outrage against the relentless forces of commerce that were denuding the region of its forests. Himalayan peasants, he said, depended on forests to meet their simple subsistence needs, but could no longer survive because non-local timber contractors were cutting them down for private profit; these contractors neither respected the sacred mountains, nor displayed any concern for the nation's security. Floods, poverty, out-migration, the every-day struggles of women in the hills seeking to collect fuelwood and fodder for household subsistence were all the inevitable consequence of reckless timber extraction by non-local forest contractors. His dramatic narrative cast the region's communities as victims of a distant and apathetic state administration, and, above all, avaricious forest contractors.[27]

Bahuguna's skilled use of government and populist rhetoric appeared to work. Politicians in New Delhi lauded the movement as the moral conscience of the nation, and urged the government to immediate action in the nation's interest. The sympathetic response from national-level politicians gained wider media coverage for Bahuguna and the movement, which in turn spawned support from environmental scholars and activists in other parts of the country. He was feted as the leader of the Chipko movement, the ecological Gandhi, the voice of the grassroots that cried out for protection of the simple, peasant ways of life so as to restore the harmony between humans and nature in the Himalayas. Chipko was hailed as the response of Indian civilisation to the ecological crisis in the Himal-ayas. Environmentalists from India and abroad visited Bahuguna and praised Chipko, claiming that the ideals it inspired across the world were far more important than the aims it had initially set out to achieve.[28] Following its rise to fame Chipko achieved hallowed status with several pieces of legislation aimed at forest protection in the Himalayas.

FELICITOUS COINCIDENCES AND LEGISLATIVE VICTORIES

The celebration of Chipko as exemplar of grassroots environmental-ism in India diverted attention from the various pressures bringing about the national government's apparent capitulation to the move-ment's demands. As the story of Chipko and its brave foot-soldiers rapidly commuted around the globe, it seemed unnecessary to delve into contextual details or to draw attention to the fact that Bahu-guna's virulent criticism of non-local forest contractors fortuitously coincided with an unprecedented period of nationalisation in India.[29]

Nationalisation began after an internal power struggle led to a division in the Indian National Congress in 1969. Indira Gandhi assumed leadership of the newly formed Congress (I) (Indira) with the support of party members representing the interests of two dominant classes, the administrative (government employees) and the rural elites. She sought reelection as Prime Minister on a popul-ist platform – encapsulated in the famous Hindi slogan, *Garibi Hatao!* (Remove Poverty!) – that promised a government that would work towards full employment and development of all regions in the country. Continuing problems of interregional disparities and lack of expansion in industrial employment provided her with ample ammunition and the rhetoric to challenge the power of the indus-trial elites.[30] Mrs Gandhi allied herself with the masses by calling for extensive state intervention in various sectors of the economy, arguing that her government, as opposed to the narrow self-nterested motives of private enterprise, would be more socially responsible in serving the public interest.[31] Her party emerged vic-torious in the parliamentary elections of 1971 which followed soon after India's successful war against Pakistan and the creation of Bangladesh.[32]

By the mid-1970s, the national government, under Mrs Gandhi's leadership, had intervened in both the sphere of circulation, that is to say, banking, credit, insurance, transport, distribution, and foreign trade, and the sphere of industrial production by directly controlling the manufacture of most basic and capital goods.[33] By the 'eighties, both national and state governments

> owned more than 60 percent of all productive capital in the industrial sector, directly employing two-thirds of all workers in the organised sector, held more than 25 percent of the paid-up capital of joint-stock companies in the private sector through nationalised financial insti-tutions, and regulated the patterns of private investment down to industrial product level and choice of technology extending to scale, location, and import content.[34]

Chipko's criticism of commercial timber extraction by non-local forest contractors emerged within this broad climate of political boosterism for nationalisation and state intervention in all economic sectors. Bahuguna's appeals were received favourably by Mrs Gandhi because they appeared to provide additional support and popular endorsement for her political and economic agenda.[35] She urged state governments to listen to Chipko's criticism of forest contractors and respond to the recommendations of the National Commission on Agriculture, which advocated extensive afforestation on public and private lands, and creation of public-sector firms to replace private businesses engaged in forest extraction.[36]

The Congress (I) government in Uttar Pradesh responded to Mrs Gandhi's exhortations by legislating the UP Forest Corporation Act 1975. The Act authorised the creation of a state-owned corporation which was to function independently of the state's Forest Department for the efficient production and stabilisation of market prices of timber and other forest commodities. The corporation was also expected to employ locally organised, forest-labour cooperatives for carrying out its extractive operations.[37]

The following years continued to prove auspicious for Chipko-inspired forest legislation. The UP Tree Protection Act 1976 prevented felling of "protected" tree species (mainly those that were commercially valuable) on private lands.[38] Environmental scholars and activists argued that nearly 4.3 million hectares of forest areas in different parts of the country had been indiscriminately destroyed by state governments in the name of industrial and infrastructure development.[39] The Indian Parliament responded in 1976 with a constitutional amendment that required states to seek the national government's approval before embarking on any development project involving large-scale conversion of forests to other land uses.[40] Four years later, a new national Ministry of Environment and Forests (MoEF) was created alongside the passage of the Forest Conservation Act. The new Act defined the required procedures and conditions for state governments wanting to obtain permission from the ministry to convert designated forest areas to non-forest uses.[41] In 1980, the national government also imposed a fifteen-year ban on the felling of green timber above 1,000 metres in the Himalayas.[42] The 1988 amendment to the Forest Conservation Act deemed it illegal for any individual or corporate institution to engage in afforestation projects on state-owned lands without permission from the Ministry of Environment and Forests.[43]

UNWRAPPING CHIPKO'S LEGACIES

Chipko's growing fame as an environmental movement and its related legislative victories produced a number of contradictory and unforeseen outcomes, most of which corresponded with Khan *Saheb's* analysis of events following its victorious debut in 1975. By the time the UP Forest Corporation began its extractive operations in Garhwal and Kumaon (in 1980), the ban on green-felling above 1,000 metres had taken effect. Most forest-labour cooperatives in higher elevations were either disbanded or rendered ineffective. Cooperatives operating in lower altitudes were divided by political rivalries and disagreements over employment opportunities and conditions offered by the Corporation. It reverted to earlier systems of contracting labour through 'mates' (labour agents) who brought groups of skilled and unskilled workers from neighbouring regions such as Himachal Pradesh and western Nepal,[44] justifying its choice in terms of the skill, reliability, and industriousness of Nepalese labourers.[45]

The ban also increased the Corporation's operating expenditures because labour and transport costs for felling damaged trees randomly distributed across high-altitude areas exceeded the price that could be obtained for such timber in wholesale auctions. The Corporation often abandoned timber at felling sites for several years to save on costs of transportation but penalised local households if they attempted to claim it for their use.[46] The greatest irony is that, despite monopolising timber extraction and wholesale trade, the Forest Corporation has been plagued, as have other public-sector firms, by the rising costs of supporting an expanded bureaucracy and financial loss in most of its operations.[47]

Chipko's legislative victories have eroded the state Forest Depart-

ment's administrative control and its revenue-earning capacity in the
region. The Department no longer has discretionary powers to settle
local disputes over forest access or allocate use of classified forest areas
for small-scale infrastructure and development projects proposed by
village- or block-level institutions. Its revenues have grown relatively
slowly because they are now based solely on fixed royalties (periodi-
cally adjusted for inflation) paid by the Forest Corporation rather
than on market prices obtained through the auction of felling tracts.
Thus, although the Forest Department's revenues showed an average
rate of increase of about 13 percent per year between 1980 and 1990,
its administrative costs and operating expenditures on forest conservation and management rose at an annual average rate of about 18
percent during the same period.[48] The commercial value of timber
stock in Reserved forests at higher altitudes has diminished because
the ban on green-felling does not allow the Department to carry out
routine maintenance activities such as lopping, thinning, and clearing
which are necessary for enhancing the quality of timber and distribution of vegetation. The ban has also contributed to the emergence
of a "timber mafia" in Garhwal, many of whose members are
reported to be small-scale forest contractors with businesses that have
suffered under the legislation. Budgetary constraints have prevented
the Forest Department from responding to illegal felling and theft
from Reserved forests;[49] it has been unable to increase its patrolling
force or provide adequate safeguards to forest rangers and guards at
tollgates to prevent armed "mafia-men" from smuggling truckloads
of timber to markets in the plains.[50] Even with a partial relaxation of
the felling ban since 1995, the Forest Department remains financially
constrained because its revenues from extraction cannot meet the
growing costs of conservation, afforestation, and effective
regulation.[51]

Social tensions have been compounded by the fact that the timber
mafia controls a rapidly diversifying portfolio of illegal activities
which includes the production and sale of locally brewed liquor in
the hill districts. Several women's groups have been unsuccessful in
demanding prohibition of brewing and sale of liquor. The foremost,
yet understated, irritation for many is that this activity is carried out

largely by migrant labourers from western Nepal whose incomes from mafia-related employment are increasing in relation to those of local communities.[52]

Chipko's rise to symbolic and celebrity status through the 'eighties was paralleled by growing resentment among local communities over the lack of development in Garhwal and Kumaon. Village leaders argued that infrastructure development projects, such as road-building and rural electrification, had been paralysed because nearly two-thirds of the total land area in the region was classified under some forest category, and projects therefore required approval from the Ministry of Environment and Forests. They accused the ministry of speedily approving large-scale projects such as dams and hydroe-lectric power plants supported by powerful coalitions and lobbies in state governments, but ignoring small-scale development projects that did not carry a similar political clout.[53] They pointed to numerous examples of projects that had been held up or abandoned because of bureaucratic apathy: a feeder road connecting a few villages that remained unbuilt because 1 kilometre of its length passed through a Reserved forest; a minor irrigation channel through another Reserved forest that lay unfinished because the ministry had not yet processed an application submitted nine years earlier; rural electrifi-cation projects that had been abandoned because the ministry did not approve the clearing of forest areas along transmission lines.[54] Women living in villages near the Nanda Devi Biosphere Reserve (established in 1990) criticised the ministry for having further deprived them of access to areas where they previously collected medicinal herbs and other commercially valuable forest products.[55]

By the late 'eighties, regional political groups such as the Uttarak-hand Kránti Dal (Uttarakhand Revolutionary Group) began publicly exhorting communities to start a movement aimed at cutting down trees in defiance of forest laws. They declared their willingness to clear-cut areas on behalf of any community or village wishing to initiate development projects,[56] arguing that such acts were the only means by which the eight Himalayan districts of Uttar Pradesh could force the state and national governments to accede to their demand for a separate state of Uttarakhand.

THE RISE OF UTTARAKHAND

The demand for regional autonomy, apart from Uttar Pradesh, was not a new political cause. In 1952, Mr P.C. Joshi, a member of the Communist Party of India and a leading politician in Kumaon, had submitted an appeal to Prime Minister Nehru requesting the creation of a separate state of Uttarakhand. Nehru himself was against the division of Uttar Pradesh, but forwarded the memorandum to the States Reorganisation Commission which later rejected Joshi's appeal.[57] Administrative autonomy for the hill districts of Uttar Pradesh were discussed in conferences in 1966 and 1967, and a public demonstration was staged in New Delhi in 1968. The Uttarakhand Kránti Dal was formed in 1979, and its representatives met with Indira Gandhi to state their demands for a separate "hill state" of Uttarakhand.[58] While the demand was not rejected outrightly, further discussions of the subject were indefinitely postponed by the Congress (I) government in Uttar Pradesh. The issue was carefully avoided by H.N. Bahuguna and N.D. Tiwari, both of whom were elected representatives of Congress (I) from Garhwal and Kumaon and had served as cabinet ministers at the state (both had also been Chief Ministers of UP) and national levels in the 1970s and early 1980s.

The sole concession made by the UP government during the mid-1980s was to create a new state agency called the Hill Development Agency (Parvatiya Vikas Nigam, functioning through two subsidiary agencies, the Garhwal Mandal Vikas Nigam and the Kumaon Mandal Vikas Nigam) which was to be responsible for planning and providing financial assistance for regional development. The agency's efforts have centred on the promotion of horticulture and tourism through investment subsidies, price supports, and incentives. It has not, however, attempted to invest in infrastructure expansion or the creation of new institutional or marketing networks in the region. Consequently, its subsidies and price support for orchard and vegetable production have been rendered meaningless. Poor road networks and procurement planning have made it difficult for households lacking access to markets or private means of transportation to benefit from horticultural production. Such households have suffered severe financial losses from being forced to sell their highly perishable harvests at throwaway prices to local traders and merchants because they were unable to afford the costs of transporting produce to regional markets.[59]

The agency's initiatives in tourism promotion have also been limited to a few cities in the lower elevations. This is the result, in part, of poorly developed road and electricity supply networks, and in part of environmental legislation and regulations which limit conversion of forest areas for non-forest uses. Since these laws do not apply to municipal and urban localities, in areas falling within the expanded boundaries of the Mussoorie–Dehra Dun Urban Development Authority, Nainital, Almora, and existing transportation corridors between these towns and cities, tourist hotels have mushroomed.[60] But, in most cases, the economic incentives, subsidies, and low-interest finance offered by the Hill Development Agency for tourism have been exploited by wealthy businessmen and entrepreneurs from within and outside Garhwal and Kumaon for land speculation in these towns and cities, or for building large vacation homes euphemistically named "hotels". Between 1990 and 1991, real-estate prices for residential land in the Mussoorie–Dehra Dun Urban Development area doubled, while land zoned for commercial use increased its value by about 80 percent. Land prices in these cities have continuously risen, albeit at a slower rate (in Dehra Dun–Mussoorie, residential land prices in 1997 were approximately three times 1991 prices), making it extremely difficult for poorer urban households to find affordable housing or commercial space for setting up small businesses.[61]

Regional political groups and elected village and block representatives point to these trends as typical examples of how development in Uttarakhand has suffered from both bureaucratic apathy and the "plains" mentality of administrators who, they claim, are ignorant about the region, display superficial understanding of its economy and society, and lack a genuine commitment to solving the problems faced by local communities.[62] They repeatedly use these arguments in their rallies and protests against the UP government, and in negotiations with national political parties and the Indian government to gain support for their demands for statehood.

The simple reason for the reluctance to grant statehood to Uttarakhand is rooted in the electoral arithmetic of Indian politics. For most national political parties, the attraction of ruling UP, one of India's most populous states (sending the largest numbers of elected representatives to the nation's Parliament), outweighs all other concerns. Arguments for dividing Uttar Pradesh into two, three, or four states for purposes of administrative efficiency or effective regional development pale in comparison with the prospect of benefiting from the votes of a massive, consolidated electorate.[63] Ruling political parties at both national and state level have, therefore, routinely played on local sentiments, expressing solidarity with the idea of Uttarakhand during parliamentary or state elections, but ignored the issue soon after assuming office. Between 1985 and 1997, almost all national political parties supported the idea by including the creation of Uttarakhand in their manifestos, but only two ever went beyond passing resolutions in its favour. The Hindu fundamentalist party, BJP (Bharatiya Janata Party), supported demands for a separate hill state during the 1991 and 1993 elections in UP, but did little more than change the name of the Hill Development Department to the Uttaranchal Development Department when it assumed control of the state legislature.[64]

In 1993, a coalition government in UP formed by SP–BSP (the Samajwadi Party represents the interests of "kulak" farmers belonging to the official category of 'Other Backward' castes; the Bahujan Samaj Party represents those groups categorised as "Scheduled" castes, which means 'untouchable' castes; both parties have their main support base in the Indo-Gangetic plains of Uttar Pradesh and Bihar) supported the creation of Uttarakhand and commissioned two reports which examined some of the details and practicalities of statehood for the region. But the coalition government proceeded to alienate itself from regional political groups and alliances when it proposed a 27 percent increase in the number of government jobs reserved for "Other Backward" castes across UP. Local leaders and political groups in Garhwal and Kumaon argued that only 2.5 percent of the population in Uttarakhand fell within the category of "Other Backward" castes and asserted that this was a ploy by the coalition government to further diminish employment opportunities for hill communities.[65] In 1994, as Uttarakhand activists travelled to New Delhi in large numbers to reiterate their demand for statehood, the UP Provincial Armed Constabulary (PAC) was ordered by the coalition government to intimidate them. Several men were killed when the police fired into the crowd and charged at demonstrators; many women were molested and even raped.

The coalition government justified its action by arguing that the Uttarakhand movement was less a grouping in favour of statehood than a front for upper castes that were determined, through violence and other means, to prevent oppressed castes achieving social equality in Indian society. National political parties attempting to uphold their secular identity against the BJP's overt Hindu fundamentalist and upper-caste stance were cautiously silent when the coalition government in UP repeatedly chose to characterise the Uttarakhand agitation of 1994 as "anti-Backward caste", "anti-reservation", and against social upliftment of oppressed groups.[66]

The struggle for statehood continues. Each cycle of appeals, promises, protests, inconclusive negotiations, and reversal of fortunes has only increased support for the Uttarakhand movement among diverse groups within the region. But as protests routinely erupt and subside without achieving much success, new militant voices from local communities and student organisations have emerged to accuse the movement and regional political parties of incompetence and an inability to force the national and state governments to accede to their demands. Their views are expressed through graffiti on public buildings and banners which announce, in Hindi, "Today, we ask for Uttarakhand with affection; Tomorrow, we'll demand it with guns!" Rumours of young men raiding remote police outposts for rifles and ammunition trickle into the towns; government buildings have been torched and vandalised. There is, in the words of a national newspaper, a regional social movement that is "slowly but surely taking on the dimensions of a bloody stir".[67]

POSSIBLE ALTERNATIVES

The Uttarakhand movement, unlike Chipko, has gained widespread support from diverse caste, class, ethnic, and religious groups within the region. Yet the leaders of the Uttarakhand movement have faced hostility from ruling coalitions at the state level when they have used the discourse of devolution of power and effective governance to argue their cause. Although the movement's leaders have consciously avoided using the vocabulary of national defence and criticised the global rhetoric of environmental protection, they have been unable to make persuasive use of other 'global' discursive strategies – cultural identity, economic development, administrative efficiency, and social justice – to articulate their demands for regional autonomy. It appears that the travails of the Uttarakhand movement are due to the fact that its concerns about regional economic development have not yet found a sympathetic audience outside the sphere of party politics.

The question of regionally relevant development might be approached by forging new forms of institutional collaboration between administrative agencies and the region's communities. Forestry remains the dominant economic sector in Garhwal and Kumaon, and it is this sector that requires fundamental reform, with a reworking of relationships with other sectors of the regional economy. Current pressures for reform of state agencies offer possibilities for alternative forms of collaborative resource management between regional agencies and local communities that can create opportunities for employment in resource-based extraction and manufacturing.[68] This approach would require a state agency such as the Forest Department – whose management practices have, until recently, been actively influenced by the region's communities – to regain some of the administrative powers that have been appropriated by the national Ministry of Environment and Forests.[69]

One does not need to look outside India to find examples of such alternative approaches to improving access to regional resources for marginalised and disadvantaged groups and creating the possibility of broad-based regional development. The process of Joint Forest Management in the Indian state of West Bengal was initiated as part of a regional reform agenda by a Left-Front Coalition government that was voted into office nearly two decades ago. The Left-Front Coalition came to power in 1977 following a period of violent struggles and protracted guerilla warfare waged by socially disadvantaged groups and indigenous communities against landlords and merchants in rural areas of the state.[70]

The Coalition government approached the question of agrarian reform in ways that would not have been prescribed by any Marxist text at the time. Rather than engaging in forced redistribution of land, the government undertook a systematic enumeration of sharecropping and landless households and used the registration as the basis for extending access to credit and capital inputs for cultivation. It sought to strengthen local levels of governance and accorded village and district councils increased powers of decision-making for rural development. It fostered reforms in the forestry sector by encouraging the state's Forest Department to collaborate on projects with village communities.[71]

The collaborative forestry projects came to be known as Joint Forest Management (JFM). Beginning with financial incentives for tree protection, the experiments expanded to include joint decisions regarding the choice of tree species, and their plantation and maintenance. These initiatives were later extended to include sharing by the Forest Department and village councils of net profits from sales of forest products. Between 1980 and 1986, the Left-Front government reemphasised the importance of ensuring equitable access to forest resources. It created a statutory body called the Forest and Land Protection Society and issued directives that safeguarded the rights of socially disadvantaged groups and indigenous communities (classified by the Indian Constitution as Scheduled Castes and Scheduled Tribes), and expanded their role in JFM committees. The JFM committees were required to identify economically disadvantaged households within these populations and include them as member beneficiaries. The state-sponsored West Bengal Tribal Cooperative became the intermediary institution for marketing forest products traditionally harvested by indigenous communities, sharing 25 percent of net profits with its members. The share of net profits accruing to JFM committees was renegotiated with the Forest Department and increased from 25 to 50 percent in new forest plantations.[72]

In sum, the West Bengal Forest Department and local communities have collaborated to find ways of expanding access to forest resources for disadvantaged social groups, improving forest quality and management systems, and negotiating the shares of net income earned from harvesting resources produced through their shared efforts. JFM is a process that directly involves the state forestry agency and forest-dependent communities without always requiring the mediating presence of 'external' non-governmental organisations. JFM committees comprise regional and local forest officers, elected village representatives affiliated with regional and national political parties, representatives of economically and socially disadvantaged groups, and members of local non-political voluntary institutions, as well as individual households which hold membership in forest protection committees. They are responsible to each other, their cultural affiliations, political constituencies, and state institutions at all levels.[73]

The Left-Front government's approach to agrarian and forestry reform has, over the past twenty years, contributed to modest, yet sustained, increases in agricultural productivity and incomes of landless cultivators in West Bengal.[74] It has steadily expanded access to forest resources for local populations without resulting in resource degradation. The JFM process has, of course, run into many routine and unavoidable problems that are part of any endeavour involving diverse actors within civil society. It encounters new problems with distribution and unforeseen conflicts arising from the multiple political affiliations and social identities of its members. It appears to work well in some areas of the state but not in others.[75] Despite these mixed outcomes, JFM continues to function as a pragmatic approach that promotes direct interactions between diverse institutions of government and regional civil society for negotiating members' needs and demands in relation to changing political configurations and broader economic conditions.

The point I want to emphasise is that JFM is part of a larger institutional process initiated by an elected state government that translated its commitment to substantive democracy by expanding access to resources for regional development. The approach was developed within the context of existing frameworks of national and state administration and political processes in India. A similar strategy could, indeed, form the first step of a broad-based regional development strategy for Garhwal and Kumaon. But such possibilities have been overwhelmed by the current preoccupation with achieving statehood for Uttarakhand.

The question of regional development in Uttarakhand, however, requires a great deal more than the achievement of statehood. Whatever the political outcome, the region's future will continue to be shaped by broader national economic policies as well as the geopolitical concerns of the Indian government. The current processes of economic liberalisation and structural reform have yielded mixed results, but ongoing patterns of foreign-direct and national investment show little indication of extending into Garhwal and Kumaon. Improved diplomatic relations with its neighbours in the Himalayas, mainly China and Pakistan, could offer new economic opportunities for households and communities in the region.[76] But recent military conflicts with Pakistan and belligerent jingoism on the part of national political parties like the BJP has again ensured that the prospects for regional development in this part of the Indian Himalayas may continue to languish in the years to come.

EIGHT

REGIONAL QUESTIONS AND SUSTAINABLE DEVELOPMENT

It was a hot day, and I faced a long, steep climb of about 10 miles from the road to the village. Benson, the taxi driver, had dropped me off at a tea shack near the road. I was lucky to find a pack-horse owner there who'd agreed on a sum of money to carry my luggage and food supplies to the Forest Rest House above the village. He walked up the slope with ease and was soon far ahead, his sporadic calls to his horse becoming fainter in the distance.

I gave up trying to keep pace after spotting a welcoming patch of shade near a stream. I gulped down the cold water and lay back to rest. As I morosely contemplated the rest of my journey Kamla appeared with a bundle of wood on her back.

"Back again," she observed, setting it down. She scooped some water into her palms, drinking and splashing her face.

"Yes," I answered. Kamla sat staring at the water, absent-minded, snapping a twig.

"I haven't heard from him in four months," she said.

"Your husband?"

She nodded. "Yes, it's him I'm talking about."

My stomach churned in a moment of fear as I remembered a story I'd heard a month or so before, of a Garhwali man's body that had been found abandoned in the outskirts of Delhi. I shook the thought out of my head.

"He should have come back to help with the harvest. He should have come back two months ago with some money. Nothing. I don't know where he is."

"He'll probably come back soon." I tried to sound confident. "He must have been held up by his employers. You know how they are in Delhi. Those rich families. They want their servants to work all the time and never leave the house."

"I have some money to pay for the bus ticket to Delhi," she mused, "but then where do I go to find him? I don't know where his employers live. I can't leave my mother-in law either. She's old and worried sick about him. I'd take my son along with me, but she'll say no, leave him here, I'll look after the child. I can't just leave and go away like that, you know, not like you or him."

I stared at the stream, my thoughts scrambling for some reassuring words that would melt away her worries. She plucked a blade of grass and shredded it to bits.

"I didn't want him to go away," she continued with a faint tremor in her voice. "I told him, listen, that city, it chews up people like us alive, don't go! But he said" – and she paused for a moment – "he said, no, Kamla, I can't stay. My heart is heavy because there's nothing here. No work, no money. Our son must grow up better, with education, a proper job. And so he went a year ago."

"He came back once, didn't he?"

She nodded. "But he hasn't since. No message, no news for four months. I don't know what to do."

Kamla's predicament is not unique. There are any number of households within the Uttarakhand Himalayas and other rural regions in India that have similar stories to tell. Even the most cursory survey of ongoing struggles in the Indian subcontinent – whether they be called ecological, ethnic, caste-based, or separatist movements[1] – would reveal that they are occurring largely in those geographical regions that are regarded as 'economically backward', where households and communities are marginalised by lack of access to resources and opportunities for their social well-being. It makes little sense, in such contexts, to quibble over whether the struggles emerging from these regions are about environmental protection, cultural identity, economic development, or popular democracy. They are not about any one thing. The struggles are part of a 'regional question', produced from the interaction of all these dimensions of social practice.

Social movements are, in effect, *regions in protest*, emerging from particular geographical histories of social practices. But most scholars, policy-makers, and activists do not view social protests as such, because the idea of regions having agency seems utterly absurd. For them, regions are geographical structures, spatial settings containing a fixed set of physical features and population attributes. Geography is seen to be static, but social history is dynamic; regions are spatial settings from which social struggles can emerge, but for these struggles to have agency they need contexts independent of their spatial settings. Hence, from this analytical perspective, social struggle is seen as opposition to other spatially independent agencies – colonialism, modernisation, globalisation – which cause outcomes such as ecological degradation, social inequality, cultural marginalisation, or economic 'backwardness'.

But such an analysis faces a fundamental dilemma when it encounters living geographies instead of mere spatial settings. These *regionalities*, the lived dimensions to social life, are produced and reproduced through social and material practices; they exist in time and space, but can have fluid and permeable boundaries. The analysis that regards geography as inert space hits the ground, quite literally and metaphorically, when it confronts regionality. This startling encounter leads scholars, policy-makers, even activists, to do what they think is conceptually right. They try to solve 'the geographic problem' through simple arithmetic functions, mainly by dividing space according to sets of biophysical or population attributes. Witness the long train of policies and 'solutions' that have responded to 'ethnic' or 'religious' conflicts, environmental degradation, struggles over social inequality, or unequal access to resources. The principal means employed for solving 'the problem' inevitably involves spatial division: creating 'nature reserves'; partitioning space by ethnic or religious categories; establishing exclusive ownership over regional resources; dividing people's identities on the basis of where they were born in space, rather than where and how they make their lives and livelihoods. Divide and rule is, indeed, a social metaphor that constantly makes its presence felt in spatial life. It arises from analytical perspectives that ignore geographical histories and regionalities, but which need to manipulate space to achieve their desired outcomes. These outcomes appear in the form of ghettoes, nature parks, native reservations, apartheid, 'partition', or 'ethnic cleansing'. But they never 'resolve' the 'regional' question.

The point I wish to emphasise is that the different geographies we see around us are relational spaces that people *make*, and *with which* they do various things. These geographies sustain social life, and are sustained by social and material practices. Seen in this way, regions are not just 'spatial settings', but geographical histories that carry both the sense and the sensibility of the lived dimensions of social life. We make distinctions between these lived dimensions by calling them cities, towns, countryside, agglomerations, villages, localities. But the names we give these geographies are unstable and contradictory because the order implied in their naming is constantly disturbed or called into question by shifts and changes in social practices.

A region is best understood as a fluid and permeable dimension of social experience that is produced and reshaped by the practices of everyday life.[2] The interactions between what Braudel has called the habitual rhythms of social and material life, and the diverse fluctuations, or *conjunctures*,[3] of demographic and capital movements and bio-geophysical processes, create regions that become palimpsests upon which overlapping geographical histories are repeatedly inscribed and incompletely erased. Regional landscapes appear as 'structured dispositions' that carry the tension between 'objectification' and 'embodiment',[4] between 'structure' and 'coherence'. Their identities are institutionalised through what Bourdieu calls 'officialising strategies' and 'non-official' customary practices.[5] These processes create shared places that people reshape in familiar ways, and from which they attempt to familiarise, customise, or challenge the changes brought about by conjunctures and events. Regions, in this sense, are overlapping geographical histories of common access that encompass known practices and knowable activities. They become regionalities through the lived dimensions that are sustained and problematised by social practices.[6]

There are four particular interlinked dimensions of social practice, that enable us to understand the geographical histories of regional change and regionality. I have explored each of these dimensions in preceding chapters, and also presented them as comprising the analytical framework for political ecology. But it is worth summarising them again. First, households need to be understood as regional actors, instead of being classified as urban or rural on the basis of their 'official' residence. As the narratives in this book show, households engage in diversified livelihood strategies which are not only confined to particular localities, but carried out within broader institutional and transregional networks of social and material activity. The livelihood strategies of households are shaped by the gender and age composition of their members, and may involve, in varying combinations and degrees, activities that are generally classified as urban and rural, agricultural and non-agricultural, waged and non-waged. Social differentiation of households in these regions is produced from the mix of livelihood strategies pursued, which both influence and change alongside the reconfiguration of regional economies, institutional networks, and transregional interactions.

Second, it is necessary to understand state actions as processes that create and sustain regional differentiation through a wide range of administrative and political practices. The character of the state is ambiguous and depends on how governance occurs at different spatial levels, how the processes of policy-making and governing are shaped by varied economic and political necessities, as well as conjunctures and events occurring within and beyond the administrative reach of state agencies. The actions of different state institutions may appear well coordinated or, at times, intensely contentious; some may tend towards authoritarian control, or conversely, be open to capture, reform, or manipulation by social groups and classes that live both within and outside their jurisdictions.

Third, it is necessary to understand management and use of natural resources not merely as outcomes of legal ownership or property status, but by looking at how various social groups and institutions both within and beyond the region exercise control over a wide array of regional resources. Juridical rights of property are only part of a wide variety of access regimes that shape the ways in which natural resources are used, managed, or traded for profit. State agencies, and market and community institutions, employ differentiated ensembles of instruments and modes of control – or *access regimes* – for controlling extraction, use, maintenance, and sale of natural resources within and across regions. These access regimes and instruments of control are routinely open to contestation and renegotiation.

Finally, it is necessary to focus on the discursive strategies employed in social protests and disputes that emerge within regions. Discursive strategies are political tools used in the process of contestation and negotiation between institutions of state, market, and civil society. They may succeed in transforming particular, localised, disputes into broader social movements by redefining the identities and roles of participants in ways that gain political support for their agendas beyond their immediately known communities. But while discursive strategies may gain the attention and support of wider audiences, they may not always yield the outcomes desired by the people whose interests they claim to represent. The success or failure of any discursive strategy – that is to say, whether or not it succeeds in gaining official recognition or altering existing institutional practices – is contingent upon the malleability of administrative domains, the flexibility of dominant policy approaches espoused by national and provincial governments, and the electoral arithmetic of political parties at both these levels of power.

The 'regional question', then, emerges from the interactions of these four interlinked dimensions of social practice. Seen from this perspective, social movements are, indeed, *regions in protest*, calling attention to crises and problems encountered in sustaining regions and regionality within the context of prevailing administrative and political configurations.

DISCURSIVE STRATEGIES AND MATERIAL OUTCOMES: CHIPKO AND UTTARAKHAND

It becomes fairly clear, when viewed in the context of the preceding discussion, that the Chipko and the Uttarakhand movements have been preoccupied with the problems of sustaining the region within the prevailing political configurations and administrative identity of the 'eight Himalayan districts' of Uttar Pradesh. Both movements have argued for increased access to local resources and infrastructure, and enhancement of regional ecological resources, and have protested against the marginalised social and political status of the region's communities within Uttar Pradesh. In their effort to draw attention to the problem of regional sustainability, both movements have voiced what they regard as legitimate claims to an expanded moral economy – espoused by the Indian government and established in popular imagination as their constitutional right – which includes access to development, democratic political engagement, and social justice. Both movements have employed discursive strategies that have called on the national government to directly intervene in state-level politics on their behalf.

Yet, despite these commonalities and shared concerns regarding regional sustainability, the two movements evolved along different pathways to their present existence. Chipko became a symbol of popular environmentalism by invoking discourses of 'global environmental protection' and 'national defence', which successfully gained the active sympathy and support of national political parties, urban-based environmentalists, academics, and international environmental lobbies. Its fortuitous rise to fame occurred through events and conjunctures that withdrew attention from demands for regional development and directed it towards 'defending the environment'. The story – along with its bucolic ending of harmony between local communities and nature – that Chipko's advocates conveyed to their global audiences never really reflected the living realities of the region. The solutions that emerged in response to the Chipko movement have, in fact, intensified regional problems. Localities now have less access to state-controlled forests than before. They can no longer contest and negotiate with the UP State Forest Department because its discretionary powers have been appropriated by the national Ministry of Environment and Forests. New environmental legislation has effectively curtailed economic activity by imposing further restrictions on forest-based extraction and infrastructure development in the region. Nor have these laws necessarily improved the ecological condition of forests. They have, instead, created the space for the emergence of a timber 'mafia' that organises illegal felling of timber in state-controlled forests. Many impoverished households have, as a result of a convolution of old and new laws, become 'criminalised' in the process of trying to eke out their livelihoods in the region by poaching in Reserved forests. In addition, ethnic tensions have heightened between local communities and migrant workers from neighbouring regions. The seasonal presence of migrant herders who have traditionally moved cattle between the Indo-Gangetic plains and Himalayan forests are no longer tolerated by localities. It is not surprising, given these outcomes, that many village leaders, including the much-celebrated women of Chipko stories, voice their resentment when they hear words such as "environmental protection",[7] and that several political groups in Uttarakhand brandish their axes instead of hugging trees.[8] Their responses must be understood in the context of successive policy outcomes that further constrain their ability to sustain and be sustained by the geographies of their everyday life.

One may, of course, argue that the regional question conveyed by Chipko's activists and supporters was co-opted by the national government and international environmental groups in order to further their own political agendas. But this argument would be disingenuous because it fails to acknowledge the conscious efforts made by Chipko's advocates to create a discursive space which endorsed the idea of intervening to restrict access to regional ecological resources in the name of protecting Himalayan nature. Chipko's transformation into myth was achieved by narratives that consciously linked the movement to an imagined state of environmental purity and harmony, and in the process regional demands for greater access to forest-based extraction, improved social and economic infrastructure, and support for industrial development were abandoned by the wayside. Chipko's local and global advocates chose, for political reasons, to tell stories that presented the movement as the symbolic outcome of the conflict between "environment" and "development".[9] In so doing, they effectively devalued concerns about regional sustainability and, instead, privileged a fetishised notion of the Himalayas as a globalized 'eco-cultural' commodity; in essence, the region as an objectified sample of pristine nature, an ecological museum to be maintained for the pleasures of contemplation and mystic exploration by well-fed elites.

The Uttarakhand movement, on the other hand, has also received widespread support across existing social divisions of caste, class, ethnicity, gender, and religion in the eight Himalayan districts of Uttar Pradesh. Its demands are repeatedly endorsed and validated by people in the region. Local officials point out how the conditions and problems faced by the Himalayan region are different from those of the Indo-Gangetic plains of Uttar Pradesh. Village leaders argue that development projects devised for this region are based on assumptions that are more applicable to the plains than the mountains; that these projects repeatedly fail because they do not take into account the region's distinctive systems of land ownership and patterns of institutional access to resources. Regional political parties claim that the state of Uttar Pradesh is too large and populous to be effectively administered as a single entity, that it should instead be divided into three or four states. Yet, despite all the reasoned arguments and rhetoric that form part of the discursive strategies adopted by the movement, the goal of statehood for Uttarakhand appears almost impossible to achieve for the time being because of the electoral arithmetic that shifts and drives political party coalitions at the state and national levels. Thus even though the Uttarakhand movement has managed to keep its focus on the regional question and make persuasive use of other 'global' discursive strategies – cultural identity, sustainable development, devolution of power, and local governance – the prevailing political configurations constantly deflect or postpone the realisation of statehood.

Faced with the current political impasse, the Uttarakhand movement has reinforced its discursive strategy with the threat of escalating violence, partly in the hope that this may galvanise both national and state governments to grant statehood. But the threats of violence have, so far, been either peremptorily dismissed or ruthlessly punished

by the UP state government. Many of the region's inhabitants fear
that the repeated frustrations experienced by the Uttarakhand movement, compounded by problems arising from the policy outcomes of
Chipko, may make it increasingly violent, resembling the trajectories
of struggles occurring in the Indian states of Kashmir and Assam.
Although the struggles in each of these 'border' states carry their
distinctive geographical histories of confrontation with the Indian
government and evolution towards violent conflict, they, too,
emerged out of debates about access to and control over regional
resources, and the uneven distribution of economic benefits and
social costs at the regional level.[10] In each case, the escalation of
animosity was met with violent suppression by the Indian government, justified as being in defence of the nation's political and
territorial integrity. If demands for a separate state of Uttarakhand
were to escalate in violence, it is likely that similar rhetorical
ammunition – of defending the Indian nation from internal and
external threat – and military force will be used by ruling political
parties or coalitions at the national level to suppress protest and
exercise greater centralised control over this Himalayan region. And,
again, this response, were it to occur, is not likely to resolve the
question of regional sustainability.

THE FUTURE OF UTTARAKHAND

What are the possible futures for this Himalayan region now called
Uttarakhand? Its dimensions and boundaries have neither been static,
nor contained an unchanging set of social features and practices over
time. The region has been bestowed with a variety of official
identities and histories: the independent kingdoms of Garhwal and
Kumaon; satrap kingdoms of the Mughal Empire; western colonies
of the Nepalese Gurkha kingdom; as British Garhwal and Kumaon,
administrative regions of the North-west Provinces and the United
Provinces of Agra and Oudh; and as eight mountain districts (five
under Garhwal Regional Commission, three under the Kumaon
Regional Commission) incorporated within the Indian state of Uttar
Pradesh. Each of these official designations has represented the efforts

of administrators and political actors – past and present – to spatially demarcate the variations made to existing patterns of social networks and material practices through economic conjunctures and political events. Although each attempt at demarcating and renaming the region has proved partial and provisional, the repeated inscriptions and incomplete erasures have created overlapping geographical histories that continue to live through people like Kamla in numerous households in Garhwal and Kumaon, people who struggle to sustain their everyday lives in the region and hope to sustain this lived dimension to their social life in the future.

The struggle for statehood marks yet another stage in the administrative redefinition of the region and the links between its existing social practices and prevailing political configurations. One approach might involve according formal statehood to the region. But the establishment of new administrative boundaries for this Uttarakhand state will undoubtedly be problematised by disputes and conflicts over which areas should be included or excluded, who should be allowed in or kept out. The regional question of sustainability will persist, even if it is phrased differently: how will this new spatial configuration called Uttarakhand enable households and localities to sustain themselves through social practices and interactions within and beyond the region? Will their activities be frustrated by new administrative barriers, will they be further isolated by new fortifications? Or will this new political configuration expose the region to increased exploitation by a few powerful provincial, national, or transnational elites? How will the boundaries of this new administrative entity affect the mobility of marginalised migrant groups and nomadic communities which have depended on the region's resources for their tenuous livelihoods over long periods of time?

I pose these questions quite broadly to all those critical scholars who have deconstructed and discredited the idea of development, and to those activists who currently advocate statehood for Uttarakhand. The idea of development continues to hold enormous significance for most households and localities in this region. They see development as state-supported, public actions aimed at increasing access to regional resources, improving shared physical infrastructure, and creating institutional mechanisms that enable them to enhance their material conditions and sustain the lived dimensions of their social life. Even the most virulent critics of 'development' would find it hard to argue that such modest desires are grossly misguided or irrelevant. And advocates of statehood for Uttarakhand will also need to address these concerns if their claims are to be taken seriously.

Even if the Uttarakhand movement achieves its goal of statehood in the forthcoming decade, there is little likelihood that political autonomy, independent of Uttar Pradesh, would automatically resolve the regional question of sustainability or sustainable development. The region's elites – new and old – may be able to gain political control of the newly formed state, but will be limited in their ability to alter existing constitutional laws that vest the national government with the power to determine and control the trajectories of development in the region's key economic sectors. Unless they somehow succeed in radically altering these controls, specifically involving changes to environmental legislation and the creation of broader economic policies, the formal recognition of Uttarakhand state will have few benefits for those groups among regional elites who aim to gain control of the forestry sector. In effect, the new administrative 'solution' may have some degree of success only by reworking social and material practices and institutional linkages between various sectors of activity, and by redefining the political control that will be exercised by the new ruling elites. Statehood will have little meaning for the larger proportion of the region's households and communities unless it improves their access to resources and related economic and political power.

The question of sustainability remains uppermost in the minds of the region's households who fear that they are doomed to remain marginal and poor, to fill their bellies, as Khan *Saheb* remarked, with myths. A quick survey of the discussions and debates around environmental issues over the past decade would lead us to believe that a different question of sustainability has preoccupied the minds of intellectuals and policy-makers. Part of this intellectual discourse about sustainability has, of course, involved protracted argument over the meaning of the term, the imprecision, ambiguity, and contradictions inherent in its usage.[11] It is not my intention to retrace these debates and pronounce judgement on their accuracy. Rather, I am interested in exploring the kinds of narratives used by the dominant participants[12] in this particular arena of social discourse to see if there are any concurrences with the question of regional sustainability as it has been articulated in the Uttarakhand Himalayas.

SUSTAINABILITY AND THE GLOBAL-LOCAL . . .

There are two distinctive features that characterise the intellectual discourse on sustainability. First, there is a shared assumption that sustainability is primarily about the bio-geophysical environment and, hence, environmental sustainability. Second, that it is necessary to establish some sort of connection between the spaces of the particular and the universal for articulating the problems related to environmental sustainability. The ensuing narratives generally follow one of two trajectories, starting with a description of how 'the local' and 'the global' are linked in the context of environmental problems, then following different pathways in their critique of prevailing practices among states, markets, and civil societies, before finally arriving at their respectively envisioned destinations of global-local sustainability.

The narratives beginning from a 'global' perspective start by outlining a range of environmental processes identified as problems by scientists, phenomena such as global warming, global population growth, and global climate change. These are seen as threatening the very survival of human life on earth. The earth is variably described as a living organism, a delicately balanced ecosystem with limited carrying capacity, a whole entity whose various parts are intricately connected to support life up to a certain level beyond which survival is severely jeopardised, even impossible. Environmental problems are caused by the exponential compounding of human activities in various parts of the world: population growth creates pressures on the earth's resources as people clear forests and encroach on fragile ecosystems to cultivate more land for food; industrial development aimed at meeting the needs of a rapidly expanding world population results in increased exploitation of minerals and burning of fossil fuels. Hence local actions cause the global crisis of sustainability.[13] Since sustainability represents a common good for all humans, it requires solutions that are conceived of and implemented at the global scale. It requires all governments of the world to set aside or check their national interests in favour of global environmental security, which involves endorsing policies developed by multilateral institutions and diligently seeking their implementation. Governments are thus expected to work towards the collective aim of restoring the health of the earth or the balance of the global ecosystem by reducing the rate of population growth, ending deforestation, preserving biodiversity, limiting the burning of fossil fuels, and protecting the fragile habitats of endangered species within their jurisdictions.

The 'local' narratives, on the other hand, begin by identifying the crisis of sustainability as stemming from economic activities – production, consumption, exchange, and waste – that occur at a global scale. In their view, the insatiable drive of global commerce and competitive pressures between countries for political and economic dominance are seen as causing irreversible damage to localities and fragile ecosystems in every part of the world. The delicate balance of the earth's ecosystem is irrevocably harmed by governments that provide succour to global forces of commerce in the name of economic development, threatening the very survival of local communities and ecosystems by allowing rampant exploitation of natural resources within their jurisdictions. Global processes exacerbate local problems, which, in turn, contribute to crises of environmental sustainability of global proportions. Hence threats to the sustainability of life on earth need to be confronted by bringing about a change in human values and reasserting the importance of preserving local communities and ecosystems. Sustainability, in this case, requires governments to limit the powers of global commerce and organise social life within localities that are bound together by a subsistence ethic and communal sharing of political and ecological responsibility.[14]

The visions of sustainability provided by these two narrative genres may seem to offer radical alternatives to present conditions in the world. But do they really? I find at least two problems with their visions of sustainable futures. First, and this should be apparent from my preceding discussion, is that there is absolutely no conception of region or regionality in these narratives. Descriptions of 'the global' and 'the local' are essentially about two spatial scales that have been stripped of geographical history. The link between global and local is tenuous at best, particularly when there is no attempt to describe how these links have been made and remade over time. Although there is little ambiguity about the spatial scope of 'the global', 'the local', despite bearing a warm fuzzy feeling, remains a poorly articulated spatial entity. What exactly is 'the local'? Is it merely a mini-container of people at the bottom of a great pyramid of spatial hierarchies? Are individual localities linked directly to 'the global' through abstract space, or are they linked with other localities? And, in either case, how are these links made? The failure to articulate the meaning of 'local', to explain how this space of 'the local' is, in fact, made by social practices that are part of a broader, more fluid dimension of regionality, results in a fetishised notion of 'locality' which resembles an exclusive country club. This fetishised locality is contrasted with an equally fetishised notion of 'the global', represented as inexorable and faceless economic processes that materialise like barbarians at its gates.

The second problem pertains to the role of the state. Both global and local narratives of sustainability expect states to act in both minimalist and highly interventionist ways. The global narrative requires national governments to relinquish their decision-making and legislative powers to multilateral agencies, to refrain from responding to apparently populist demands and local interests, and yet somehow to maintain the political and economic power to regulate and micro-manage their populations according to globally negotiated environmental policies.[15] The local narrative requires governments to function in exactly the opposite manner. It expects national governments somehow to maintain the political and economic power to impose strict constraints on transnational corporations and global financial institutions, but requires them to withdraw from localities so as to allow them to manage their environments in sustainable ways.[16]

So, on the one hand, the global narrative conjures the image of states that derive their power and legitimacy from being loyal and obedient functionaries of transnational environmental regimes,[17] rather than responding to the varied needs and competing demands of the populations within their jurisdictions. They are to function as faithful executors of a global mission to save the world. On the other hand, the local narratives invoke the image of states that are suffused with benevolence and utterly devoted to securing social justice for each individual and ensuring the ecological and social welfare of localities and communities while keeping predatory forces of global-ization at bay. In this case, states are expected to behave like benign parents, providing protection without imposing an overbearing authority on their offspring. The alternative futures are not only confusing, but also limited in what they offer: authoritarian 'eco-imperialism' or protective 'eco-parentalism'.[18]

The idea of national governments functioning as executors of the global will or as amiable parents (or both) for the sake of ecological sustainability may sound appealing, but practical questions remain. How are states to muster the necessary resources to perform either or both of these roles? Will they be provided with financial resources and powers of enforcement by global environmental organisations for ensuring effective implementation of policies? Conversely, will each local, self-governing community generate the resources needed, with the assistance of a benevolent state, to protect itself from the rampaging forces of global commerce?

Global and local narratives seem persuasive because they present sustainability as a future state of being, a myth abstracted from present conditions. They fetishise 'the local' and 'the global', and they ignore regions and their geographical histories in order to reinforce their myth of sustainability. The two kinds of narratives authenticate each other through a shared vocabulary – such as environmental security, democracy, citizenship, cultural identity – to present the global and the local as 'two sides of a coin' or as 'mutually reinforcing entities'. Yet their visions of sustainability are curiously narrow, conservative, and exclusionary, as well as blind to the lived dimensions of social life. Global-local narratives sketch out the idea of a sustainable future with descriptions of a contemporary world faced with narrow or absolute limits – human and ecological. They employ the language of restriction, exclusion, and authoritative control for the 'future survival of the planet', or for bestowing a profitable legacy (earth as property) for future generations. Such narratives seem, in fact, to speak to propertied audiences that easily understand the exercise of power through the language of exclusive rights to protect their material interests and those of their progenies. Associating sustainability with words such as 'survival' and 'legacy' suggests the exclusion of some people (usually those without property) more than others. It restricts their access to the 'commons', and demarcates boundaries that constrain their mobility and ability to pursue their livelihoods. This kind of discourse about sustainability has little meaning to most households in marginalised regions like Uttarakhand that barely make a living from day to day in their present circumstances. How are they to go about ensuring the future survival of the planet? What property do they pass on to future generations as their legacy?

SUSTAINABILITY AS REGIONAL DEVELOPMENT

Any discussion of sustainability must begin by addressing the regional questions of improved access to resources and social well-being in the *present continuous*, and not as a state that might be restored by return to an idyllic past or miraculously created in the distant future. Sustainability needs to be redefined in terms of social practices that enable the continuation of the lived dimensions of social life through diverse pathways that are open-ended and changeable. Sustainable development then becomes a process involving active, direct, and continuing collaboration between regional institutions and communities to ensure that all social groups, including those that are currently impoverished, transient, and politically marginalised, gain improved access to regional resources and institutional networks.

The question of sustainable regional development must, therefore, be approached from a political-ecology perspective that examines the

way varied dimensions of social practice produce overlapping geographical histories: how households and communities actually engage
in livelihood activities; how governance actually occurs through
formal and customary practices; how these formal and customary
practices actually transform regional landscapes; and how the claims
of diverse localities and social groups in regions assume authority or
illegitimacy through various discursive strategies that, in turn, influence ecological, social, and distributional outcomes.

My attempt to redefine sustainability and sustainable development
may appear both naive and unworkable to those who would argue
that the processes of globalisation have steadily eviscerated the
abilities of national and regional governments to expand and
strengthen the spaces that are accessible to all inhabitants within their
jurisdictions. But it is necessary to remind ourselves that governments
and their constituents have always been mutually dependent in the
process of creating and maintaining spaces of production and political
life, and legitimising cultural identities. In the more recent past, many
nation-states and their constituents emerged from colonial domination by mutually reshaping and legitimising their roles and identities
on the basis of ideas of freedom, self-rule, and democracy. These
experiences suggest that while globalised processes of accumulation
and consumption can generate tremendous economic uncertainties
and environmental risks, they can also open up possibilities that
compel states and civil societies in different regions of the world to
reexamine and actively renegotiate the meanings of glibly used terms
such as global democracy, neoliberalism, freedom, universal citizenship, 'private' property, and 'public' domain in the context of their
distinctive geographical histories. There is no better time than the
continuing present for governments and their constituents to rework
these concepts in enabling, rather than exclusionary, ways to sustain
regions.

There are many examples of such activity in different parts of the
world, where institutions of state and civil society are engaged in
sustaining regional communities and households. The process of
Joint Forest Management in the state of West Bengal is one example
where attempts to address the question of regional sustainability have

locked diverse institutions of state and civil society into a bitter-sweet liaison that requires them to constantly negotiate, accommodate, and readjust their practices as they deal with economic conjunctures and political events.[19] Such collaborative strategies are integral to sustainable regional development because they assume sustainability as part of the practices of social institutions which grapple with questions of enabling access to resources, redistributive justice, and political representation. In so far as they remain committed to practices that do not seek to exclude those that are poor and politically marginalised, they ensure that sustainable regional development continues to be facilitated by substantive, rather than symbolic, democracy.[20]

Which brings me back to Chipko, the movement and the myth. I do not wish to suggest that the ecological, ecofeminist, peasant-populist representations of Chipko are untrue, but rather that these are narratives about a selected group of social actors in a spatial setting that just happens to be the Garhwal Himalaya. They carry very little sense of the overlapping geographical histories that gave rise to this regional protest. Most narratives about Chipko do not help us understand the regional question that has caused both Chipko and Uttarakhand, that has made households in Garhwal and Kumaon rush out to hug trees, and then threaten to chop them down, burn some forests but protect others, argue for greater integration with the national economy while simultaneously demanding regional autonomy from the state of Uttar Pradesh. The inability of these narratives to convey that such contradictory actions are part of a larger regional question has led to repeated failures of analysis and politics which have had serious consequences for the region. Chipko as myth has itself contributed a new layer to the region's geographical history which has resuscitated the movement for statehood for Uttarakhand. Chipko's narrators, however well meaning in their intent, have unwittingly contributed to discursive strategies and policies that have called for regional isolation and social exclusion, and for the setting up of new regulatory barriers and administrative fences in the name of environmental protection. In so doing, Chipko's narrators have reinforced the link, as Khan *Saheb* observed, between poverty and myth. They have contributed yet another layer of geographical history that has kept the Garhwal and Kumaon Himalayas in their state of 'backwardness' and their inhabitants routinely embroiled in cycles of protest, violence, exhaustion, and despair.

My insistence on rewriting Chipko as a struggle over the regional question of sustainable development does not prevent the possibility of seeking commonalities and differences with other regional movements occurring around the world. I am also aware, having earlier in this book explored the relationship between myth and narrative, that my narrative, too, may be interpreted as a myth about this Himalayan region or about regional sustainability. Some readers may feel that I am replacing the fetish of 'the global' and 'the local' with the fetish of 'the region' in my discussion of sustainability. I would say that my narrative does not seek to mythicise regions, but offers, instead, a set of parables about regionality and the question of regional sustainability. It is exceedingly difficult, if not impossible, to fetishise the geographies that my narratives describe as fluid and permeable, involving shared terrains of common access which allow habitual movement and familiar interactions of people within and beyond their horizons. As lived dimensions to social life, these geographies will always resist being fetishised or enclosed. At worst, they will be ignored or abandoned because they make myth-making extremely difficult; in which case serious political, ecological, social, and economic consequences will follow. The narratives contained in this book can serve as parables for motivating people to engage in political actions that both recognise and challenge the geographical histories of social practices, resist the inane nostrums of global-local discourses, and attempt to transform 'official' meanings of property, citizenship, and democracy by expanding access for sustaining livelihoods and the lived dimensions of social life.

Chipko was a movement that emerged nearly twenty-five years ago in the Garhwal Himalaya. It exists today as myth. In this book I have attempted to bring Chipko back from the realm of symbolic nature into geographical history. I have done so in the hope that the Chipko movement will not only continue to inspire people to action, but also make them aware of the challenges involved in the collaborative social practices of sustaining regional development and regionality. My narrative does not celebrate Chipko as a multifaceted social movement aimed at recovering the idyllic world that was once the Garhwal Himalaya. My narrative does not end happily ever after, but it does provide a sense of the determined efforts of this region's inhabitants to continue their struggle for sustainable development and substantive democracy. Chipko yesterday, Uttarakhand today. Who knows what name tomorrow's struggles will take?

NOTES

PREFACE

1. White (1990), quoted in Harvey (1997).

1 MYTH AND MARGINALISATION

1. Barthes 1972, p. 143.
2. Naipaul 1990.
3. See Agarwal and Narin 1982; Bahuguna 1981, 1987; Berreman 1978; Bhatt 1987, 1991; Dogra 1980; Guha 1989; Shiva 1989; Shiva and Bandyopadhyay 1986a, 1986b, 1987; Weber 1988.
4. Hartley 1984, p. 7.
5. For analyses of myths, see Campbell (ed.) 1970, and his other writings; Cassirer 1979; Coupe 1997; Eliade 1963; Frye 1957; Hillman 1978; Lévi-Strauss 1972, 1978; Malinowski 1954.
6. Baeten 1996, p. 24.
7. Barthes 1972, p. 109; also see Calvino 1997.
8. McNeill 1986, p. 23.
9. *Ibid.*, p. 13.
10. Why do I choose to contrast this particular interpretation of myth with history, particularly when historians themselves have underscored the similarities between the two? William McNeill, (*ibid.*), argues that one person's history may be regarded as myth by another, and that it might be more appropriate to refer to historical narratives as "mythistories". M.I. Finley observes that without myth, the earliest (Greek) historians could never have begun their work. How else could they have made sense of the past? "Long before anyone

dreamed of history, myth gave an answer. That was its function, or rather one of its functions; to make the past intelligible and meaningful by selection, by focussing on a few bits of the past which thereby acquired permanence, relevance, and universal significance" (1965, p. 283). Raphael Samuel states that "[h]istory has always been a hybrid form of knowledge, syncretizing past and present, memory and myth, the written record and the spoken word" (1994, p. 453).

I do not find these arguments contradicting my interpretation of myth, in part because they allude to myth in conventional ways, namely, as classical legends, or as false or unreal narratives, and also because they refer to the sort of historical writing that postmodernists call "metanarrative", which has perhaps aspired to provide history with universal, near-mythic significance. My conception of geographical history is derived from the recognition that it is a product of social and material practices – that is to say, economic, cultural, and political actions of people – in relation to their ecological surroundings and over time. See also Earle 1992; Harvey 1996.

11. For examples, see Wilmsen 1989; Hecht and Cockburn 1989; as well as numerous writings on post-Columbian representations, particularly those produced in the sixteenth and seventeenth centuries, of the Americas and American Indians.

12. See Wolf 1982.

2 PASSAGES FROM HISTORY TO NATURE

1. Weber 1988, p. 10.

2. *Ibid.*, pp. 128–9.

3. Kuyek 1993, p. 21, quoted in Garb 1995. This chapter has benefited from a number of discussions and arguments between Yaakov Garb and myself, and from a joint attempt to resolve our differences over how Chipko could be understood in Rangan and Garb 1996.

4. Garb 1995.

5. *Ibid.*

6. Cronon 1992. I have drawn extensively on Cronon's essay for developing the theoretical argument in this section.

7. I cannot do justice to these debates or to the voluminous literature produced on this subject in a note. But interested readers may wish to explore these debates in R. Williams 1977; H. White 1987; Jameson 1981; Said 1983; Clifford and Marcus 1986; Ahmad 1992.

8. Cronon 1992, pp. 1349–50.

9. *Ibid.*, p. 1368.

10. *Ibid.*, p. 1375.

11. For an illustration of this point, see Harvey 1974.

12. I have borrowed the ideas of Benedict Anderson to make this argument. Anderson is not, of course, discussing environmental narratives, but attempting to explain the paradoxical entity we call the modern "nation-state". He argues that the nation-state is a curious amalgam of legitimate fictions and concrete illegitimacies. See Anderson 1980, 1983.

13. Government of India 1985, p. 70.

14. This brief biographical sketch of Chandi Prasad Bhatt is based on his writings, as well as those provided in other Chipko narratives. See Bhatt 1982, 1987, 1991; Dogra 1980, pp. 46–8; Shepard 1982, pp. 91–102; Weber 1988, pp. 34–42.

15. Mishra and Tripathi 1978, p. 8.

16. Bhatt 1987, p. 250.

17. *Ibid.*, p. 254.

18. *Ibid.*, quotes from pp. 249–53.

19. *Ibid.*, quotes from pp. 252–3.

20. *Ibid.*, p. 249.

21. *Ibid.*, quotes from p. 262.

22. *Ibid.*, quotes from p. 261.

23. *Ibid.*, quotes from p. 262.

24. *Ibid.*, quotes from p. 263.

25. *Ibid.*, p. 264.

26. Bhatt 1991, p. 17–19.

27. Bahuguna's biographical sketch is based, like Bhatt's, on his own writings and those provided in other narratives on the Chipko movement. See Bahuguna 1987; Weber 1988, pp. 33–5; Mishra and Tripathi 1978, pp. 6–12; Dogra 1980, pp. 46–8, 54–64.

28. There are records of timber contracts awarded by the Forest Department to Bahuguna's cooperative in the 1960s. This information was obtained from interviews with Forest Department officials during my field research in Garhwal.

29. His mentor, Mira Behn (which means sister in Hindi; Mira is the name of a well-known woman poet–saint of medieval India), previously known as Madeleine Slade, was a European disciple of Mahatma Gandhi. She established an ashram in Tehri Garhwal as Bahuguna later did himself. Mira Behn's concerns regarding changes

in Himalayan ecology were expressed in her book, *The Spirit's Pilgrimage*, published in 1960.

30. Quoted in Weber 1988, p. 34.
31. *Ibid.*, p. 246.
32. *Ibid.*, p. 238.
33. *Ibid.*, p. 239.
34. Bahuguna 1987, p. 246.
35. *Ibid.*, quotes from pp. 241–2.
36. *Ibid.*, p. 246.
37. *Ibid.*
38. Shiva 1989, p. 38.
39. *Ibid.*, p. 40.
40. *Ibid.*, p. 61.
41. *Ibid.*, p. 63.
42. *Ibid.*, p. 4.
43. *Ibid.*, p. 5. The italics in this quote are mine.
44. *Ibid.*, p. 67.
45. *Ibid.*, p. 77.
46. *Ibid.*, pp. 70, 73.
47. *Ibid.*, pp. 76–7.
48. I do not wish to imply that Shiva's arguments regarding the work and responsibilities of village women in Garhwal are entirely baseless. However, her assertion that these women have no desire to engage in the cash-based economy is simply inaccurate. Several studies of the household economies and women's work in Garhwal indicate that women are responsible for managing their families at home while their menfolk migrate in search of employment. Their activities involve a combination of subsistence cultivation of their land-holdings (which are usually less than or about 1 hectare in size), maintaining a small herd of goats or a few cows (depending on their class/caste status), collection of minor forest products, fuelwood, and fodder for both household needs and sale in local markets, and fetching water if a piped-water supply is not available in the village. See Agarwal 1986, 1990, 1994.

My field interviews indicate that apart from the fact that there were more women at any given time in these villages, their motivations for participating in Chipko protests were twofold. First, the demands for forest-based industry, if met, offered the possibility that their kinsmen might be employed closer to home. Second, the demands for increased rights of local access to state-controlled forests and greater concessions for small-scale commercial extraction (which had originally been part of the demands made by Chipko's leading activists, Bhatt and Bahuguna) may have offered women the possibility of adding to their meagre incomes and insuring themselves from potential crisis if remittances ceased or became intermittent.

49. Mies and Shiva 1993, p. 303.

50. Critical perspectives on Shiva's representation of gender roles in the household economies of Garhwal can be found in Agarwal 1992; Jackson 1993.

51. Guha, 1989, p. xiv. He identifies his work as following the tradition of Teodor Shanin, James Scott, Barrington Moore, Ranajit Guha, Sartono Kartodirdjo, and E.P. Thompson, sociologists and historians renowned for their theoretical contributions and empirical research on peasants and peasant resistance.

52. *Ibid.*, quotes from pp. xi–xii.

53. *Ibid.*, pp. 2–3.

54. *Ibid.*, pp. 27–8.

55. *Ibid.*, pp. 33–4.

56. *Ibid.*, pp. 56–7.

57. *Ibid.*, Chapter 4: "Rebellion as Custom", pp. 62–98; Chapter 5: "Rebellion as Confrontation", pp. 99–137. Guha employs the concept of "moral economy" and "everyday resistance" from the works of James Scott (1976, 1985); E.P. Thompson (1971); and Eugene Genovese (1973).

58. Guha, 1989, p. 153.

59. *Ibid.*, p. 172.

60. *Ibid.*, p. 174.

61. *Ibid.*, p. 178.

62. Clark 1986, p. 6.

63. See Bailey 1991.

64. Guha 1993, pp. 45–6.

65. See Aryal 1994b; Mawdsley 1997.

66. See Mitra 1993b; Rangan 1996.

67. Mitra 1993b, pp. 50–1. Italics in the original (translated from Hindi).

3 NATURALISED HIMALAYA

1. *Times of India*, 25 February 1991; *Himachal Times*, 30 May 1990.

2. *Hindustan Times*, 30 June 1990.

3. Bhatt 1987.
4. Dogra 1980.
5. Bahuguna 1987; Ramachandra Guha 1989; Shiva 1989.
6. Moorcroft and Trebeck 1841, p. 6.
7. Rawat 1989a, p. 74; Tucker 1983.
8. Rawat 1989, pp. 46–70.
9. Prasad and Verma 1982.
10. The placename Gómukh is often pronounced and written as Gau-mukh, and is consequently translated from Sanskrit as "the cow's mouth" (*Gau* = cow, *mukh* = mouth). A priest at the pilgrimage shrine for the Ganges river at Gangotrí, however, informed me that its correct pronunciation was Gómukh (*Gó* = earth, *mukh* = mouth).
11. Sir Thomas Holdich, quoted in Woodman 1969, p. 7.
12. The statement is by T.V.R. Murti, and is quoted by Bharati 1987. Idealising wilderness as sacred is not unique to Hindu thought. English Romantic poets such as Shelley, Wordsworth, Coleridge, and Southey, and American transcendentalists such as Thoreau, Emerson, and Muir consciously argued for the need to recognise wilderness as sacred space. See R. Williams 1980, pp. 67–80; Thomas 1983; Pepper 1984; Chase 1987; Sears 1989; Cartmill 1993.
13. According to John Keay, the largest number of gold medals awarded by the Royal Geographical Society during the eighteenth and nineteenth centuries went to explorers who travelled through Central Asia and the Himalayas. See Keay (ed.) 1991.
14. See Keay 1983, for the avid interest in Himalayan exploration shown by the British government, and the heroic exploits of Sir Francis Younghusband. Also see Rennell 1788; Turner 1800; Moorcroft and Trebeck 1841; "Pilgrim" Barron 1844; Landon 1906; and Smythe 1937, p. 16, who describes the attempts to ascend Mount Everest as a national duty comparable with attempts to reach the North and South Poles.
15. William Moorcroft died mysteriously during his travels in the western Himalayas; his travel diaries were recovered and posthumously published by the Royal Society. See also Keay 1983; Turner 1800.
16. R. Williams 1973, pp. 120–6.
17. See Khan and Tripathy 1976; Government of India 1985; Dobhal 1987; Bora 1987. This mode of explanation also conveniently allows the governments of India and Bangladesh to shift blame across political borders and avoid having to address the inadequacies of

their flood-management policies. They usually invoke the image of a small number of peasants in Nepal and the Indian Himalayas wreaking environmental havoc and destroying the prospects of economic stability and progress for the bulk of populations in the plains. See Ives and Messerli 1989 for a critique of this politically expedient explanation.

18. See for example, Dogra 1980; Shiva and Bandyopadhyay 1986a and b, 1987, 1989; Weber 1988; Berreman 1989.

19. Blaikie and Brookfield 1987; Guha 1983, 1985, 1986, 1989; Guha and Gadgil 1989; Somanathan 1991; Pathak 1997.

20. McNeill 1986, p. 18. He is not referring to ecosystem models but to "truths" which, he claims, are general rather than particular. The methods of science attempt to do the same.

21. O'Neill et al. 1986, p. 4. The first section of their book offers a remarkably accessible and thorough summary of concepts of ecosystems and how they have changed as a result of debates between ecological scientists with opposing views.

22. See Weiss (ed.) 1971; Huxley 1943.

23. R.L. Lindeman, quoted in O'Neill et al. 1986; also see Odum 1971.

24. This was the view adopted by naturalists and geographers such as Alexander von Humboldt; see Colinvaux 1973, for a detailed discussion of the static view of changes in the geographic distribution of organisms.

25. This is the dynamic view of change proposed by F.E. Clements, also known as the theory of succession; see ibid. for more details. The concept of equilibrium has exercised a powerful influence on naturalists and geographers since antiquity. See Glacken 1967; Egerton 1976.

26. Botkin 1990; Crossley 1996.

27. Wiens 1984.

28. Siciliano 1978, pp. 8–11.

29. A.G. Tansley, quoted in Chase 1987, p. 315.

30. Strong 1984, pp. viii–ix.

31. See Nebel and Wright 1998, pp. 23–39, for definitions of these categories.

32. O'Neill et al. 1986, pp. 26–30.

33. Thompson and Warburton 1988, p. 5. They give an example of one key variable – the per capita rate of fuelwood consumption – that is used to evaluate rates of deforestation.

A survey of these estimates at the national level for Nepal over the last 26 years reveals a range from 60 kilograms to 4000 kilograms per capita per annum. Both these amounts are separated by a factor of 67, and even if the upper outliers are deleted, the range still differs by a factor of 26. The range of expert opinion is very instructive for those trying to assemble previous research data on the Himalayan region. Uncertainty of this magnitude on a crucial system variable is quite rare in the systems with which we are familiar. Even the vast uncertainties associated with estimating oil and gas reserves pale into insignificance when compared with this.

s   And, as they point out, in the case of fuelwood consumption, there is at least *something* that can be measured; with oil and gas reserves estimation, there is nothing that can be directly measured; see pp. 5–6.

34. See Turner 1800; Moorcroft and Trebeck 1841; G.R.C. Williams 1874; Atkinson 1882, Vols I and III; Landon 1906; H.G. Walton 1910, Rawat 1989a.

35. Thompson 1988; Thompson and Warburton 1988.

36. See Atkinson 1882, Vols I and III; H.G. Walton 1910; Von Fürer-Haimendorf 1975, 1981; Fisher 1986.

37. Thompson and Warburton 1988.

38. See Ludwig *et al.* 1993, pp. 17, 36.

39. Kuhn 1970, p. 52.

40. Thompson and Warburton 1988, p. 21.

41. See Douglas 1986.

42. See references to the work of A.S. Watt and others in O'Neill *et al.* 1986, pp. 30–4.

43. Holling 1986.

44. Kay 1991; Crossley 1996.

45. Rapport 1992.

46. Vayda 1983; Norton 1992.

47. Kellert and Wilson (eds) 1993; also see Saegert and Winkel 1990.

48. See Williams and Patterson 1996.

49. Sack 1992.

50. Allen and Gould 1986.

51. For an overview of this literature, see Bryant 1992; Friedmann and Rangan (eds) 1993; with respect to Latin America, see Buttel and Sunderlin 1988; for a similar assessment of political ecology in the Asian context, see Peluso 1992.

52. Blaikie and Brookfield 1987, p. 17.

53. *Ibid.*, p. 239.
54. Peet and Watts 1996, p. 8.
55. *Ibid.*, p. 6.
56. *Ibid.*, p. 8.
57. Their critical assessment of political ecology is perhaps the best to date, yet their edited book, despite its ambitious title and claims regarding liberation ecology, reproduces the problems they find in the political ecology literature; it remains a collection of essays written by diverse scholars with interests in similar areas of inquiry. My point is well illustrated by comparing the essays of Escobar and Yapa, with those written by Carney and myself. The analytical approaches adopted by the two former authors are remarkably different from that adopted by the latter two authors.
58. For geography's enduring interest in understanding the mutual shaping of nature and social life, see C.J. Glacken 1967.
59. Gould 1987, p. 13.

4 HIMALAYAN BACKWARDNESS

1. Keay 1983, p. 5. Keay adds that this distinction was in spite of the fact that the Royal Geographical Society was not involved in Himalayan exploration in any active manner as it was in Africa.
2. Quoted in Woodman 1969, p. 7.
3. Keay 1983, p. 7.
4. Walton (1910) states that the rulers of Garhwal had succeeded only once, and for a short period of time towards the end of the fourteenth century, in bringing fifty-two principalities under their control. See p. 114.
5. Rawat 1989, pp. 79–80.
6. Capt. Thomas Hardwicke, a military officer of the East India Company, carefully recorded the various streams of revenue collected by the king of Garhwal prior to invasion by rulers of the neighbouring kingdom of Nepal in 1804: the Garhwali ruler had received 12,000 rupees as rent from the duties collected at Kotdwar, one of the passes linking his territory with the plains. With at least nine major passes falling within Garhwal, the duties realised at points along trade routes ranged anywhere between 70,000 to 100,000 rupees which comprised 50 percent of the total revenue. See *ibid.*, p. 85; also see Atkinson 1882, Vol. III, Part I, p. 283.
7. Rawat 1989, p. 83.

8. G.R.C. Williams 1874, p. 109.

9. Traill 1828, p. 193.

10. Atkinson 1882, Vol. I, Part II, pp. 845–6.

11. Walton (1910) noted that the pilgrim economy in 1900, "must on the most modest computation be worth not less that five lakhs [500,000 rupees] a year to the inhabitants". See p. 73.

12. *Ibid.*, pp. 80–1; Rawat 1989, p. 82.

13. Walton 1910, pp. 87–8; Atkinson 1882, Vol. III, Part I, p. 264.

14. Walton 1910, pp. 89–90.

15. These proportions have been estimated based on the figures given by Traill 1828 and Atkinson 1882, Vol. III, Part I, pp. 289–91. Atkinson records the total revenue collected in 1815, the year when the Company established control over Garhwal, as 117,730 rupees, and indicates that land revenue amounted to 36,074 rupees. This proportion seems to have remained relatively constant over the following eighteen years despite eight consecutive reforms made to the revenue system during the Company's rule in Garhwal.

16. Traill 1828, p. 193.

17. *Ibid.*

18. Rawat 1989; Saklani 1986.

19. In addition to these increases, several new taxes were imposed on timber and forest products, on the sale of children, a marriage tax, a ferry tax, and excise on the sale of drugs and liquor. See Walton, p. 89; Atkinson, Vol. III, Part I, pp. 283–4.

20. Walton 1910, p. 126–7; Atkinson 1882, pp. 252–3.

21. Chetan Singh (1991) quotes Francisco Pelsaert, a Dutch traveller in India during the sixteenth century, who was struck by the high cost of firewood and the use of dried cow dung as fuel substitutes by peasants in the region.

22. Keay 1983, pp. 17–34.

23. Moorcroft and Trebeck 1841.

24. The work of Richard Tucker, John Richards, and Chetan Singh are exceptions. See Tucker 1983, 1988, 1991; Richards 1987; C. Singh 1991.

25. Max Weber's definition of states as "compulsory associations claiming control over territories and the people within them" does not, as Peter Evans notes, reduce the complexities of analysing what they do. See Evans 1995, pp. 5–6.

26. See Polanyi 1944; Braudel 1973, 1977, 1979a and 1979b.

27. See Bourdieu's (1977) discussion of structures, power, and practices, particularly Chapter 4.

28. Foucault (1991) uses the term "governmentality" in his discussion of the evolution of the modern nation-state in Europe. He identifies governmentality, which is the term he uses for the actual practices of governing, describing the modern nation-state as the 'daemonic coupling' of 'city-game' and 'shepherd-game': the invention of a form of secular political pastorate which couples 'individualization' and 'totalization'. Also see Gordon 1991, p. 8.

29. See Abu-Lughod 1989; Arrighi 1994; Braudel 1977; Chaudhuri 1986; Ghosh 1995.

30. See Braudel 1966; Foucault 1991; Gordon 1991.

31. See Lawson 1993.

32. Wrigley 1978, p. 21.

33. See Heckscher 1935; Wrigley 1978 (p. 23) notes that although, "its name descends from the Middle Ages, the typical expression of the 'staple' policy was in the English Navigational Acts, and it constituted the 'mercantile system' which was denounced by Adam Smith in Book Four of the *Wealth of Nations*. Its beneficiaries are merchants, together with shipbuilders, dockers, hoteliers, and others whose living depends on an active foreign commerce."

34. Wrigley 1978, p. 24.

35. The Company was granted the district known as the 24 Parganas in present-day West Bengal in recognition of the military support given to the Mughal emperor for subduing the economic and political ambitions of the Nawab of Bengal.

36. Wrigley 1978, pp. 23-6.

37. In 1813, Lord Grenville gave an impassioned speech attacking the East India Company's monopoly:

> It is the glory of our ancestors, that in the first moments of recovered freedom, in the hour when commerce and legislation were but as yet beginning to dawn on Europe, they recognized the rights of commercial interchange between mankind, proclaimed to foreign nations a secure and unmolested intercourse with ports and markets of our country, and sanctified this just and beneficent principle to all succeeding times by incorporating it into the great charter of their liberties. By what different rule shall we, their descendants, in this more liberal and enlightened age, with morals humanized by knowledge, and benevolence animated by purer religion, administer the

interests of this vast empire, which the unsearchable decrees of Providence have subjected to our dominion?

Quoted in Hopkins 1978, p. 1.

s38. From the time of its earliest acquisition of territory in Bengal following the battle at Plassey in 1757, the Company's expansion proceeded steadily across northern India. Benares was acquired as an adjunct to Bengal in 1793, providing it with its first foothold in the Indo-Gangetic plains. In 1801, the Nawab of Oudh ceded areas north of Benares, the central Doáb (Doáb is a specific geographical term referring to the land lying between the Ganges and its major tributary, the Yamuna), and Rohilkhand; the Company conquered the Upper Doab in 1803, and gained control over large parts of the subcontinent by the time Garhwal was ceded in 1815 after its war with Nepal. Three years later the Mahratta War was settled to the Company's advantage. By 1846, following the war with the Sikh rulers of Punjab, the whole coastline of India, excluding the Indus delta, was under its control, with native states reduced to dependent powers. By 1856, a year before the Mutiny, the Company had complete control over northern India, after having deposed Wajid Ali Shah, the Nawab of Oudh. The entire territory which now comprises the state of Uttar Pradesh was called the United Provinces of Agra and Oudh.

39. The following decades saw escalation of Anglo-Russian rivalry in Asia. The Great Game, as it was called, preoccupied foreign policy in both Britain and India for most of the nineteenth and early twentieth centuries. See Moorcroft and Trebeck 1841; Keay 1983.

40. Atkinson 1882, Vol. I, Part II, pp. 799–802.

41. See official correspondence on "Papers regarding the cultivation of hemp in Garhwal", *Collectorate Records: Pre-Mutiny 1816–1857*, Serial No. 89, File No. 35, Dehra Dun: U.P. State Regional Archives.

42. Between 1815 and 1833, land revenues increased from 36,074 to 70,198 rupees. See Atkinson 1882, Vol. III, Part I, p. 289.

43. See Stokes 1959, pp. 37–9.

44. Wrigley 1978; Dewey 1978; Alavi 1980.

45. Woodman 1969, pp. 37–41.

46. Quoted in Atkinson 1882, Vol. I, Part II, pp. 889–90.

47. Quoted *ibid.*, pp. 893–4.

48. These were Koth, Ráma Serai, and Gadoli in Garhwal, Lachmesar,

Bhartpur, Hawalbágh, Rasiya, and Bhim Tál in Kumaon, and Kaulagir in Dehra Dun.

49. Annual Report to the Government, dated 28 February 1844, published in the *Journal of the Agri-Horticultural Society of India*, quoted in Atkinson, 1882, p. 895.

50. Quoted *ibid.*, pp. 901–2.

51. G.R.C. Williams 1874, p. 314.

52. *Ibid.*, p. 317. The entire venture is described on pp. 314–32. I have essentially summarised his detailed account of related events, arguments, and outcomes.

53. Tucker 1983, p. 151.

54. Many of the contemporary debates regarding the virtues and disadvantages of large infrastructure projects such as dams and irrigation canals were carried out in the context of the Ganges Canal project. Some argued that the canal would undermine the existing hydrology of the region and result in desertification and increase in waterborne diseases; others questioned the economic viability of the project, stating that the water-based transportation of goods would be jeopardised by the proposed canal network. But most of these arguments were settled in favour of those who emphasised the importance of canal irrigation for securing agricultural commodity production. See Cautley 1860, p. 25. Sir P. Cautley, who served as the Chief Engineer for the Ganges Canal works, outlines the various debates and criticisms surrounding the project and its subsequent resolution.

The Company's approach to agrarian reform had, by this time, undergone substantial change based on its earlier experiences in the Bengal, Madras, and Bombay Presidencies, where land reforms had not been able to achieve the expected levels of agricultural production. As a result, its interventions in the Northwest Provinces were focused less on altering prevailing social relations of agricultural production but rather on enhancing commodity production by improving the infrastructure for cultivators. For the failures and successes of earlier land reforms, see Ranajit Guha 1962; Frykenberg (ed.) 1961; Metcalfe 1976; Stokes 1978.

55. The signing of the Treaty of Lahore between the British Indian administration and the Sikh rulers of Punjab in 1846 established a phase of relative peace that assisted the progress of canal construction.

56. The equivalent of £150,000, the exchange rate at the time being 10 rupees to £1. The estimate was based on proposed levies on

irrigation charged at an average rate per acre of land, excluding revenues that were to be collected from watermills, transit duties, and miscellaneous sale of canal produce. See Cautley 1860, p. 28.

57. See Whitcombe 1972, p. 8.
58. Cautley 1860, p. 66.
59. See G.R.C. Williams 1874, pp. 253–4; Atkinson 1882, Vol. I, Part II, pp. 863–4.
60. G.R.C. Williams 1874, p. 324.
61. *Ibid.*.
62. *Ibid.*, pp. 314, 332.
63. C.W. McMinn, quoted by Whitcombe 1972, p. 97.
64. See Woodman 1969, Chapters. 2 and 3.
65. *Ibid.*, pp. 37–41.
66. Atkinson 1882, Vol. III, Part I, p. 259.
67. Walton 1910, pp. 44–5.
68. *Ibid.*, p. 64.

5 BIOGEOGRAPHY OF CONTROL

1. During my visits to Chakrata, the Forest Officer in charge considered it prudent to ensure that a single woman be accompanied by a person who knew his way through the forest ranges and was recognised in the villages within his Division. I would request the Range Officer to spare Saar Singh from his regular duties, which he generously consented to each time I visited the area.

2. Sharecropping was not uncommon in the village. The village comprised thirty-five families that owned land in Konain; at least fifteen of these had migrants, usually from the western districts of Nepal, cultivating some portion of their lands. I was initially puzzled by their presence because I could not understand why, given the relatively small landholdings (averaging roughly 1 hectare per household), these families found it necessary to establish sharecropping relations with migrants from Nepal. Through interviews with families in Konain and other villages in the district, I learned that sharecropping arrangements were often made when male members of households belonging to the villages migrated in search of waged employment.

Typically, lands owned by village households in this region are distributed at varying altitudes; one plot may be located at a lower altitude along the edges of a stream or a river, the second nearer the village settlement, and the third might be located at a higher elevation. Some plots may be located within the boundaries of other villages. The crops cultivated in these plots vary according to soil quality, micro-climatic conditions, the level of rainfall or the availability of water for irrigation. See Berreman 1972; S.D. Pant 1935; Atkinson 1882, Vols I and III; Walton 1910.

Migrant households are often given rain-fed plots located at the edge of villages or adjacent to Forest Department lands for cultivation. The sharecropping arrangements between a village household and that of the migrant may extend over a three- to five-year period, after which it may be renewed, or the migrant family may move to another area within the region. Most migrant households from Nepal comprise a husband and wife in their late twenties or thirties, with two or three children. Their children often work as casual labour in their localities, and move to other regions in their mid-teens.

3. UP Forest Department 1989.
4. See Champion and Seth 1968a, p. 4. They divide the forest vegetation of India into four major groups corresponding to the main temperature-based climate zones: tropical, subtropical, temperate, and alpine. These are further divided into sixteen type-groups on the basis of rainfall and the distinctive morphological features of vegetation; further classification of subgroups within these type-groups yields 221 "ecologically stable" vegetation types. All of Champion and Seth's books are considered classic texts by Indian foresters, and form part of the basic training in silviculture for newly recruited officers to the Indian Forest Service.
5. See Champion and Seth 1968b; Lal 1989, pp. 44 ff.; Negi 1990.
6. See, for example, Brandis 1897; Webber 1902. Authors such as Vandana Shiva, Ramachandra Guha, and Madhav Gadgil place great emphasis on the cultural and symbolic meanings of forests for various communities. See Shiva 1989; Gadgil and Guha 1992.
7. These estimates have been based on information provided in the *Annual Progress Reports of Forest Administration in the United Provinces* for various years. I was able to examine the reports for 1920–21, 1934–35, 1954–55. The most recent information on land-use distribution was found in the *Forest Statistics* of the UP Forest Department published in 1989; State Planning Organisation 1984; Singh and Berry 1990, p. 9.
8. Neoclassical economists often assume that state ownership of forests

tends towards being nominal (*res nullius*) and thereby results in overuse of resources (i.e. the tragedy of the commons). Based on this assumption, free-market advocates assert that state control of forests is, in effect, a monopoly that results in price distortions, inefficient markets, and consequent misuse of resources. See, for example, Hyde *et al.* 1991; World Bank 1991. Critics who adopt a populist perspective assume that state control over forests is exclusive and functions as corporate/private property by keeping the common people out. See Shiva and Bandyopadhyay 1986b; Shiva 1989; Ramachandra Guha 1989; Gadgil and Guha 1992. For a similar, yet more nuanced, perspective in the context of Indonesia, see Peluso 1992.

9. A version of this analysis has been previously published in Rangan 1997.

10. Ribot 1998, p. 310. Ribot's theoretical analysis of access is by far the most challenging and original discussion in the contemporary literature on forestry and forest management.

11. Marxist scholars such as Macpherson (1978) have argued that property is a relational concept and that it is inaccurate to represent it as a thing in itself; that the very fact that it is a socially defined right vested in particular individuals and entities imputes some measure of control within its definition. I agree with their arguments, but wish to emphasise the fact that although property is defined as relational, it is not very often that one sees analyses of how social actions and practices redefine the relational concept. Take for example, a person who says, "This is my property, I'll do what I like with it." The focus of attention is often on the person's assertion of a socially approved individual right with which the private property is imbued, and much less on exactly what that person actually does with it after the initial assertion. My concern is to look at what sort of actions and practices, or, more precisely, how the exercise of control shapes or redefines the character of prescriptive rights vested in particular forms of possession or ownership.

12. Ribot 1998, p. 312.

13. See Hardin 1968.

14. See Bromley 1989; Bromley and Cernea 1989.

15. Bromley 1989, pp. 33–4; also see Ciriacy-Wantrup and Bishop 1975.

16. Macpherson 1978, p. 5.

17. McGranahan 1991, p. 1277.

18. Macpherson 1978, p. 5.

19. Bromley and Cernea 1989, p. 35.
20. Ribbentrop 1900, pp. 68–9.
21. *Ibid.*, p. 69.
22. *Ibid.*, pp. 65 ff.; Brandis 1897, pp. 82 ff.; Smythies 1925.
23. Ribbentrop 1900, pp. 66, 71.
24. Brandis 1897, p. 107.
25. Ribbentrop 1900, pp. 70–3. He quotes Dr Wallich on p. 72.
26. *Ibid.*, p. 73.
27. *Ibid.*, p. 71. See also Webber 1902.
28. The Company found it necessary to develop a fiscal system that would form the foundation for governing its newly acquired territories in Bengal. The aim was to establish a formal machinery of social and territorial control through laws that defined how land revenue was to be assessed and collected. See Whitcombe 1972, p. 3.
29. See Ranajit Guha's (1962) rich analysis of the debates surrounding the idea of 'permanent settlement' in Bengal. All three proponents believed that the Company's rule in India would be strengthened by the loyalty of its beneficiaries, the new landowning class. The Permanent Settlement of 1793 was implemented in Bengal under Lord Cornwallis. It represented an early victory for the free-trade lobby, which had begun pressing the British Parliament to abolish the Company's commercial monopoly over Indian trade. See pp. 11–19.
30. This view continued from the early years of the Company's rule in Bengal. Replying to the accusations made by free-trade proponents in Britain of "lax and arbitrary rule" in India, Warren Hastings retorted that "the people of this country do not require our aid to furnish them with a rule for their conduct, or a standard for their property". See Stokes 1959, p. 3.
31. John Shore (Lord Teignmouth), quoted in Ranajit Guha 1962, p. 190. The main objection expressed by administrators such as Shore, Lord Elphinstone, Sir Charles Metcalfe, Sir John Malcolm, and Sir Thomas Munro was that the Permanent Settlement of 1793 would create a class of *zamindárs* (landlords) similar to the British aristocracy who would not necessarily undertake improvement of their property and increase production. Following a physiocratic line of reasoning, they argued instead that the *raiyat* (the peasant cultivator) would be far more productive if he was spared from the parasitic influence of this intermediary class that stood between the cultivator and the government. See Stokes 1959, pp. 15–47.

32. John Malcolm and Charles Metcalfe later served as Governor-Generals of the North-West Provinces (Garhwal was part of this administrative division), and supervised the adoption of *raiyatwári* and *bhaichára* (loosely translated as the "brotherhood" and village collectives) settlement in these regions. See Stokes 1959.

33. Despite these adaptations and modified approaches to property settlements in agriculture, constant criticism from Britain restrained the Company from throwing caution to the winds and abandoning private property. It was only after the Indian Mutiny and the establishment of Crown rule in India that administrators could boldly venture forth and proclaim sovereign ownership as the natural and legitimate continuation of traditional rights exercised from times immemorial by rulers of Asiatic societies. See Maine 1876; Baden-Powell 1892.

34. Ribbentrop 1900, p. 97.

35. *Ibid.*, p. 73.

36. *Ibid.*, p. 74.

37. Rawat 1989b, p. 11.

38. See McClelland 1835. The appointment of several medical officers as Conservators of Forests occurred prior to the establishment of the Imperial Forest Service in 1862. They were, in essence, the men of science in the Company's employ, and were seen as having the skills to address the problems relating to agriculture and forestry. The need for officers trained specifically in the profession of forestry emerged with the creation of the Imperial Forest Service. In the initial stages, German foresters such as Berthold Ribbentrop and Dietrich Brandis were recruited to develop an appropriate system of conservancy and management of Indian forests. British foresters serving in India were mainly trained in Germany and France until the establishment of a School of Forestry in the Coopers Hill College of Engineering at Oxford in 1884. A Forestry School for Indian forest-rangers was established earlier in 1878 in Dehra Dun. Later, the Imperial Forest Research Institute was also established in Dehra Dun. See Ribbentrop 1900, pp. 175–85; Brandis 1897, pp. 115–16, 129–31.

39. Ribbentrop 1900, pp. 53–65. Such disagreements regarding climate change continue to the present day.

40. See Cleghorn *et al.* 1851; Stebbing 1922, pp. 214–15. We continue to have these arguments, nearly 150 years later, over similar issues relating to the environment and development in the tropics.

41. Rawat 1989, p. 12.

42. Another reason for bringing forests under state control was eloquently argued by Ribbentrop: ". . . our Indian forests were thus exposed at the same time to the legitimate demands of a rapidly spreading modern civilization and the waste which accompanies a more primitive state of society" (pp. 61–2). This line of reasoning continues to echo in the neo-Malthusian statements made by planners and policy makers in the central ministries at New Delhi; and similar arguments are stated, perhaps more subtly these days, by governments of advanced industrial countries at global environmental meetings.

43. The Company's demise marked a shift from the policy of protection to that of provision. Canal and road construction was soon augmented by the introduction of railways into the subcontinent. Economic policies of the colonial government focused on increasing the production of raw materials for British industry and expansion of transport infrastructure – roads and railways – for ensuring efficient movement of goods to ports. See Whitcombe 1972, pp. 91–7. Railway construction required steady supplies of iron and durable timber species, both of which were imported during the early years of railway-building from Norway. The reason for importing timber in the initial stages was partly because the colonial government was reluctant to use teak, an extremely valuable commodity, for the production of railway sleepers, and also because the newly established Forest Service did not have a comprehensive inventory of timber species that could be used for such purposes. Forest surveyors and botanists explored the Himalayan forests for substitutable species, and in due course found appropriate varieties such as *sal* (*Shorea robusta*), *chir* (*Pinus roxburghii*), and deodar (*Cedrus deodara*), in Garhwal, Kumaon, and other parts of the North-West Provinces and British Punjab. See Ribbentrop 1900; Stebbing 1922; Smythies 1925; Troup 1919.

44. Wastelands were defined in legal terms as unsurveyed lands that "had relapsed into jungle or had never been cultivated before" and which were the property of the government. See Stowell 1907; Baden-Powell 1892; G.B. Pant 1922.

45. Ribbentrop 1900, pp. 99 ff.; Stebbing 1932; G.R.C. Williams 1874.

46. See Ribbentrop 1900, p. 76; Stebbing 1922, p. 456. Readers may be interested in exploring Hays (1959) for descriptions of similar processes which led to increased state involvement in forestry and

conservation towards the end of the nineteenth century in the United States. Also see Koppes (1987) for a discussion of ideas shaping the forestry and conservation movement during the Progressive Era in the United States.

47. See Mann and Dickinson 1978; Mann 1990, especially Chapter 2 and Appendix II. By comparing production processes in agriculture and manufacturing, Mann and Dickinson argue that agriculture is not as profitable as manufacturing because it is constrained by natural factors such as seasonality, catastrophic variability, and the time required for maturation of crops. Productivity of labour in agriculture is also constrained because work schedules are often limited to daylight hours, and because there are several subsidiary tasks in cultivation that cannot be performed in the manner of industrial assembly lines.

48. See Lal 1989; Troup 1919. For an interesting discussion of the problems of plantation experiments in another part of the world, see Hecht and Cockburn 1989.

49. For a similar argument in the context of agriculture, see Mooney 1978. He argues that the natural or ecological constraints limiting profitability in agriculture are often overcome through an array of production relations that include contract farming, corvée labour, wage labour, tenancy, and sharecropping. Also see Brass 1986, for contemporary examples of how agriculture is made profitable through the use of indentured and bonded labour.

50. Ribbentrop 1900, p. 97; Stebbing 1922, pp. 205–30.

51. When Dietrich Brandis was appointed as the Superintendent of Forests in Pegu, he set himself three objectives: "(1)To protect, and as far as possible, to improve the forests, to arrange the cuttings so as to keep well within their productive powers, in order to ensure a permanent and sustained yield. (2) To make the inhabitants of the forests and the people in the vicinity my friends and allies. (3) As soon as possible to produce an annual surplus revenue." Brandis 1897, p. 108. He proceeded to establish systems of enumeration and organisation of forest extraction. Conditions were imposed on quantities of timber that could be extracted so that the prices charged by firms would stabilise. Since shifting cultivation was a widely adopted practice by communities living in the forested provinces of Burma, Brandis proposed that the most efficient mode for artificial regeneration of teak as well as protection and improvement could be implemented by encouraging cultivators to plant teak in their

newly cleared plots; *ibid.*, pp. 109 ff. This system of artificial regeneration is still widely practised as *taungya* on Forest Department lands in northeastern India and has been introduced into other parts of the country as an afforestation strategy involving local communities (the tree species planted in this manner are not always teak, though this has been tried, somewhat unsuccessfully in the forests of Madhya Pradesh). Similar strategies have been adopted in Southeast Asia; in Indonesia, the system goes by the name of *tumpang sari*; see Peluso 1992. Most of the systems developed in Burma by Brandis formed the broad principles for forest management and conservancy by the Forest Service in India. See Ribbentrop 1900, pp. 74 ff.; Stebbing1932.

52. I went into the field assuming that *haq-haqooq* referred to a bundle of entitlements accorded by the Forest Department to all households living in villages near its forests. This is how, for example, Ramachandra Guha (1989) describes them. He states that "through the mechanisms of the forest act, the state preferred to deal directly with individual households rather than with village communities as such"; p. 55. My interviews and discussions with village leaders and Forest Department officials indicated that Guha's account is flawed. Inalienable rights and concessions are negotiated between a village or a group of villages and the Forest Department, so that households can meet their consumption needs for fuelwood, fodder, and timber for construction and repairs from its forests. For instance, the Forest Department grants timber each year to villages which present their need, through a formal application, based on requests made by individual households to their village representatives; fodder and fuelwood collection by village households in Reserved forests is generally allowed without any formal application. These rights and concessions are, of course, limited to stipulated amounts established by the Forest Department: a fixed volume of 9 cubic feet of round-timber (not sawn into planks) is allocated annually to each household that receives concessions; members of villages are allowed to collect one head-load of fuelwood and one of fodder from the forests on a daily basis. See UP Forest Rules, Appendix XII, Chapter II, Item 5b, in Upadhyay (ed.) 1990, p. 1012.

53. Needless to say, Mr Brandis's systems of forest management were not enthusiastically received by native traders and mercantile firms in Burma. These firms had enjoyed the advantage of free access to Government forests in the past and benefited from the low duties

on timber extracted for sale. As their share of profits began to fall under the new system that came into force following 1856, groups of timber traders and mercantile firms pressured the government to open more forested areas for timber extraction by private entrepreneurs. By 1862, the government acceded to their demands. But unlike previous leases and permits given to merchants, the new system established by Mr Brandis imposed more stringent conditions on the lessees so that forests would not suffer damage and depletion. See Ribbentrop 1900, pp. 75 ff.

54. Private contractors are generally permitted to carry out selective, rather than coupe (uniform or clear) felling; the Forest Service controls the selection of trees to be felled and supervises their girdling. This is seen as necessary for ensuring better production practices and less financial loss for the Department. Selective felling aims at maintaining a mixed composition of age classes within all areas of the forest, as opposed to the clear- or uniform- felling system in which demarcated tracts in the forest are harvested in their entirety so that even-aged stands can be formed either by natural or artificial regeneration. Clear-felling is not extensively practised in India. The Forest Department generally allows this practice for only those tree species that are identified as naturally gregarious or, easily raised through artificial regeneration, or have entered the climax stage of succession. See Troup 1919; Lal 1989, pp. 112–19.

55. UP Forest Department 1983.

56. See Tucker 1983, 1988.

57. G.B. Pant 1922, p. 36.

58. Tucker 1983, pp. 157–8.

59. The colonial Forest Department paid back 80 percent of all the profits generated from forest extraction to the ruler. See Walton 1910, pp. 211–13; Rawat 1989, pp. 90–1.

60. There is very little by way of historical evidence to support Ramachandra Guha's claim that state control over forests in Garhwal and Kumaon was not exercised by pre-British rulers, and that this occurred with the entry of the colonial Forest Service. Guha (1989, pp. 56–7) invokes Marx's concept of alienation to argue that state control over forests was

a negation of the communal appropriation of nature in Uttarakhand. Not only did forests constitute an important means of subsistence, but their products were treated, as in other peasant societies, as a free gift of nature to which all had equal access. The assertion of state monopoly ran contrary to traditional management practices. These practices were at once an affirmation of communal action oriented towards production and of the unity between humans and nature.

s   While Guha's argument has romantic appeal, it fails to be supported by historical evidence either from Garhwal or Kumaon, or for that matter, from Burma. There is also no basis for his claim that all peasants had equal access to forest resources. Guha makes the common error of assuming that the management of forest and grazing areas near village settlements extended across the region as a whole, an assumption which clearly has no historical validity. While forests near villages may have been (and still are) managed as common-access areas, access to other forested areas was mediated by the level of taxation imposed by the ruler on the extraction and sale of various forest products.

61. Ribbentrop 1900, pp. 98–109; Stebbing 1922, pp. 205 ff.

62. Estimates based on the statistical overview provided in the UP Forest Department's *Annual Progress Report of Forest Administration in the United Provinces* for various years.

63. Ribbentrop 1900, pp. 109–13. The analysis is based on my interpretation of the history of experiences in regional forest administration recorded by colonial forest officers, reports on forest problems prepared by political leaders during colonial rule, government orders, and Forest Working Plans that make note of important changes in forest classifications in the region.

64. Brandis 1897; Stebbing 1922.

65. See Rawat 1989b, pp. 17–20.

66. G.B. Pant 1922, pp. 40–60.

67. Rawat 1989b, p. 18; Stebbing 1932.

68. G.B. Pant 1922; Stebbing 1932.

69. Tucker 1988.

70. The rajah of neighbouring Tehri Garhwal faced virulent opposition from his subjects when his Forest Department made a similar request. See Saklani 1986; Rawat 1983, 1989b; G.B. Pant 1922.

71. In 1921, the Forest Service reported 317 fires in Kumaon and Garhwal that destroyed 830 square kilometres of Reserved forests and ruined plantations that had been established over two decades. Forest officers estimated that nearly 24,300 hectares of Reserved

forests set aside for natural regeneration and soil management were severely damaged by arson. Rawat 1989b; Stebbing 1932.

72. See Upadhyay (ed.) 1990, for references to the Forest Act 1927, pp. 1087–97.

73. G.B. Pant 1922, pp. 91–2.

74. *Ibid.*, pp. 84–91.

75. Guha 1989; Rawat 1983, 1989b; Saklani 1986.

76. Tucker 1988.

77. The reports were published under the title of "An Investigation into the Villagers' Rights in the Reserved Forests of Kumaon"; see Rawat 1989a and b.

78. See Upadhyay (ed.) 1990, for text of the *Government Order No. 145-AF/XIV-308–1936*, 1941.

79. See Stebbing1932; Champion and Osmaston 1962; Guha 1989.

80. Champion and Osmaston 1962.

81. Lal 1989, pp. 25, 31; Tucker 1988. Also see passing references to the effects of the *Zamindári* Abolition Acts in Champion and Osmaston 1962, and Rawat 1989b.

82. UP Forest Department 1956.

83. Colonial "rule of law" has been studied by social historians of India, many of whom take part in a forum of debate called the Subaltern Studies Group on South Asian history. Their interpretations of resistance to colonial rule, by and large, centre on contrasting European norms and ideas of social control with indigenous values and consciousness of 'the subaltern natives' to explain the various protests and conflicts that emerged under British colonialism. For critical assessments of these debates, see Gupta 1985; Bayly 1988. I am of the view that while foot-dragging, petty thieving, and arson might plausibly represent 'everyday forms of resistance' engaged by peasants for defending their 'moral economy', these were not the only expressions or forms of protest. (For descriptions of concepts such as 'moral economy' and 'everyday forms of resistance', see Scott 1976, 1985, 1990; E.P. Thompson 1993. Ramachandra Guha's accounts of peasant protest in Garhwal are based on Scott's conceptualisation of moral economy and everyday resistance.) If anything, differentiation within South Asian peasantry across regions and by caste and class indicates that village leaders, who were often better off in terms of economic status and caste, contested the colonial state through the legal system. For example, a case cited in the compila-

tion of Indian forest laws centres on a dispute over the legal definition of 'forest' between a landowner and the Divisional Forest Officer of Raigarh in 1951. The Full Bench of the Nagpur High Court delivered the following judgement:

> The term 'forest' has not been defined anywhere in the Forest Act. In the absence of such a definition the word 'forest' must be taken in its ordinary dictionary sense. The Shorter Oxford English Dictionary, Vol. I gives the following meaning to it − 1) an extensive tract of land covered with trees and undergrowth, sometimes intermingled with pasture . . .; 2) a woodland district, usually belonging to the king, set apart for hunting wild beast and game; 3) a wild, uncultivated waste.
>
> Sub clauses (ii), (iii), and (iv) of Clause (4) (b) of Section 2 of the Indian Forest Act would indicate that the word 'forest' has been used in the definition in its widest significance.

s   See *Laxman Ichharam* v. *D.F.O. Raigarh*, AIR 1951, Nag. 51, (FB), in Upadhyay (ed.) 1990, p. 17.

84. Forest officers found themselves constantly referring forest laws and rules for settling disputes with village leaders and defending the agency in the courts. They rarely enjoyed the luxury of conducting experiments according to the scientific principles of applied ecology in the isolated calm of their forest jurisdictions. See accounts of legal wrangles and desires to work in less litigious circumstances, described in Stebbing 1922, 1932; Champion and Osmaston 1962; Atkinson 1882.

85. Ribbentrop 1900, p. 120. Forest Service officers routinely pointed to the political nature of their work when their superior authorities demanded, in typically magisterial fashion, to know why production targets were not being achieved, or why scientific methods were not being adequately pursued in forest management.

86. UP Forest Department 1989.

87. Bayly 1988, p. 145.

88. Women and children were eased out of these activities because they rarely had access to, or control over household finances. The process was similar to what happened to women and young adults following enclosure of the commons in England. As Humphries (1990) shows, before the enclosures, women and children were able to substantially contribute towards the household income by either engaging in small-scale extraction of commercially valuable common-access

resources, or maintaining milch cattle on these lands. Enclosures effectively erased their rights of access and, as a result, accelerated the pace of proletarianisation in rural England.

89. Tucker 1983, pp. 162–3.

90. Berreman 1972; Rawat 1983, p. 100.

91. Ribbentrop 1900, p. 61.

92. Forest officers often criticised the severity of controls imposed on extraction within Village forests, noting that the legal authority vested in villages over their forests was, in fact, quite illusory because the Forest Department retained control over commercially valuable timber species within these forests. Ramachandra Guha cites the correspondence between the Superintendent of Forests in Dehra Dun and the District Commissioner of Meerut Division in 1897, where the former laments that this was one main reason for the poor maintenance of Village forests. See Guha 1983; see also Government of India, *G.O. No. 526/IV-A-244, Dec. 10, 1900; G.O. No. 786/XIV-403, Dec. 11, 1903; G.O. No. 234-Special/XIV-217, Sept. 19, 1918*; and references to Mr Clutterbuck's *Working Plan for the Government Forests in Jaunsar-Bawar, 1900–01 to 1929–30*, in the Working Plan documents of the Chakrata Forest Division.

93. Military cantonments in colonial hill stations such as Lansdowne, Nainital, Mussoorie, and Chakrata in Garhwal and Kumaon created demand for goods and services in the region. Walton 1910, pp. 73–4, notes that Lansdowne became the centre for recruiting and training soldiers for the Garhwal Rifles and Gurkha Regiments. Woodyatt 1922, p. 86, observed that nearly 90 percent of men in the Gurkha battalions under his command were either from Garhwal or Kumaon. During my field research, I interviewed several retired soldiers who recounted stories of their participation in military campaigns in Mesopotamia during the First World War, and in Burma and Malaya during the Second World War when some had been captured by the Japanese army and interned in camps until the end of war.

94. Tucker 1988, p. 96.

95. Walton 1910, pp. 71–2. He estimates that land-based revenue fell to approximately 1 percent of the total value assessed for cultivable lands by the 1920s.

96. Based on interviews held with Afghan households in the village of Bhatti, and with Nepalese sharecroppers and labourers in the villages of Konain, Budyar, Bhujkoti, Dharagad, and Mundali, and in the

towns of Sahiya, Tiuni, and Kalsi, all in the Chakrata Division of
Dehra Dun district; in the town of Pauri and the villages of Khirsu,
Dudatoli, and Bhainswara in Pauri Garhwal district; the town of
Uttarkashi in Uttarkashi district, and in the village of Chamoli and
town of Gopeshwar in Chamoli district. Labour recruiters and
contractors are generally from western Nepal and are called 'mates'.
They usually make annual trips lasting two or three months to their
villages to recruit labour for forest-based activities such as timber-
felling and resin-tapping. Nepali-speaking households form an amor-
phous community in this region. Not all are migrants; some have
lived in Garhwal for decades without ever returning to Nepal.
Nevertheless, households are generally perceived as 'outsiders' by
village communities in Garhwal. In most of the villages where I
conducted interviews, Nepali households rarely owned land, but
gained access to it through sharecropping or leasing arrangements
with landowning households.

6 DEVELOPMENT IN THE MARGINS

1. Jaunsar-Bawar is the *pargana* (subdistrict) that comprises the northern
   reaches of the district of Dehra Dun. The military cantonment of
   Chakrata is located within this area. Jaunsar-Bawar, along with the
   western subdistricts of Uttarkashi, is classified by the national and
   UP state government as a Backward and Tribal Area.
2. *Amar Ujala*. 1991.
3. The critical literature is enormous, and would be impossible to list
   here. Good overviews of the critiques may be found in Apter 1987;
   Sachs (ed.) 1992; Friedmann 1992; Hettne 1990; Crush (ed.) 1995;
   Brohman 1996; Peet and Watts (eds). 1996; Ferguson 1990; Kothari
   1988; Kitching 1980.
4. See, for example, Shiva 1989; Mies and Shiva 1993; Esteva 1987;
   Escobar 1995a and b; Trainer 1989; Parajuli 1991; Yapa 1993;
   Marglin and Appfel-Marglin (eds). 1990.
5. Escobar 1992, p. 22.
6. This, again, is an enormous body of literature and cannot be
   comprehensively cited here. But see, for example, hooks 1984;
   Spivak 1987; Bhabha 1990; Haraway 1988; Nandy 1989; Minh-ha
   1989; Rabinow 1986.
7. A comprehensive compilation of critical views regarding development can be found in Sachs (ed.) 1992.

8. R. Williams 1983.

9. For a similar discussion, see Watts 1993.

10. Bailey 1996.

11. Naipaul 1990.

12. Rushdie 1991, p. 33.

13. It has managed to whittle away at the caste system, which, as Bardhan 1985, observes, remains "one of history's most well-entrenched and ornately elaborate ideological systems of legitimizing inequality and exploitation" (p. 82). Also see Naipaul 1990, pp. 516–18.

14. Naipaul 1990, pp. 95–118.

15. Chatterjee 1986; Ramachandra Guha 1983.

16. Chatterjee 1986. See also Bailey 1983, 1991.

17. See Bayly 1996; Herring 1989; Rudolph and Rudolph 1987.

18. Ambedkar 1945; Nehru 1946.

19. Interactions between the colonial government and the Indian National Congress have also shaped subsequent modes of political alliance-building in postcolonial India. See Bardhan 1985; S.K. Mitra 1992.

20. Given the diverse forms of coalitions among the dominant elite in different regions, the strength and stability of the ruling political party at the national level integrally depends on ensuring a elected majority in the states. Political control at the state level is equally complex because it requires national-level parties to depend on alliances with village leaders and local elites to gain votes. This strategy is necessary because the majority of the population in almost every state in India continues to be rural, and largely poor; they rarely have the economic power to influence decisions at the national or state level, but they do have the right to vote in the elections. And their votes matter. See Bardhan 1985, particularly Chapters 6 and 9.

21. These processes are not exclusive to India. Scholars of social change in Latin America argue that rural and urban protests in Latin American countries are interlinked with development processes and policies. See for example, Smith 1989; J. Walton 1984; Bebbington 1996; Pezzoli 1993.

22. Chakravarty 1987.

23. The colonial administration argued that industrial development in India was necessary because growing military competition between European powers threatened the flow of trade between India and

Britain, added to the cost of manufactured goods imported from Britain, and rendered the internal economy extremely vulnerable to external factors. See Dewey 1978.

24. Nehru 1946, pp. 410–15.

25. *Ibid.*, pp. 412–13.

26. *Ibid.*, pp. 395–403.

27. *Ibid.*, pp. 495–99. Also see Woodhead 1945; Sen 1981.

28. States have been preoccupied with industrialisation in one form or another ever since the last quarter of the nineteenth century. Germany, Japan, and Russia were all seen as latecomers to industrialisation; as were countries such as South Korea, Taiwan, and other East Asian 'NICs'. What was common to them, as opposed to "early industrialised" countries such as Britain was the necessity for state institutions to be centrally involved in promoting industrialisation so as to remain prosperous through competition within the global economy. See Gerschenkron 1962; Johnson 1982; Amsden 1989; Wade 1990; Fishlow 1990.

29. There has been a long debate among Indian scholars over Nehruvian vs. Gandhian models of development. A recent version of this debate can be found in Gadgil and Guha 1992, 1995.

30. Chakravarty 1987, p. 9.

31. *Ibid.*, p. 3.

32. Forestry was initially classified as a 'state subject' in the Indian Constitution. This meant that state governments, rather than the central government, held authority over the forests within their jurisdiction. Forest officers, however, continued to be recruited through the Indian Forest Service. Officers were selected through national competitive examinations, similar to those for recruitment to the Indian Administrative Service, and began their careers as Divisional Forest Officers in different states. Lower-ranking officials such as Range Officers and Forest Rangers were recruited at the state level, but were expected to pass various examinations for subsequent promotions.

33. See Government of India 1956; Chakravarty 1987, pp. 21–3. Chakravarty argues that Indian planners were not, at least in the first three five-year plans, thinking in terms of surplus extraction from agriculture for financing investment in industry, even though this emerged as the generally accepted view by the third five-year plan. By viewing agriculture as a low-investment sector, planners drastically underestimated the extent and nature of the political mobilis-

ation required for achieving institutional changes such as land reform.

34. See Woodman 1969, pp. 279–301.

35. The Indian government entered into an agreement with the United States for importing wheat prior to the monsoon failures of 1965 and 1966. PL 480 allowed wheat to be exported to India partly as food aid and partly under a soft loan that could be repaid in Indian currency. The rupee payments were utilised by the US government for funding development projects and research in India through the Indo-US Fund. My dissertation research fellowship was supported through this fund by the American Institute of Indian Studies in Chicago and New Delhi.

36. Chakravarty 1987, p. 23.

37. Government of India 1961.

38. Government of India 1970.

39. See Byres 1972; Harriss (ed.) 1982; Raj 1973; Srinivasan 1979; Subramaniam 1979; A.K. Sen 1960, 1984. According to Amartya Sen, an interesting feature of the Green Revolution in India was that much of the capital intensity was *landesque* rather than *labouresque*. This meant that the Green Revolution in India did not lead to large-scale displacement of labour from agriculture. Chakravarty (1987) notes that during the 1970s, capital intensity in agriculture helped achieve an increase in output per unit of land as well as per agricultural worker despite severe land constraints and rising agricultural population; see p. 25, and p. 113, Table 15: "Labour, Land, Capital and Output in Indian Agriculture, 1950–51 to 1979–80".

40. Government of India 1976.

41. Resin-tapping from *chir pine* (*Pinus Longifolia*) became increasingly profitable when innovative methods for distillation and creosoting railway sleepers were developed around the beginning of this century.

42. See Tucker 1988, p. 98; Stebbing 1932, pp. 594–9. The Indian Turpentine and Resin Factory at Bareilly is still a public-sector enterprise and continues to be the major supplier of resin products for Indian industry.

43. The Forest Research Institute was established in 1926, and was considered to be the premier institution for forestry research in the British Empire. It served as the model for other research institutes that were later established in other British colonies. See Tucker 1988, p. 99.

44. *Ibid.*, p. 95; also Stebbing 1932, p. 531.
45. Tucker 1988, p. 102.
46. See Dobhal 1987; Khan and Tripathy 1976; Joshi (ed.) 1983; Swarup 1991.
47. This was considered urgent because the Chinese government had, prior to the war, built a road through Aksai-Chin, the eastern part of Indian Kashmir, and had subsequently claimed the area as Chinese territory. A war was also fought with Pakistan in 1965 over territories in western Kashmir. See Woodman 1969, pp. 311–13.
48. These figures have been calculated based on data provided in UP Forest Department 1983, Table 1.16. The table indicates the extent of deforestation (i.e. forest areas converted to non-forest uses through land transfers or forest clearing) in the whole state during successive five-year plans. Of the total area deforested, nearly 42 percent occurred through land transfers to state and central government departments for hydroelectric power generation and other national projects (though not explicitly stated in the table, this figure includes lands transferred for defence-related purposes; several forest officers indicated that defence-related transfers of forest areas were included in the category National Projects); 34 percent through land titling and conversion to agriculture; 2 percent for road construction, 10 percent through land allocation for establishment of industries; and about 12 percent for miscellaneous purposes (which includes urban development). The data do not reflect the transfers and conversion of forest areas in Garhwal and Kumaon, but offer a rough estimate of the extent of the area set aside for defence-related purposes.
49. Pangtey and Joshi 1987; Singh and Berry 1990.
50. See Chapter 5 of this book; also see Bora 1987; Khanka 1988.
51. Mountainous terrain, lack of infrastructure, and fragmented land-holdings distributed across different ecological and altitudinal zones were hindrances to the spread of Green Revolution strategies in the region; the techniques were, however, adopted by landowners with access to capital and credit in the sub-Himalayan tracts of Garhwal and Kumaon. See Swarup 1991.
52. Dobhal 1987; Khan and Tripathy 1976; Swarup 1991.
53. See Government of India 1976. The section on "Forest Policy" reiterates that forests must be regarded as national resources and hence not open to reckless exploitation by local communities. State Forest Departments were expected to be firm in limiting the number

of requests or demands for additional rights and concessions within their jurisdictions. The Government of India's attitude towards communities located near forests is less severe now compared to when this report was written.

54. See UP Forest Department 1983, Tables 13.8 a, b, and c. The data provide trends in annual changes in real prices for major and minor forest products between 1950 and 1970 for the state of Uttar Pradesh. Tables 3.14 through 3.17 indicate that the value of construction timber rose at about 7 percent per annum, fuelwood at 2.5 percent, resin at 14 percent, pulpwood, bamboos, and grasses at 10 percent; *tendu* leaves, used for making local varieties of cigarettes (*beedis*) and cigars (*suttas or cheroots*), rose by 21 percent each year.

55. See Chapter 5 of this book. This point was repeatedly emphasised during my field interviews with village leaders and organisers of labour cooperatives.

56. See Dogra 1980.

57. Dogra 1980; Bahuguna 1981; Bhatt 1987. In my interviews, several Divisional Forest Officers observed that given the directives of the national forest policy, they would have risked disciplinary action and faced suspension from their jobs if they had agreed to the demands made by village leaders. They also could not have mandated the use of locally organised labour groups for felling operations in the region, because this would have violated the Forest Department's policy of obtaining market prices through public auctions.

58. See Jain 1984; Shiva and Bandyopadhyay 1987; Ramachandra Guha 1989, pp. 180–1; Berreman 1988; Weber 1988.

59. The view that these protests were primarily against non-local contractors and labourers is countered by the fact that some contractors were locally-based, and had been hired by firms to carry out the felling. Amit Mitra (1993I, p. 31) reports his interview with one such subcontractor, Jagadish Prasad Nautiyal, now an elected official representing a village near the town of Mussoorie in Dehra Dun district:

> "I was a sub-contractor of Symonds [a sporting goods manufacturer]. Earlier, I had worked as a labourer. In 1973, I got the contract for felling trees in Pangarbasa forest near Mandal village. That was the first time I got a contract and, as it turns out, the last. Bhatt said he would not allow the felling and the villagers threatened to hug the trees.
>
> I got scared and did not go to the forest. Instead, I met district

forest officer Narinder Singh Negi, who asked me to wait till he could pacify the DGSM workers. After three months, I was permitted to fell trees in Phata in the Kedarnath [Reserved forest] division. But the DGSM got there, too. I lost Rs. 32,000 in payments to 17 labourers. The DGSM didn't *chipko* any tree, but it put up posters against me all over Gopeshwar even though I had not engaged any Nepalese labourers. The workers were from my village."

7 CHIPKO'S MOVEMENTS

1. See, for example, the classic by Charles Mackay (1841) which has been reprinted several times since its original date of publication. In an introduction to the 1932 edition of the book, Bernard Baruch comments that "[t]he value of all this literature [on crowds and popular delusions] lies in its emphasis on forces that are, at all times, functions – and that, at some times, seem to become controlling factors – of national or even racial life. No preventive is anywhere suggested, but accurate knowledge and popular recognition of them and their early symptoms should lighten and may even avoid the more harmful of their full effects" (p. xiv).

2. Classic works on this subject are by Polanyi 1944; Banfield 1958; Moore 1966; Hobsbawm 1965; E.P. Thompson 1966.

3. There are numerous studies on rural struggles for almost every region in the world. The best analysis of a political movement that attempted to preserve the power of rural landlords is by Gerschenkron 1943; for an example of religious millenarian movement, see Michael 1966, in which the leader of the peasant rebellion in China saw himself as the younger brother of Jesus Christ.

4. See Skocpol 1982; Paige 1983.

5. Wolf 1969.

6. Scott 1976.

7. Scott 1985, 1990.

8. Popkin 1979.

9. Paige 1976, 1983.

10. Touraine 1981; Castells 1983; Offe 1985.

11. See Sklair 1998.

12. See Ranajit Guha 1983. Ranajit Guha delineates the social category of "subaltern" as a means of referring to particular oppressed groups, and their consciousness and motivations for protest. His writings have established a genre of revisionist historical literature that is now

known as Subaltern Studies, various volumes of which have been published by Oxford University Press, New Delhi. The genre has contributed to the rise of a new interdisciplinary area of research called Postcolonial Studies. See Gandhi 1998, for a good introduction to this literature.

13. Ramachandra Guha 1985, 1989.

14. Mies and Shiva 1993.

15. For a critique of the Subaltern Studies literature, see Gupta 1985; Bayly 1989; Bahl 1997.

16. Brass 1991, 1994.

17. Omvedt 1990, 1993.

18. Castells 1997, p. 7.

19. The process of establishing and legitimising congruence between identity and particular roles can be long, arduous, and incomplete. For example, with reference to national identity, see E. Weber 1976; Anderson 1983.

20. If 'class' is seen as referring to the position of a person in relation to the process of capital accumulation and associated social power, then class identity (with respect to the means, relations, and conditions of production, consumption, and accumulation) can be used to mobilise people around the idea of class as shared experiences, rather than as a formal identity; on the other hand, if class is rigidly defined in terms of particular roles or purely in terms of economic status, then mobilisation may privilege ethnic, caste, race, or gender identity roles. See Harvey 1996.

21. This point is made somewhat differently by Migdal 1974; Gramsci 1971, pp. 229–30. See also Chatterjee 1986; Ranajit Guha 1983.

22. S.K. Mitra 1992, pp. 210–11. One of the major achievements of the Indian government has been the legislation of *Panchayati Raj* (loosely translated as village self-governance), which essentially transformed the nature of politics at the village level. In the past, village *panchayats* were organised as committees of five persons who either held these positions on the basis of their hereditary status, or were selected by village elders. They were, in most cases, representatives of the dominant castes in the village. Gaining their political support and loyalty required national parties to ensure their continued dominance in the village, or create alternative relations of patronage by opening *panchayats* to elections. Elected representation has created more uncertainties – in terms of political strength and stability for the ruling party – in the short term, but has also created opportunities

for political parties to adopt a variety of strategies for garnering the majority of rural votes. These can range from supporting the dominant castes, pitting local elites against one another, or promoting representatives of lower-caste groups as agents of economic progress and social justice.

23. See S.K. Mitra 1992.

24. These arguments were revisited in my interviews with various village leaders and small-scale timber contractors in the region. See also Agarwal and Narain 1982, pp. 42-3; Aryal 1994, pp. 8-23; Bahuguna 1981; Berreman 1989; Bhatt 1988; Dogra 1980; Government of India 1985.

25. Field interviews with forest officers, 1990-91.

26. See A. Mitra 1993a, p. 30. He quotes a former lawyer and Chipko activist, P.C. Tiwari: "Bahuguna, too, favoured granting the local people the right to fell trees for commercial exploitation. On April 4, 1977, he performed a ceremony to worship the axe, the major instrument of survival of the forest labourer. He was not a conservationist then."

27. See Bahuguna 1981, 1982, 1987; Weber 1988.

28. See for example, Dogra 1980; Shiva 1989, Shiva and Bandyopadhyay 1986a and b, 1987; T. Weber 1988.

29. Bardhan 1985, 1991.

30. Mrs Gandhi argued for nationalisation by linking it to the recommendations of the fourth (and later, the fifth) five-year plan which stressed the need to engage in poverty alleviation, accelerated development of the agriculture sector and rural areas, reduction of interregional disparities, and expanded employment creation.

31. I am following Pranab Bardhan's analysis of class formations in post-independence India. He argues that three elite classes emerged in the decades following independence: the administrative, the business, and the rural elites. These class categories also tend to overlap with elite caste divisions. Thus if we look beyond the economic arguments provided by Mrs Gandhi's party, nationalisation was largely used to strengthen Congress (I)'s political support among the dominant administrative classes (who also happen to be the dominant castes in India) by expanding the job security and employment prospects and security of professionals, while simultaneously attempting to gain the support of workers in the organised industrial sector. See Bardhan 1985, p. 58; Bardhan 1991; Chakravarty 1987; Rudolph and Rudolph 1987.

32. The Partition of India resulted in the creation of West and East Pakistan (now Bangladesh). In 1970, following the elections in Pakistan, Sheikh Mujibur Rahman, the leader of the Awami League and from East Pakistan, won by a large majority, and was expected to form a new government. The incumbent rulers in West Pakistan led by Mr Zulfikar Ali Bhutto sought to prevent this from happening (because it was seen as eroding the traditional power base controlled by elites of West Pakistan's Punjab and Sind regions), which led to demands for independence in East Pakistan. The Indian government offered its support for Sheikh Mujibur Rahman and helped the rebel army, Mukti Bahini, fight against the Pakistani army. The Indo-Pakistan war was fought on both eastern and western fronts, and ended when Pakistani troops in the East surrendered to the Indian army in 1970. On gaining independence, East Pakistan became Bangladesh.

33. See Bardhan 1991.

34. Bardhan 1985, pp. 37–8.

35. A. Mitra 1993, p. 32, describes Mrs Gandhi's subsequent views regarding Chipko:

> Reacting to Chipko in 1980, Indira Gandhi told *Nature* magazine in an interview, "Well, frankly, I don't know all the aims of the movement. But if it is that trees should not be cut, I'm all for it." When informed that Chipko was concerned also about poverty in the region, she replied, "Naturally, anybody who lives in a backward country has to be concerned about that, too." But clarifying that trees are important in themselves, she added, "The cutting of trees has immediately brought havoc because it has increased our drought, it has increased our floods and has made vast areas much more difficult to live in."

s36. Government of India 1976; Lal 1989.

37. Government of Uttar Pradesh 1975.

38. This legislation overruled earlier regulations which allowed land-owners to sell trees harvested on their property after paying a nominal tax to revenue authorities. See Government of Uttar Pradesh 1976.

39. Agarwal and Narain 1982, p. 41.

40. Upadhyay (ed.) 1990.

41. According to Clarification on Sub-Clause 2 (iv) of the Act [Section 1.8 (iii)], "The regional office [of the Ministry of Environment and

Forests] will however, seek prior clearance of the Ministry whenever the proposal involves clear-felling of forest areas having density above 0.4 irrespective of the area involved. Also prior clearance would be required when the proposal is for clear-felling of an area of size more than 20 ha. in the plains and 10 ha. in the hilly region, irrespective of density." See Government of India 1997, p. 30.

42. Upadhyay (ed.) 1990, pp. 452–9; Lal 1989, pp. 33–4; Agarwal and Narain 1991a.

43. Forest (Conservation) Rules, 1981, substituted by Notification No. GSR 14, dated December 14, 1987. See Upadhyay (ed.) 1990, p. 457. The amendment aims to restrict individuals and private corporations from claiming the right of access to public lands by planting trees. Section 4.3.2 of the National Forest Policy of 1988 broadly indicates that the regulatory role of the ministry as well as relevant state forestry agencies is necessary for preventing introduction of exotic species without long-term scientific trials "undertaken by specialists in ecology, forestry and agriculture [who] have established that they are suitable and have no adverse impact on native vegetation and environment." See Government of India 1997, pp. 67–8.

44. It is interesting to note that despite being a smaller country and receiving substantial amounts of foreign aid, most of the economic growth in Nepal has occurred in the districts surrounding Kathmandu and along the *terai* region bordering India. Nepal's western, eastern, and northern districts are extremely poor. Most of the Nepalese labourers and migrants to India and Bhutan arrive from these impoverished regions. (Nepal receives approximately US$16 foreign aid per capita as opposed to about US$2 in India; see Lipton and Toye 1991, p. 3.)

45. Interviews with regional and divisional managers of the Forest Corporation, 1990–91. Some managers justified their recruitment of migrant labourers by arguing that tensions and rivalries between local leaders in charge of labour cooperatives in the region resulted in inefficient felling and conversion of timber, poor management of finances, and increased costs of production. Their justifications for recruiting migrant labour from outside the region stem from the fact that during the early phase of mobilisation, Chipko activists criticised private forest contractors for not employing local labour. Some officials of the Forest Corporation were more forthright about their decision to hire labour from other regions, stating that they preferred

contract labour from western Nepal because the Nepalese were willing to work for lower wages and more likely to submit to the disciplinary control exercised by the labour agents.

46. Interviews with village leaders, Chakrata Block, Dehra Dun district, 1990–91; see also A. Mitra 1993a and b.

47. Field interviews, 1990–91. See also *Amar Ujala*, 18 February 1991; *Hindustan* 1990.

48. UP Forest Department 1989.

49. *Amar Ujala*, 5 July 1991.

50. Interviews with forest guards in Garhwal, Chakrata, and Tons Forest Divisions, 1990–91. Forest guards are not allowed to carry arms; this was legislated in earlier forest Acts under colonial rule so that local communities would not feel threatened by Forest Department staff. The Divisional Forest Officer was, however, permitted an arms licence; this was perhaps a concession to senior officers in the colonial forest service (who were mainly British) and in recognition of their keen interest in hunting as sport. See Webber 1902, which, while being extremely informative about forests in the Himalayas, reads like a memoir of sporting excursions for hunting rare animals. Also see Stebbing 1920.

51. See *Himachal Times* 1990; *Indian Express* 1990. In a brief interview in 1997, the Forest Conservator of the Yamuna Circle told me that he was unsure of whether the green-felling ban had effectively ended in the region, and whether this had led to an increase in legal and illegal timber extraction (he admitted that this was more than likely to occur). Relaxation of the ban has made some difference for village communities in Chakrata because they can now apply to the Forest Department to obtain undamaged trees (concessional timber) for building repairs. See pp. 114–35 above for explanations of rights and concessions accorded to village communities by the Forest Department.

52. This issue was repeatedly raised by village residents during my field interviews in 1990–91 and, later, in 1993, 1994, and 1997. See also Jain 1984; *Amar Ujala*, 5 March 1991, 20 April 1991, 12 June 1991.

The diversification of illegal activities is not restricted to the new timber and liquor mafia. Over the past ten years or more, increased government restrictions on the cultivation of opium and Indian hemp (*cannabis sativa*) have made it illegal to engage in petty commodity production of these crops. Households that have continued small-scale cultivation of these crops can be charged and punished for engaging in their production under the national Drugs and Psychotropic Substances Act. It may be useful to remember that both hemp and opium cultivation played a role in the region's agricultural economy (see p. 81–3 above), even though most of the large-scale, commercial production of opium occurred in the Indo-Gangetic plains and parts of central India.

India continues to be one of the largest suppliers of legally grown opium for the world's pharmaceutical industry. The government issues permits to farmers for cultivating the crop, and purchases their entire harvest. Some of the district administrators I interviewed said that permits for opium cultivation in the region were withdrawn because they found it difficult – given the mountainous terrain, land-use patterns, and cultivation practices – to effectively monitor the growers and control illegal sales (to non-government buyers).

53. During my field interviews in 1990–91, village leaders and block representatives from various parts of the region repeatedly pointed to this example, and also commented on Maneka Gandhi's (the Minister of Environment at the time) marked silence regarding the debates raging over construction of the Tehri Dam, an obvious contrast to her usually voluble support for wildlife preservation and forest conservation. I found it interesting that most village leaders interviewed were not opposed to the Tehri Dam project; they felt that it would supply much-needed electricity to the region and would result in improved living conditions and local economic development. Also see Agarwal and Narain 1991a.

54. Field interviews, 1990–91, 1994; Agarwal and Narain 1991a; A. Mitra 1993a, p. 35.

55. One woman from Reni – the village celebrated in almost every account of Chipko – stated that she had since come to hate the word *paryavaran* (environment), and is quoted to have said, "We took part in Chipko and we've been left dangling ever since; we've had enough, we don't want to attempt anything else." See A. Mitra 1993b, p. 35. The original quote is in Hindi, "*Chipko karke hum latak gaye, bas ab aur kuchh nahin karna.*"

56. Field interviews, 1990–91; Agarwal and Narain 1991a; A. Mitra 1993b, p. 35, quotes one activist as saying: "We cut trees in 111 places, where the government was using the Forest Conservation Act to hold up development projects. After all, we had to consider whether the trees are for the people or if it's the other way around. Nearly 4,500 development schemes in the hills are held up due to

environmental reasons. The hill people want trees, but they want development, too."

57. Dhoundiyal *et al.* (eds) 1993.

58. *Sunday*, 6–12 November 1994; Aryal 1994b; Mawdsley 1997.

59. Field interviews, 1990–91, 1994.

60. Most of the tourist facilities along pilgrimage, mountaineering, and remote trekking routes have been established and are run by the Hill Development Agency. Their services are fairly minimal, and the hotels are unable to deal with the demand generated during the peak seasons May–June and mid-August through mid-October.

61. Interviews with property agents and developers in Dehra Dun and Mussoorie, 1990–91, 1993, 1994, 1997.

62. Several village leaders and elected block representatives offered examples where the Hill Development Department – staffed predominantly by bureaucrats from the plains and located in Lucknow (the state capital which is in the plains) – set up a credit scheme for purchasing tractors without any recognition of the fact that these were inappropriate for terrace cultivation on steep mountain slopes. Another oft-quoted example was a scheme promoted by the Hill Development Department for ferry boats without, again, any knowledge that such transport would be both dangerous and impossible to use for fording mountain rivers and rapids. I am inclined to think that many of these anecdotes have become well-embellished stories through repeated telling, but I do believe they reflect the general sense of disenchantment among local communities towards the 'plains' government of Uttar Pradesh and the 'plains-orientated' mentality of its administrators. See also Dhoundiyal *et al.* (eds) 1993.

63. The population of Uttar Pradesh is anywhere between 170 and 200 million. The bulk of this population is concentrated in the Indo-Gangetic plains.

64. *Sunday*, 1994. The BJP's strategy was confined to playing on the politics of regional identity. It argued for the creation of a state named 'Uttaranchal' rather than 'Uttarakhand' (in Hindi, the former word means "northern province" while the latter refers to a "northern region") thereby distinguishing itself from other regional political parties which had been mobilising support for the creation of Uttarakhand. Mawdsley 1997, notes that when the issue of Uttarakhand was raised in the Indian Parliament in 1993, only one MP from the BJP chose to be present for the discussion.

65. The proposal outlined reservation of 50 percent of all government

jobs and access to higher education for Scheduled Tribes (7.5 percent), Scheduled Castes (15 percent), and Other Backward Castes (27 percent). Caste surveys indicate that the majority of the population in Uttarakhand does not fall within these categories, and would thus have been denied access to government jobs and higher education. As Mawdsley 1997 points out, in the absence of any significant employment in manufacturing or other tertiary service sectors in the region (excluding the cities of Dehra Dun and Nainital), government jobs provide the bulk of salaried employment in the region. This is perhaps why access to education is seen as extremely important among communities in Uttarakhand, which has a high level of literacy compared to the plains (about 60 percent in Uttarakhand compared to about 40 percent for the plains).

66. For media reports of the 1994 events surrounding the Uttarakhand agitation, see *Frontline* 7 October and 4 November 1994; *Sunday*, 1994. For a good, detailed analysis of evolving caste-centred politics and their effects on the continuing agitation for Uttarakhand statehood, see Mawdsley 1997; Aryal 1994b. Mawdsley notes that the confrontation between Uttarakhand activists and the UP state police was "successfully 're-worked' into a pro- and anti-reservation format that distracted attention from the real issues at the heart of the Uttarakhand movement – regional development; cultural (as opposed to caste) unity; and the desire for greater devolution of political power in the context of an under-developed area." Both Mawdsley and Aryal note that caste identities in Uttarakhand differ substantially between districts even though they broadly appear to fall within two officially designated upper-caste categories. They differ from those that exist in the plains and are consequently the source of much confusion, resentment, and misrepresentation outside the region.

There is, in my view, a great degree of confusion even *within* Uttarakhand regarding the distribution of its resident population by caste categories. This is because the issue of caste has been the object of contention among various political parties since Independence, and partly because it has been introduced as a factor, since 1994, into the Uttarakhand movement which had previously maintained its focus on issues of regional development and devolution of political power. While the Constitutional Order of 1950 and the subsequent amendment of the Schedule Castes and Scheduled Tribes Act 1796 identify those castes specified in Parts 1 through

19 of the Schedule (1950) on the basis of untouchability (caste) and tribal affiliation (tribes), there is no mention of "Other Backward" castes. The Schedule identifies sixty-six different 'untouchable' castes for Uttar Pradesh. Mawdsley cites the Mandal Commission Report as well as her interviews with protestors in Mussoorie, stating that the proportion of upper castes (Brahmins and Rajputs) in the region is about 80 percent, with Other Backward castes between 2 and 3 percent; the remaining 17 to 18 percent of the Uttarakhand population presumably falls within the category of "Scheduled" or untouchable castes. These figures are in stark contrast with those for the plains region of UP, where 16 percent of the population falls within the upper-caste category, while Other Backward castes comprise 50 percent; this means that, according to her statistics, the population of Scheduled castes in the plains is about 34 percent. However, according to another set of statistics provided by the Director of the UP Harijan and Social Welfare Department, the proportion of Scheduled castes in the plains is about 21 percent; see Upadhyay (ed.) 1990, pp. 97–8. These statistics indicate that approximately 16 percent of the population in Uttarakhand falls within the Scheduled caste category. The creation of the relatively new category of Other Backward castes by the 1990 Mandal Commission Report has not only caused a great deal of confusion, but also contributed to heightened insecurity among Scheduled caste groups in Uttarakhand, because they fear becoming victims of the general resentment towards Other Backward castes. The politics of reservation (affirmative action) and identity are, as one can readily observe in India, extremely unpredictable and not altogether benign.

67. *Sunday* 1994, p. 44.

68. The emergence of Joint Forest Management strategies in various parts of India are an indication of such collaborative efforts. These have stemmed from the efforts of state Forest Departments (rather than the Ministry of Environment) to collaborate and negotiate forest management practices with village communities through differing arrangements and incentives for maintaining and enhancing their resource base. State Forest Departments in India have been leaders in social forestry – with the adjective "social" being used in both a descriptive and a normative sense – and similar experiments with Joint Forest Management are being tried in diverse countries and regions of the world such as Canada, northern California, Sri

Lanka, Thailand, and parts of west Africa. See Corbridge and Jewitt 1997; Poffenberger and McGean (eds) 1996; Tiwary 1998.

69. See discussions of natural resource management in references cited above; see also B. Agarwal 1997; Dréze and Sen (eds) 1997.

70. See Banerjee 1984; for rural discontent in neighbouring states, see Anderson and Huber 1988.

71. G. Williams 1997; Dréze and Sen (eds) 1997.

72. Government of West Bengal 1996; Poffenberger and McGean (eds) 1996; Poffenberger 1994.

73. Society for the Promotion of Wastelands Development 1993.

74. See Lieten 1992, 1996; Dréze and Sen (eds) 1996.

75. For critical analyses of ongoing experiments, see Corbridge and Jewitt 1997; Rahul 1997; Tiwary 1998.

76. The borders between India and China (between Uttarakhand and Tibet) were to be gradually opened to regional trade, beginning in 15 July 1992, allowing for barter, exchange, and commerce in freely convertible currency. See Naqvi 1992.

8 REGIONAL QUESTIONS AND SUSTAINABLE DEVELOPMENT

1. For example, see Corbridge 1988; Hauser 1993.

2. See Braudel 1973, 1977; Bourdieu 1977.

3. See Braudel 1977, pp. 5–7; Braudel 1966, pp. 651–6.

4. Bourdieu (1977) uses these terms to describe the relationship between structures and 'habitus'. See Chapter 2, particularly pp. 86–95.

5. *Ibid.*, p. 35.

6. I am, in a sense, trying to rearticulate what many scholars in the disciplinary traditions of geography and regional development have been saying about regions and regionality. See, for example, Harvey 1996; Friedmann 1988; McGee 1997.

7. A. Mitra 1993a and b; see, in particular, pp. 32, 35, 50–1.

8. See Agarwal and Narain 1991a; Aryal 1994a.

9. See the comments of leading Indian environmentalists such as Jayanto Bandyopadhyay, Ramachandra Guha, Madhav Gadgil, and Anupam Misra in "Crosscurrents", *Down to Earth*, 30 April 1993, pp. 45–7; also see Mies and Shiva 1993.

10. Both Kashmir and Assam share borders with neighbouring countries.

The conflict in Assam initially erupted over demands for adequate compensation for the petroleum resources extracted in the region, and increased investment in regional development; it escalated over time and was further complicated by the steady influx of impoverished refugees from Bangladesh attempting to settle in the region. The conflict in Kashmir has a long and complex geopolitical history that reaches back into the colonial period, and remains intractable because of the continuing bellicosity between India and Pakistan over territories in the western Himalayas. In both these instances, the conflicts have been represented as being primarily motivated by religious or ethnic differences, rather than as crises of regional sustainability that emerged in the context of geopolitical strategies and economic policies pursued by the Indian government.

11. See for example, Daly 1991. A detailed discussion of debates on sustainable development can be found in Mitlin 1992; Redclift 1987; Bryant and Parnwell 1996.

12. See Beder 1993; for views of transnational corporations, see the Business Council for Sustainable Development 1992; Hampson 1990.

13. See Taylor and Buttel 1992; Agarwal and Narain 1991b.

14. Mies and Shiva 1993, pp. 318–22; Gadgil and Guha 1995.

15. See Peluso 1993. She argues that the rhetoric of global environmental change, deforestation, and ecological collapse has allowed "globally concerned" environmental groups to tacitly support coercive conservation tactics that weaken local claims to resource access for sustaining livelihoods. Peluso observes that some of the conservation programmes introduced by international conservation groups in Indonesia and Kenya have not merely 'armed' local non-governmental organisations with symbolic and financial support to 'empower' local users, but have directed the bulk of their efforts towards influencing state policy.

16. Mies and Shiva 1993; Gadgil and Guha 1995, pp. 123–32, 190–1.

17. See the recent collection of essays edited by Young 1997.

18. See Agarwal and Narain 1991b; Corbett 1995. Charges of 'environmental imperialism' also occasionally emerge from unlikely quarters such as the GATT and OECD, institutions not commonly renowned for viewing the world through Trotskyist lenses. See Dodwell 1992.

19. Rangan 1999.

20. See Bose and Jalal (eds) 1998; also Jalal 1995, for a good discussion of substantive democracy. For critiques of 'symbolic' democracy in the context of contemporary European and North American politics, see Wood 1995; Beck 1998.

BIBLIOGRAPHY

Newspapers and Magazines

Agarwal, A. and Narain, S. 1991. "Chipko People Driven to 'Jungle Kato' [Cut the Forests] Stir". *Economic Times.* 31 March.

Amar Ujala. 1991. "Bahuguna's Statements Criticised". 8 February.

——. 1991. "Inefficient Management of Forest Corporation Causes Wastage of Timber in Hill Regions of UP". 18 February.

——. 1991. "Women Strive Yet Again to Ban Liquor from Hill Regions". 20 April.

——. 1991. "Demonstrations Against Sale of Illicit Liquor in Uttarkashi". 12 June.

——. 1991. "Timber Mafia Thumbs Its Nose at Forest Laws". 5 July.

——. 1991. "Women Demonstrate Against Brewing of Illicit Liquor in Tehri Garhwal". 5 March.

Bardhan, P. 1991. "State and Dynamic Comparative Advantages". *Economic Times.* New Delhi edition. 19–20 March.

Dodwell, D. 1992. "GATT Issues Warning Against Environmental Imperialism". *Financial Times.* 12 February.

Frontline. 1994. "Fire in the Hills, Pulls and Pressures in UP". 7 October.

——. 1994. "Violent Games: the Uttarakhand Stir and Power Politics". 4 November.

Himachal Times. 1990. "Amendment of Forest Act for Developing Hill Areas". 2 April.

——. 1990. "Tiger Kills Forest Guard". Dehra Dun edition. 30 May.

Hindustan. 1990. "Millions of Rupees Wasted by the Forest Corporation". 31 August.

Hindustan Times. 1990. "Of Elephantine Problems". Saturday Magazine. New Delhi edition. 30 June.

Indian Express. 1990. "UP to Amend Tree Protection Act". New Delhi edition. 28 March.

Lamb, C. 1992. "Forests Set to Fire World Passions". *Financial Times.* 15 June.

Naqvi, J. 1992. "TransHimalayan Trade with China after 30 years". *India-West.* 10 July.

Sen, A.N. 1992. "Kamal Nath [Minister of Environment and Forests] Employs Street Savvy on World [Global Summit] Scene". Reprinted by arrangement with the *Times of India. India-West.* 10 June.

Sunday. 1994. "The Sound and the Fury: Is the Uttarakhand Agitation Taking a Violent Turn?" 6–12 November: 44–7.

Times of India. 1991. "Another Man-eater Roams in Kumaon". New Delhi edition. 25 February.

Note: The titles of articles from the regional newspapers *Amar Ujala* and *Hindustan* have been translated from Hindi.

GOVERNMENT DOCUMENTS AND PUBLICATIONS

Government of India. 1956. *Second Five-Year Plan.* New Delhi: National Planning Commission.

——. 1961. *Third Five-Year Plan.* New Delhi: National Planning Commission.

——. 1970. *Fourth Five-Year Plan.* New Delhi: National Planning Commission.

——. 1976. *Report of the National Commission on Agriculture, Volume IX: Forestry.* New Delhi: Ministry of Agriculture and Irrigation.

——. 1985. *National Forest Policy.* New Delhi: Ministry of Environment.

——. 1997. *The Indian Forest Act, 1927 along with Forest Conservation Act, 1980, Consolidated Guidelines for Diversion of Forest Land under* the Forest (Conservation) Act, 1980 and National Forest Policy, 1988. Dehra Dun: Natraj Publishers.

Government of Uttar Pradesh. 1975. The Uttar Pradesh Forest Corporation Act, 1974 (UP Act No. 4 of 1975). Lucknow: UP Government Press.

——. 1976. The Uttar Pradesh Tree Protection Act, 1976. Lucknow: UP Government Press.

Government of West Bengal. 1996. Status Report on Arabari Socio-Economic Project. Calcutta: Directorate of Forests, Silviculture, South Division.

Society of the Promotion of Wastelands Development. 1993. Joint Forest Management Update 1993. New Delhi: SPWD.

State Planning Organisation. 1984. Statistical Diary of UP State. Lucknow: Economics and Statistical Department.

UP Forest Department. 1922. Annual Progress Reports of Forest Administration in the United Provinces, 1920–21. Allahabad: Government Press.

——. 1936. Annual Progress Reports of Forest Administration in the United Provinces, 1934–35. Allahabad: Government Press.

——. 1956. Annual Progress Reports of Forest Administration in Uttar Pradesh, 1954–55. Allahabad: Government Press.

——. 1983. Forest Statistics: Uttar Pradesh, compiled up to 1981–82, Lucknow: Forest Administration and Development Circle.

——. 1989. Forest Statistics: Uttar Pradesh. Lucknow: Forest Administration and Development Circle.

Upadhyay, C.B. (ed.) 1990. Forest Laws, with Commentaries on Indian Forest Act and Rules, State Acts, Rules Regulations etc. 7th edn. Allahabad: Hind Publishing House.

BOOKS AND ARTICLES

Abu-Lughod, J. 1989. Before European Hegemony: The World System A.D. 1250–1350. New York: Oxford University Press.

Agarwal, A. and Narain, S. 1982. The State of India's Environment. New Delhi: Centre for Science and the Environment.

——. 1991. "Global Warming in an Unequal World: A Case

of Environmental Colonialism". *Earth Island Journal*. Spring: 39–40.

Agarwal, B. 1986. *Cold Hearths and Barren Slopes: The Woodfuel Crisis in the Third World*. London: Zed Books.

———. 1990. "Social Security and the Family: Coping with Seasonality and Calamity in Rural South Asia". *Journal of Peasant Studies*. 17 (3): 341–412.

———. 1992. "The Gender and Environment Debate: Lessons from India". *Feminist Studies*. 18 (1): 119–58.

———. 1994. *A Field of One's Own: Gender and Land Rights in South Asia*. Cambridge: Cambridge University Press.

———. 1997. "Environmental Action, Gender Equity and Women's Participation". *Development and Change*. 28 (1): 1–43.

Ahmad, A. 1992. *In Theory: Classes, Nations, Literatures*. London: Verso.

Alavi, H. 1980. "India: Transition from Feudalism to Colonial Capitalism". *Journal of Contemporary Asia*. 10 (4): 359–99.

Allen, G.M. and Gould Jr, E.M. 1986. "Complexity, Wickedness, and Public Forests". *Journal of Forestry*. 84 (4): 20–3.

Ambedkar, B.R. 1945. *Annihilation of Caste: With a Reply to Mahatma Gandhi*. Bombay: Bharat Bhushan Press.

Amsden, A.H. 1989. *Asia's Next Giant: South Korea and Late Industrialization*. London: Oxford University Press.

Anderson, B. 1980. "Old State, New Society: Indonesia's New Order in Comparative Historical Perspective". *Journal of Asian Studies*, XLII (3): 477–96.

———. 1983. *Imagined Communities: Reflections on the Origins and Spread of Nationalism*. London: Verso.

Anderson, R.S. and Huber, W. 1988. *The Hour of the Fox: Tropical Forests, the World Bank, and Indigenous People in Central India*. Seattle: University of Washington Press.

Apter, D. 1987. *Rethinking Development: Modernization, Dependency, and Postmodern Politics*. Newbury Park, Cal.: Sage.

Arrighi, G. 1994. *The Long Twentieth Century: Money, Power, and the Origins of Our Times*, London: Verso.

Aryal, M. 1994a. "Axing Chipko". *Himal*. 7 (1): 8–23.

——. 1994b. "Angry Hills: An Uttarakhand State of Mind". *Himal*, November/December: 10–21.

Atkinson, E.T. 1882. *The Himalayan Gazetteer*. Vol. I, Parts I and II. Vol. III, Parts I and II. Reprinted 1989. New Delhi: Cosmo Publications.

Baden-Powell, (Lord) B.H. 1892. *Land Systems in British India*. Oxford: Clarendon Press.

Baeten, E.M. 1996. *The Magic Mirror: Myth's Abiding Power*. Albany, NY: State University of New York Press.

Bahl, V. 1997. "Relevance (or Irrelevance) of Subaltern Studies". *Economic and Political Weekly*. 32 (23): 1333–44.

Bahuguna, S. 1981. *Chipko: A Novel Movement for Establishment of a Cordial Relationship between Man and Nature*. Tehri Garhwal: Chipko Information Centre.

——. 1982. "Let the Himalayan Forests Live". *Science Today*. March: 41–6.

——. 1987. "The Chipko: A People's Movement". In M.K. Raha (ed.) *The Himalayan Heritage*: pp. 238–48. New Delhi: Gian Publishing House.

Bailey, F.G. 1983. *Tactical Uses of Passion: An Essay in Power, Reason, and Reality*. Ithaca, NY: Cornell University Press.

——. 1991. *The Prevalence of Deceit*. Ithaca, NY: Cornell University Press.

——. 1996. *The Civility of Indifference: On Domesticating Ethnicity*, Ithaca, NY: Cornell University Press.

Banerjee, S. 1984. *India's Simmering Revolution: The Naxalite Uprising*. London: Zed Books.

Banfield, E. 1958. *Moral Basis of Backward Societies*. Glencoe, Il.: Free Press.

Bardhan, P. 1985. *The Political Economy of Development in India*. New Delhi: Oxford University Press.

——. 1991. "State and Dynamic Comparative Advantages". *Economic Times*. New Delhi edition. 19–20 March.

Barron, P. 1844. *Notes of Wandering in the Himmala*. Reprinted 1990. Nainital: Gyanodaya Prakashan.

Barthes, R. 1972. *Mythologies*. Trans. Annette Lavers. New York: Noonday Press.

Bayly, C.A. 1976. *The Local Roots of Indian Politics: Allahabad 1880–1920*. Oxford, Clarendon Press.

——. 1988. *Indian Society and the Making of the British Empire*. Reprinted 1993. Cambridge: Cambridge University Press.

——. 1989. "Rallying around the Subaltern". *Journal of Peasant Studies*. 16 (2): 110–20.

Bebbington, A. 1996. "Movements, Modernizations, and Markets: Indigenous Organizations and Agrarian Strategies in Ecuador". In R. Peet and M.J. Watts (eds). *Liberation Ecologies* pp. 86–109. London: Routledge.

Beck, U. 1998. *Democracy Without Enemies*. Cambridge: Polity Press.

Beder, S. 1993. *The Nature of Sustainable Development*. Newham: Scribe.

Behn, M. 1960. *The Spirit's Pilgrimage*. London: Longmans.

Berreman, G. 1972. *Hindus of the Himalayas: Ethnography and Change*. Berkeley: University of California Press.

——. 1978. *Himachal: Science, People, and "Progress"*. Copenhagen: IWGIA.

——. 1988. "Uttarakhand and Chipko: Regionalism and Environmentalism in the Central Himalayas". In M.K. Raha (ed.) *The Himalayan Heritage*: pp. 266–300. New Delhi: Gian Publishing House.

——. 1989. "Chipko: A Movement to Save the Himalayan Environment and People". In C.M. Borden (ed.) *Contemporary Indian Tradition: Voices on Culture, Nature, and the Challenge of Change*: pp. 239–66. Washington, DC: Smithsonian Institution.

Bhabha, H. 1990. "The Other Question: Difference, Discrimination, and the Discourse of Colonialism". In R. Ferguson (ed.) *Out There: Marginalization and Contemporary Cultures*: pp. 71–89. Cambridge, Mass.: MIT Press.

Bharati, A. 1987. "Actual and Ideal Himalayas: Hindu Views of the Mountains". In J.F. Fisher (ed.), *Himalayan Anthropology: The Indo-Tibetan Interface*: pp. 77–82. The Hague: Mouton.

Bhatt, C.P. 1982. *Ecosystem of Central Himalayas*. Gopeshwar, Chamoli: Dasholi Gram Swarajya Mandal.

———. 1988. "The Chipko Movement: Strategies, Achievements, and Impacts". In M.K. Raha (ed.) *The Himalayan Heritage*: pp. 249–65. New Delhi: Gian Publishing House.

———. 1991. "Chipko Movement: The Hug that Saves". *Survey of the Environment 1991*: pp. 17–19. Madras: The Hindu.

Blaikie, P. and Brookfield, H. 1987. *Land Degradation and Society*, London: Methuen.

Bora, R.S. 1987. "Extent and Causes of Migration from the Hill Regions of Uttar Pradesh". In V. Joshi (ed.) *Migrant Labour and Related Issues*: pp. 187–209. New Delhi: Oxford University Press and IBH.

Bose, S. and Jalal, A. (eds). 1998. *Nationalism, Democracy, and Development: State and Politics in India*. Delhi: Oxford University Press.

Botkin, D.B. 1990. *Discordant Harmonies: A New Ecology for the Twenty-First Century*. New York: Oxford University Press.

Bourdieu, P. 1977. *Outline of a Theory of Practice*. Reprinted 1992. Cambridge: Cambridge University Press.

Brandis, (Sir) D. 1897. *Forestry in India: Origins and Early Developments*. Reprinted 1994. Dehra Dun: Natraj Publishers.

Brass, T. 1986. "Unfree Labour and Capitalist Restructuring in the Agrarian Sector: Peru and India". *Journal of Peasant Studies*. 14 (1): 51–77.

———. 1991. "Moral Economists, Subalterns, New Social Movements, and the (Re-) Emergence of a (Post-) Modernised (Middle) Peasant". *Journal of Peasant Studies*. 18 (2): 173–205.

———. 1994. "The Politics of Gender, Nature, and Nation in the Discourse of New Farmers' Movements". *Journal of Peasant Studies*. 21 (3/4): 27–71.

Braudel, F. 1966. *The Mediterranean and the Mediterranean World in the Age of Philip II*. Reprinted 1992. London: HarperCollins.

———. 1973. *Structures of Everyday Life*. Republished 1981. New York: Harper and Row.

———. 1977. *Afterthoughts on Material Civilization and Capitalism*. Baltimore: Johns Hopkins University Press.

——. 1979a. *The Wheels of Commerce*. Republished 1982. New York: Harper and Row.

——. 1979b. *The Perspective of the World*. Republished 1984. New York: Harper and Row.

Brohman, J. 1996. *Popular Development: Rethinking the Theory and Practice of Development*. Oxford: Blackwell.

Bromley, D. 1989. "Property Relations and Economic Development: The Other Land Reform". *World Development*. 17 (6): 867–77.

——. and Cernea, M. 1989. "Management of Common Property Natural Resources: Overview of the Bank Experience". In L. Richard Meyers (ed.) *Innovation in Resource Management: Proceedings of the Ninth Agriculture Sector Symposium*: pp. 29–45. Washington, DC: World Bank.

Bryant, R.L. 1992. "Political Ecology: An Emerging Research Agenda in Third-World Studies". *Political Geography*. 11 (1): 12–36.

——. and Parnwell, G. 1996. *Environment and Development in Southeast Asia*. London: Routledge.

Business Council for Sustainable Development. 1992. *Changing Course: A Global Business Perspective on Development and the Environment*. Cambridge, Mass.: MIT Press.

Buttel, F.H. and Sunderlin, W. 1988. "Integrating Political Economy and Political Ecology: An Assessment of Theories of Agricultural and Extractive Industry Development in Latin America". Paper presented at the 46th International Conference of Americanists, Amsterdam, 4–8 July.

——. and Taylor, P. 1994. "Environmental Sociology and Global Environmental Change: A Critical Assessment". In M. Redclift and T. Benton (eds). *Social Theory and the Global Environment*: pp. 228–55, London: Routledge.

Byres, T.J. 1972. "The Dialectic of India's Green Revolution". *South Asian Review*. 5 (2): 99–116.

Calvino, I. 1997. *The Literature Machine*. London: Vintage.

Campbell, J. (ed.) 1970. *Myths, Dreams, and Religion*. New York: E.P. Dutton.

Cartmill, M. 1993. *A View to a Death in the Morning: Hunting and Nature through History.* Cambridge, Mass.: Harvard University Press.

Cassirer, E. 1974. *An Essay on Man: An Introduction to a Philosophy of Culture.* New Haven, Conn.: Yale University Press.

——. 1979. *Symbol, Myth, and Culture.* Ed. D.P. Verene. New Haven, Conn.: Yale University Press.

Castells, M. 1983. *The City and the Grassroots: A Cross-Cultural Theory of Urban Social Movements.* Berkeley: University of California Press.

——. 1997. *The Power of Identity.* Oxford: Blackwell.

Cautley, (Sir) P.T. 1860. *Report on the Ganges Canal Works: From their Commencement until the Opening of the Canal in 1854.* Vol. I. London: Smith, Elder.

Chakravarty, S. 1987. *Development Planning: The Indian Experience.* New Delhi: Oxford University Press.

Champion, (Sir) H.G. and Osmaston, F.C. 1962. *E.P. Stebbing's 'The Forests of India', being the history from 1925 to 1947 of the forests now in Burma, India, and Pakistan, Volume IV.* Reprinted 1983. Delhi: Periodical Expert Book Agency.

——. and Seth, S.K. 1968a. *A Revised Survey of the Forest Types of India.* New Delhi: Government of India Publication Branch.

——. and Seth, S.K. 1968b. *General Silviculture for India.* New Delhi: Government of India Publication Branch.

Chase, A. 1987. *Playing God in Yellowstone: The Destruction of America's First National Park.* San Diego, Cal.: Harcourt Brace Jovanovich.

Chatterjee, P. 1986. *Nationalist Thought and the Colonial World: A Derivative Discourse.* London: Zed Books.

Chaudhuri, K.N. 1986. *Trade and Civilisation in the Indian Ocean: An Economic History from the Rise of Islam to 1750.* Cambridge: Cambridge University Press.

Ciriacy-Wantrup, S.V. and Bishop, R.C. 1975. "Common Property as a Concept in Natural Resources Policy". *Natural Resources Journal.* 15: 713–27.

Clark, T.J. 1986. *The Painting of Modern Life: Paris in the Art of Manet and His Followers.* Ithaca, NY: Cornell University Press.

Cleghorn, (Sir) H., Royle, F., Baird Smith, (Capt.) H, and Strachey,

(Capt.) R. 1851. *To consider the probable effects in an Economical and Physical point of view of the Destruction of Tropical Forests.* Edinburgh: British Association Report.

Clifford, J. and Marcus, G.E. (eds). 1986. *Writing Culture: The Poetics and Politics of Ethnography.* Berkeley: University of California Press.

Colinvaux, P. 1973. *Introduction to Ecology.* New York: John Wiley and Sons.

Corbett, T. 1995. "The Birth of Legitimacy of Ecology within the Global Political Economy". Unpublished paper. Griffith University, Queensland.

Corbridge, S.E. 1988. "The Ideology of Tribal Economy and Society: Politics in the Jharkhand, 1950–1980". *Modern Asian Studies.* 22 (1): 1–41.

——. and Jewitt, S. 1997. "From Forest Struggles to Forest Citizens? Joint Forest Management in the Unquiet Woods of Jharkhand". *Environment and Planning A.* 29 (12): 2145–64.

Coupe, L. 1997. *Myth.* London: Routledge.

Cronon, W. 1992. "Nature, History, Narrative: A Place for Stories". *Journal of American History.* March: 1347–76.

Crossley, J.W. 1996. "Managing Ecosystems for Integrity: Theoretical Considerations for Resource and Environmental Managers". *Society and Natural Resources.* 9 (5): 465–81.

Crush, J. (ed.) 1995. *Power of Development.* London: Routledge.

Daly, H. 1991. "Sustainable Growth: A Bad Oxymoron". *Grassroots Development.* 15 (3): 39.

Dewey, C. 1978. "The End of the Imperialism of Free Trade: The Eclipse of the Lancashire Lobby and the Concession of Fiscal Autonomy to India". In C. Dewey and A.G. Hopkins (eds). *The Imperial Impact: Studies in the Economic History of Africa and India:* pp. 35–67. London: The Athlone Press.

Dhoundiyal, N.C., Dhoundiyal, V.R., and Sharma, S.K. (eds). 1993. *The Separate Hill State.* Almora: Shree Almora Book Depot.

Dobhal, G.L. 1987. *Development of the Hill Areas: A Case Study of Pauri Garhwal District.* New Delhi: Concept Publishers.

Dogra, B. 1980. *Forests and People: The Efforts in Western Himalayas to*

Re-establish a Long-Lost Relationship. Rishikesh: Himalaya Darshan Prakashan Samiti.

Douglas, M. 1986. *How Institutions Think*. Syracuse, NY: Syracuse University Press.

Dréze, J. and Sen, A. (eds). 1996. *Economic Development and Social Opportunity*. Clarendon: Oxford University Press.

——. and Sen, A.K. (eds). 1997. *Indian Development: Selected Regional Perspectives*. Delhi: Oxford University Press.

Earle, C. 1992. "Introduction: The Practice of Geographical History", in *Geographical Inquiry and American Historical Problems*. Stanford, Cal.: Stanford University Press.

Egerton, F.N. 1976. "Ecological Studies and Observations before 1900". In B.J. Taylor and T.J. White (eds). *Issues and Ideas in America*: pp. 311–51. Norman, Okla.: University of Oklahoma Press.

Eliade, M. 1963. *Myth and Reality*. New York: Harper and Row.

Escobar, A. 1992. "Imagining a Post-Development Era? Critical Thought, Development and Social Movements". *Social Text*. 10 (2/3): 20–56.

——. 1995a. *Encountering Development: the Making and Unmaking of the Third World*. Princeton, NJ: Princeton University Press.

——. 1995b. "Imagining a Post-Development Era". In J. Crush (ed.) *Power of Development*. pp. 211–27. London: Routledge.

Esteva, G. 1987. "Regenerating People's Space". *Alternatives*. 10 (3): 125–52.

Evans, P. 1995. *Embedded Autonomy: States and Industrial Transformation*. Princeton, NJ: Princeton University Press.

Ferguson, J. 1990. *The Anti-Politics Machine: "Development", Depoliticization and Bureaucratic Power in Lesotho*. Cambridge: Cambridge University Press.

Finley, M.I. 1965. "Myth, Memory, and History". *History and Theory*. IV (5): 281–302.

Fisher, J.F. 1986. *Trans-Himalayan Traders: Economy, Society, and Culture in Northwest Nepal*. Berkeley: University of California Press.

Fishlow, A. 1990. *Pathways from the Periphery: The Politics of Growth in* the *Newly Industrializing Economies*. Ithaca, NY: Cornell University Press.

Foucault, M. 1991. "Governmentality". In G. Burchell, C. Gordon, and P. Miller (eds). *The Foucault Effect: Studies in Governmentality, with two lectures by and an interview with Michel Foucault*: pp. 87–104. London: Harvester Wheatsheaf.

Friedmann, J. 1988. *Life-Space and Economic Space: Essays in Third World Planning*. New Brunswick, NJ: Transaction Books.

——. 1992. *Empowerment: The Politics of Alternative Development*. Cambridge, Mass.: Blackwell.

——. and Rangan, H. (eds). 1993. *In Defense of Livelihood: Comparative Studies in Environmental Action*. West Hartford, Conn.: Kumarian Press.

Frye, N. 1957. *Anatomy of Criticism: Four Essays*. Princeton, NJ: Princeton University Press.

Frykenberg, R. (ed.) 1961. *Land Control and Social Structure in Indian History*. Madison, Wis.: University of Wisconsin Press.

Gadgil, M. and Guha, R. 1992. *This Fissured Land: An Ecological History of India*. Berkeley: University of California Press.

——. 1995. *Ecology and Equity: The Use and Abuse of Nature in Contemporary India*. London: Routledge.

Gandhi, L. 1998. *Postcolonial Theory: A Critical Introduction*, St Leonards, NSW: Allen and Unwin.

Garb, Y. 1995. "Lost in Translation: Toward a Feminist Account of Chipko". Paper presented at the Conference on Translations, Environments, Transitions: The Meanings of Feminism in Contemporary Politics. Rutgers University/ Institute for Advanced Study. 29 April.

Genovese, E. 1973. *Roll, Jordan, Roll: The World the Slaves Made*. New York: Pantheon.

Gerschenkron, A. 1943. *Bread and Democracy in Germany*. Reprinted 1989. Ithaca, NY: Cornell University Press.

——. 1962. *Economic Backwardness in Historical Perspective*. Cambridge, Mass.: Harvard University Press.

Ghosh, A. 1995. *In an Antique Land*. New Delhi: Ravi Dayal.

Glacken, C.J. 1967. *Traces on the Rhodian Shore: Nature and Culture in*

Western Thought from Ancient times to the End of the Eighteenth Century. Berkeley: University of California Press.

Gordon, C. 1991. "Government Rationality: An Introduction". In G. Burchell, C. Gordon, and P. Miller (eds). *The Foucault Effect: Studies in Governmentality, with two lectures by and an interview with Michel Foucault*: pp. 1–52. London: Harvester Wheatsheaf.

Gould, S.J. 1987. *An Urchin in the Storm: Essays about Books and Ideas.* New York: W.W. Norton.

Gramsci, A. 1971. *Selections from the Prison Notebooks.* Ed. and trans. by Q. Hoare and G.N. Smith. New York: International Publishers.

Guha, R. [Ramachandra] 1983. "Forestry in British and Post-British India: A Historical Analysis". *Economic and Political Weekly.* 18 (45 and 46): 1892–6, 1940–7.

——. 1985. "Forestry and Social Protest in British Kumaon, c.1893–1921". In Ranajit Guha (ed.) *Subaltern Studies Volume 4.* New Delhi: Oxford University Press.

——. 1986. "Commercial Forestry and Social Conflict in the Indian Himalaya". *Forestry for Development Lecture Series.* Berkeley: School of Forestry, University of California.

——. 1989. *The Unquiet Woods: Ecological Change and Peasant Resistance in the Himalaya.* New Delhi: Oxford University Press.

——. 1993. "Chipko's Triumphs Extend Beyond the Forest". *Down to Earth.* 30 April pp. 45–6.

——. and Gadgil, M. 1989. "State Forestry and Social Conflict in British India". *Past and Present.* 123: 141–77.

Guha, R. [Ranajit] 1962. *A Rule of Property for Bengal: An Essay on the Idea of Permanent Settlement.* Paris: Mouton.

——. 1983. *Elementary Aspects of Peasant Insurgency in Colonial India.* New Delhi: Oxford University Press.

Gupta, D. 1985. "On Altering the Ego in Peasant History: Paradoxes of the Ethnic Option". *Peasant Studies.* 13 (1): 5–24.

Hampson, C. 1990. "Industry and the Environment: A Question of Balance". In D.J.R. Angell, J.D. Comer and M.L.N. Wilkinson (eds). *Sustaining Earth: Response to the Environmental Threat*: pp. 108–19. London: Macmillan.

Haraway, D. 1988. "Situated Knowledges: The Science Question in Feminism and the Privilege of Partial Perspective". *Feminist Studies*. 14 (3): 575–99.

Hardin, G. 1968. "The Tragedy of the Commons". *Science*. 164: 1243–8.

Harriss, J. (ed.) 1982. *Rural Development: Theories of Peasant Economy and Agrarian Change*. London: Hutchinson Press.

Hartley, L.P. 1984. *The Go-Between*. Harmondsworth: Penguin.

Harvey, D. 1974. "Population, Resources, and the Ideology of Science". *Economic Geography*. 50 (3): 256–78.

——. 1996. *Justice, Nature and the Geography of Difference*. Oxford: Blackwell.

——. 1997. "Considerations on the Environment of Justice". Paper presented at the Conference on Environmental Justice: Global Ethics for the 21st Century, University of Melbourne, Australia, 1–3 October.

Hauser, W. 1993. "Violence, Agrarian Radicalism and Electoral Politics: Reflections on the Indian People's Front". *Journal of Peasant Studies*, 21 (1): 85–126.

Hays. S.P. 1959. *Conservation and the Gospel of Efficiency: The Progressive Conservation Movement, 1890–1920*. Cambridge, Mass.: Harvard University Press.

Hecht, S. and Cockburn, A. 1989. *The Fate of the Forest: Developers, Destroyers, and Defenders of the Amazon*. London: Verso.

Heckscher, E.F. 1935. *Mercantilism*. Vol. II. London: G. Allen and Unwin.

Herring, R. 1989. "Dilemmas of Agrarian Communism: Peasant Differentiation, Sectoral and Village Politics in India". *Third World Quarterly*. 11 (1): 89–115.

Hettne, B. 1990. *Development Theory and the Three Worlds*. Essex: Longman.

Hillman, J. 1978. *The Myth of Analysis: Three Essays*. New York: Harper and Row.

Hobsbawm, E.J. 1965. *Primitive Rebels: Studies in the Archaic Forms of Social Movements in the 19th and 20th centuries*. New York: Norton Press.

Holling, C.S. 1986. "The Resilience of Terrestrial Ecosystems: Local Surprise and Global Change". In W.C. Clark and R.E. Munn (eds). *Sustainable Development of the Biosphere*: pp. 292–317. Cambridge: Cambridge University Press.

hooks, b. 1984. *Feminist Theory: From Margin to Center*. Boston: South End Press.

——. 1991. *Yearning: Race, Gender, and Cultural Politics*. Boston: South End Press.

Hopkins, A.G. 1978. "Imperial Connections". In C. Dewey and A.G. Hopkins (eds). *The Imperial Impact: Studies in the Economic History of Africa and India*: pp. 20–34. London: The Athlone Press.

Humphries, J. 1990. "Enclosures, Commons Rights, and Women: The Proletarianisation of Families in Late Eighteenth and Early Nineteenth Centuries". *Journal of Economic History*, 50 (1): 17–42.

Huxley, J. 1943. *Evolution, the Modern Synthesis*. New York: Harper.

Hyde, W., Newman, D. H., and Sedjo, R.A. 1991. *Forest Economics and Policy Analysis: An Overview*. Washington, DC: The World Bank.

Ives, J.D. and Messerli, B. 1989. *The Himalayan Dilemma: Reconciling Development and Conservation*. London: Routledge.

Jackson, C. 1993. "Women/Nature or Gender/History? A Critique of Ecofeminist 'Development'". *Journal of Peasant Studies*. 20 (3): 389–419.

Jain, S. 1984. "Women and People's Ecological Movement: A Case Study of Women's Role in the Chipko Movement in Uttar Pradesh". *Economic and Political Weekly*. 19 (41): 1788–94.

Jalal, A. 1995. *Democracy and Authoritarianism in South Asia: A Comparative and Historical Perspective*. Cambridge: Cambridge University Press.

Jameson, F. 1981. *The Political Unconscious: Narrative as a Socially Symbolic Act*. Ithaca, NY: Cornell University.

Johnson, C. 1982. *MITI and the Japanese Miracle: The Growth of Industrial Policy 1925–1975*. Stanford, Cal.: Stanford University Press.

Joshi, S.C. (ed.) 1983. *Kumaon Himalaya: A Geographic Perspective on Resource Development*. Nainital: Gyanodaya Prakashan.

Kay, J.J. 1991. "A Nonequilibrium Thermodynamic Framework for Discussing Ecosystem Integrity". *Environmental Management*. 15: 483–95.

Keay, J. 1983. *Where Men and Mountains Meet: The Explorers of the Western Himalayas, 1820–1875*. London: Century.

——. ed. 1991. *History of World Exploration*. London: The Royal Geographical Society/Hamlyn.

Kellert, S.R. and Wilson, E.O. (eds). 1993. *The Biophilia Hypothesis*. Washington, DC: Island Press.

Khan, W. and Tripathy, R.N. 1976. *Plan for Integrated Rural Development in Pauri Garhwal*. Hyderabad: National Institute of Community Development.

Khanka, S.S. 1988. *Labour Force, Employment and Unemployment in a Backward Economy: A Study of Kumaon Region in Uttar Pradesh*. Bombay: Himalayan Publishers.

Kitching, G. 1980. *Development and Underdevelopment in Historical Perspective*. London: Methuen.

Koppes, C. R. 1987. "Efficiency/Equity/Esthetics: Towards a Reinterpretation of American Conservation. *Environmental Review*. 2 (2): 127–46.

Kothari, R. 1988. *Rethinking Development: In Search of Humane Alternatives*. Delhi: Ajanta.

Kuhn, T. 1970. *The Structure of Scientific Revolutions*. Chicago: Chicago University Press.

Kuyek, J. 1993. "What is an Organizer? Political Organizing". *Canadian Dimension*. 27 (3): 21.

Lal, J.B. 1989. *India's Forests: Myth and Reality*. Dehra Dun: Natraj Publishers.

Lamb, C. 1992. "Forests Set to Fire World Passions". *Financial Times*. 15 June.

Landon, P. 1906. *The Opening of Tibet*. New York: Doubleday.

Lawson, P. 1993. *East India Company: A History*. London: Longman.

Lévi-Strauss, C. 1972. *The Savage Mind*. London: Weidenfeld and Nicolson.

——. 1978. *Myth and Meaning*. London: Routledge.

Lieten, G.K. 1992. *Continuity and Change in Rural West Bengal.* New Delhi: Sage Publications.

——. 1996. "Land Reforms at Centre Stage: The Evidence on West Bengal". *Development and Change.* 27 (1): 111–30.

Lipton, M. and Toye, J. 1991. *Does Aid Work in India? A Country Study of the Impact of Official Development Assistance.* London: Routledge.

Ludwig, D., Hilborn, R. and Walters, C. 1993. "Uncertainty, Resource Exploitation, and Conservation: Lessons from History". *Science.* 260: 17, 36.

McClelland, J. 1835. *Some Inquiries in the Province of Kemaon relative to Geology, and other branches of Natural Science.* Calcutta: Baptist Mission Press.

McGee, T.G. 1997. "Globalisation, Urbanisation and the Emergence of Sub-Global Regions: A Case Study of the Asia-Pacific Region". In R.F. Watters and T.G. McGee (eds). *New Geographies of the Pacific Rim: Asia Pacific.* Bathurst, NSW: Crawford Publishing.

McGranahan, G. 1991. "Fuelwood, Subsistence Foraging, and the Decline of Common Property". *World Development,* 19 (10): 1275–87.

Mackay, C. 1841. *Extraordinary Popular Delusions and the Madness of Crowds.* New York: Farrar, Straus, and Giroux.

McNeill, W.H. 1986. *Mythistory and Other Essays.* Chicago: University of Chicago Press.

Macpherson, C.B. 1978. *Property: Mainstream and Critical Positions.* Toronto: University of Toronto Press.

Maine, (Sir) H. 1876. *Village Communities in the East and West.* London: John Murray.

Malinowski, B. 1954. *Magic, Science, and Religion and Other Essays.* Garden City, NY: Anchor Doubleday.

Mann, S.A. 1990. *Agrarian Capitalism in Theory and Practice.* Chapel Hill: University of North Carolina Press.

——. and Dickinson, J.M. 1978. "Obstacles to the Development of a Capitalist Agriculture". *Journal of Peasant Studies.* 5 (2): 466–81.

Marglin, S. and Appfel-Marglin, F. (eds). 1990. *Dominating Knowledge*, Oxford: Clarendon Press, 1990.

Mawdsley, E. 1997. "The Uttarakhand Agitation and Other Backward Classes". *Economic and Political Weekly*. 31 (4): 205–10.

Metcalfe, T.R. 1976. *Land, Landlords, and the British Raj*. Berkeley: University of California Press.

Michael, F. 1966. *The Taiping Rebellion: History and Documents*. Vol. 1. Seattle: University of Washington Press.

Mies, M. and Shiva, V. 1993. *Ecofeminism*. London: Zed Books.

Migdal, J. 1974. *Peasants, Politics, and Revolution*. Princeton, NJ: Princeton University Press.

Minh-ha, T. T. 1989. *Woman, Native, Other*. Bloomington: Indiana University Press.

Mishra, A. and Tripathi, S. 1978. *Chipko Movement: Uttarakhand Women's Bid to Save Forest Wealth*. New Delhi: Gandhi Peace Foundation.

Mitlin, D. 1992. "Sustainable Development: A Guide to the Literature". *Environment and Urbanization*. 4 (2): 111–24.

Mitra, A. 1993a. "Chipko: An Unfinished Mission". *Down to Earth*. 30 April: 25–51.

——. 1993b. "There can be no development without women: Interview with Gayatri Devi". *Down to Earth*. 30 April pp. 50–1.

Mitra, S.K. 1992. *Power, Protest and Participation: Local Elites and the Politics of Development in India*. London: Routledge.

Mooney, P. 1978. "Labour Time, Production Time, and Capitalist Development in Agriculture: A Reconsideration of the Mann–Dickinson Thesis". *Sociologia Ruralis*. 20 (3/4): 279–92.

Moorcroft, W. and Trebeck, G. 1841. *Travels in the Himalayan Provinces of Hindustan and the Panjab from 1819 to 1825*. Vol. I. London: John Murray.

Moore Jr, B. 1966. *Social Origins of Dictatorship and Democracy: Lord and Peasant in the Making of the Modern World*. Boston: Beacon Press.

Naipaul, V.S. 1990. *India: A Million Mutinies Now*. London: Minerva.

Nandy, A. 1989. "Shamans, Savages, and the Wilderness: On the

Audibility of Dissent and the Future of Civilizations". *Alternatives*. 14 (3): 263–78.

Naqvi, J. 1992. "TransHimalayan Trade with China after 30 Years". *India-West*. 10 July.

Nebel, B.J. and Wright, R.T. 1998. *Environmental Science: The Way the World Works*. New York: Prentice-Hall International.

Negi, S.S. 1990. *Himalayan Forests and Forestry*. New Delhi: Indus Publishing.

Nehru, J. 1946. *The Discovery of India*. New Delhi: Oxford University Press.

Norton, B.G. 1992. "A New Paradigm for Environmental Management". In R. Costanza, B.G. Norton, and B.D. Haskell (eds). *Ecosystem Health: New Goals For Environmental Management*: pp. 23–44. Washington, DC: Island Press.

Odum, P. 1971. *Fundamentals of Ecology*. 3rd ed. Philadelphia: W.B. Saunders.

Offe, C. 1985. *Disorganized Capitalism: Contemporary Transformations of Work and Politics*. Cambridge, Mass.: The MIT Press.

Omvedt, G. 1990. *Violence against Women: New Movements and New Theories in India*. New Delhi: Kali for Women.

——. 1993. *Reinventing Revolution: New Social Movements and the Socialist Tradition in India*. Armonk, NY: M.E. Sharpe.

O'Neill, R.V., DeAngelis, D.L., Waide, J.B. and Allen, T.F.H. 1986. *A Hierarchical Concept of Ecosystems*. Princeton, NJ: Princeton University Press.

Paige, J.M. 1976. *Agrarian Revolutions*. New York: Free Press, 1976.

——. 1983. "Social Theory and Peasant Revolution in Vietnam and Guatemala". *Theory and Society*. 12: 699–737.

Pangtey, Y.P.S. and Joshi, S.C. (eds). 1987. *Western Himalaya: Environment Problems and Development*. Vols I and II. Nainital: Gyanodaya Prakashan.

Pant, G.B. 1922. *Forest Problems in Kumaon*. Reprinted 1987. Nainital: Gyanodaya Publishers.

Pant, S.D. 1935. *Social Economy of the Himalayans*. London: Allen and Unwin.

Ribbentrop, (Sir) B. 1900. *Forestry in British India*. Calcutta: Government Press.

Ribot, J.C. 1998. "Theorizing Access: Forest Profits along Senegal's Charcoal Commodity Chain". *Development and Change*. 29 (2): 307–41.

Richards, J.F. 1987. "Environmental Changes in the Dehra Dun Valley: 1880–1980". *Mountain Research and Development*. 7 (3): 299–304.

Rudolph, L. and Rudolph, S.H. 1987. *In Pursuit of Lakshmi: The Political Economy of the Indian State*. Chicago: University of Chicago Press.

Rushdie, S. 1991. *Imaginary Homelands: Essays and Criticism, 1981–1991*. London: Penguin.

Sachs, W. (ed.) 1992. *The Development Dictionary: A Guide to Knowledge as Power*. London: Zed Press.

Sack, R.D. 1992. *Place, Modernity, and the Consumer's World: A Relational Framework for Geographic Analysis*. Baltimore: The Johns Hopkins University Press.

Saegert, S. and Winkel, G.H. 1990. "Environmental Psychology". *Annual Review of Psychology*. 41: 441–77.

Said, E. 1983. *The World, the Text and the Critic*. Cambridge, Mass.: Harvard University Press.

Saklani, A. 1986. *The History of a Himalayan Princely State: Change, Conflicts and Awakenings: An Interpretive History of the Princely State of Tehri Garhwal, 1811–1949*. Delhi: Durga Publications.

Samuel, R. 1994. *Theatres of Memory*, London: Verso.

Scott, J.C. 1976. *The Moral Economy of the Peasant*. New Haven, Conn.: Yale University Press.

——. 1985. *Weapons of the Weak: Everyday forms of Peasant Resistance*. New Haven, Conn.: Yale University Press.

——. 1990. *Domination and the Arts of Resistance: Hidden Transcripts*. New Haven, Conn.: Yale University Press.

Sears, J. 1989. *Sacred Places*. New York: Oxford University Press.

Sen, A.K. 1960. *Choice of Techniques*. Oxford: Blackwell.

——. 1981. *Poverty and Famines: An Essay on Entitlements and Deprivation*. Oxford: Clarendon Press.

——. 1984. "Peasants and Dualism". In A.K. Sen. *Resources, Values and Development*: pp. 37–72. Cambridge, Mass.: Harvard University Press.

Sen, A.N. 1992. "Kamal Nath [Minister of Environment and Forests] Employs Street Savvy on World [Global Summit] Scene". Reprinted by arrangement with the *Times of India*. *India-West*. 10 June.

Shepard, M. 1982. "Chipko: North India's Tree Huggers". In S.S. Kumar (ed.) *Hugging the Himalaya: The Chipko Experience*. Gopeshwar, Chamoli; Dasholi Gram Swarajya Mandal.

Shiva, V. 1989. *Staying Alive: Women, Ecology and Development*. London: Zed Books.

——. and Bandyopadhyay, J. 1986a. "Environmental Conflicts and Public Interest Science". *Economic and Political Weekly*. 21 (2): 84–90.

——. and Bandyopadhyay, J. 1986b. *Chipko: India's Civilisational Response to the Forest Crisis*. New Delhi: Intach.

——. and Bandyopadhyay, J. 1987. "Chipko: Rekindling India's Forest Culture". *The Ecologist*. 17(1): 26–34.

——. and Bandyopadhyay, J. 1989. "The Political Economy of Ecology Movements". *IFDA Dossier*. 71 (May–June): 37–60.

Siciliano, A.V. 1978. *Entropy Considerations in Environmental Planning*. Monograph No. 25. University of California, Berkeley: Institute of Urban and Regional Development.

Singh, C. 1991. "Humans and Forests: the Himalaya and the *terai* during the Medieval Period". In A.S. Rawat (ed.) *History of Forestry in India*: pp. 163–78. New Delhi: Indus Publishing.

Singh, S.P., and Berry, A. 1990. *Forestry Land Evaluation: An Indian Case Study*. Dehra Dun: Surya Publications.

Sklair, L. 1998. "Social Movements and Global Capitalism". In F. Jameson and M. Miyoshi (eds). *The Cultures of Globalization*. Durham, NC: Duke University Press.

Skocpol, T. 1982. "What Makes Peasants Revolutionary?" In R. Weller and S. Guggenheim (eds). *Power and Protest in the Countryside*: pp. 157–79. Durham, NC: Duke University Press.

Smith, G. 1989. *Livelihood and Resistance: Peasants and the Politics of Land in Peru*. Berkeley: University of California Press.

Smythe, F.S. 1937. *The Valley of Flowers*. [Reprint not dated.] Dehra Dun: Natraj Publishers.

Smythies, E.A. 1925. *India's Forest Wealth*. London: Humphrey Milford.

Somanathan, E. 1991. "Deforestation, Property Rights and Incentives in Central Himalaya". *Economic and Political Weekly*. 26 (4): 37–46.

Spivak, G. 1987. *In Other Worlds: Essays in Cultural Politics*. London: Methuen.

Srinivasan, T.N. 1979. "Trends in Agriculture in India, 1949–50 to 1977–78." *Economic and Political Weekly*. 21 (2): 30–2.

Stebbing, E.P. 1920. *The Diary of a Sportsman Naturalist in India*. London: Bodley Head.

——. 1922. *The Forests of India*. Vols I and II. London: Bodley Head.

——. 1932. *The Forests of India*. Vol. III. London: Bodley Head.

Stokes, E.T. 1959. *English Utilitarians and India*. Oxford: Oxford University Press.

——. 1978. *The Peasants and the Raj*. Cambridge: Cambridge University Press.

Stowell, (Sir) V.A. 1907. *A Manual of the Tenures of the Kumaon Division*. Reprinted 1938. Allahabad: Government Press.

Strong Jr, D.R. 1984. *Ecological Communities: Conceptual Issues and the Evidence*. Princeton, NJ: Princeton University Press.

Subramaniam, C. 1979. *The New Strategy in Indian Agriculture*. New Delhi: Vikas.

Swarup, R. 1991. *Agricultural Economy of the Himalayan Region: With Special reference to Kumaon*. Nainital: G.B. Pant Institute of Himalayan Environment and Development.

Taylor, P.J. and Buttel, F.H. 1992. "How Do We Know We Have Global Environmental Problems? Science and the Globalization of Environmental Discourse". *Geoforum*. 22 (3): 405–12.

Thomas, K. 1983. *Man and the Natural World: A History of the Modern Sensibility*. New York: Pantheon Books.

Thompson, E.P. 1966. *The Making of the English Working Class*. New York: Vintage Books.

——. 1993. 'Moral Economy of the English Crowd in the Eighteenth Century'. In E.P. Thompson, *Customs in Common: Studies in*

Traditional Popular Culture. New York: The New Press: pp. 185–258.

Thompson, M. 1988. "Uncertainty and Its Uses". In Piers Blaikie and Tim Unwin (eds). *Environmental Crises in Developing Countries*. Monograph No. 5: pp. 125–41. London: Developing Areas Research Group, Institute of British Geographers.

——. and Warburton, M. 1988. "Uncertainty on a Himalayan Scale". In J.D. Ives and D.C. Pitt (eds). *Deforestation: Social Dynamics in Watersheds and Mountain Ecosystems* pp. 1–53. London: Routledge.

Tiwary, M. 1998. "Participatory Forest Management in West Bengal: Ground-Breaking Triumph or Dilemma in the 'Commons'?" Unpublished paper presented at the *Workshop on Participatory Natural Resource Management*, Oxford, England, 6–7 April.

Touraine, A. 1981. *The Voice and the Eye: An Analysis of Social Movements*. Trans. A. Duff. Cambridge: Cambridge University Press.

Traill, G.W. 1828. "A Statistical Sketch of Kumaon". *Asiatic Researches*. Vol. XVI. Reprinted 1980. New Delhi: Indus Publishing.

Trainer, F.E. 1989. *Developed to Death: Rethinking World Development*. London: Green Press.

Troup, R.S. 1919. *Silviculture of Indian Trees*. Vol. I–III. Reprinted 1976. Dehra Dun: Forest Research Institute. 127–46.

Tucker, R.P. 1983. "The British Colonial System and the Forests of the Western Himalayas, 1815–1914". In R.P. Tucker and J.F. Richards (eds). *Global Deforestation and the Nineteenth Century World Economy*: pp. 146–66. Durham, NC: Duke University Press.

——. 1988. "The British Empire and India's Forest Resources: The Timberlands of Assam and Kumaon, 1914–1950". In J.F. Richards and R. P. Tucker (eds). *World Deforestation in the Twentieth Century*: pp. 91–111. Durham, NC: Duke University Press.

——. 1991. "The Evolution of Transhumant grazing in the Punjab Himalaya". In A.S. Rawat (ed.) *History of Forestry in India*: pp. 215–40. New Delhi: Indus Publishing.

Turner, (Capt.) S. 1800. *An Account of An Embassy to the Court of Teshoo Lama in Tibet*. London: Bulmer and Row.

Upadhyay, C.B. (ed.) 1990. *Forest Laws, with Commentaries on Indian Forest Act and Rules, State Acts, Rules Regulations etc.* 7th edn. Allahabad: Hind Publishing House. Upadhyay, H.C. 1990. *Harijans of the Himalaya.* Nainital: Gyanodaya Prakashan.

Vayda, A.P. 1983. "Progressive Contextualization: Methods for Research in Human Ecology". *Human Ecology.* 2 (3): 265–81.

Von Fürer-Haimendorf, C. (ed.) 1981. *Asian Highland Societies in Anthropological Perspective.* New Delhi: Sterling Publishers.

——. 1975. *Himalayan Traders: Life in Highland Nepal.* London: John Murray.

Wade, R. 1990. *Governing the Market.* Princeton, NJ: Princeton University Press.

Walton, H.G. 1910. *British Garhwal: A Gazetteer, being Volume XXXVI of the District Gazetteers of the United Provinces of Agra and Oudh.* Allahabad: Government Press.

Walton, J. 1984. *Reluctant Rebels: Comparative Studies in Revolution and Underdevelopment.* New York: Columbia University Press.

Watts. M.J. 1993. "Development I: Power, Knowledge, and Discursive Practice". *Progress in Human Geography.* 17 (2): 257–72.

Webber, T. 1902. *Forests of Upper India and their Inhabitants.* London: Edward Arnold.

Weber, E. 1976. *Peasants into Frenchmen: The Modernization of Rural France, 1870–1914.* Stanford, Cal.: Stanford University Press.

Weber, T. 1988. *Hugging the Trees: The Story of the Chipko Movement.* New Delhi: Viking Press.

Weiss, P.A. (ed.) 1971. *Hierarchically Organised Systems in Theory and Practice.* New York: Hafner.

Whitcombe, E. 1972. *Agrarian Conditions in Northern India: The United Provinces under British Rule, 1860–1900.* Vol. I. Berkeley: University of California Press.

White, H. 1987. *The Content of Form: Narrative Discourse and Historical Representation.* Baltimore: Johns Hopkins University Press.

White, J.B. 1990. *Justice as Translation: An Essay in Cultural and Legal Criticism.* Chicago: University of Chicago Press.

Wiens, J.A. 1984. "On Understanding a Non-Equilibrium World: Myth and Reality in Community Patterns and Processes". In D.R.

Strong Jr *et al.* (eds). *Ecological Communities: Conceptual Issues and the Evidence*: pp. 439–51, Princeton, NJ: Princeton University Press.

Williams, D.R. and Patterson, M.E. 1996. "Environmental Meaning and Ecosystem Management: Perspectives from Environmental Psychology and Human Geography". *Society and Natural Resources*. 9 (5): 507–21.

Williams, G. 1997. "State, Discourse, and Development in India: the Case of West Bengal's *Panchayati Raj*". *Environment and Planning A*. 29 (12): 2099–112.

Williams, G.R.C. 1874. *Historical and Statistical Memoir of Dehra Doon*. Reprinted 1985. Dehra Dun: Natraj Publishers.

Williams, R. 1973. *The Country and the City*. Oxford: Oxford University Press.

——. 1977. *Marxism and Literature*. Oxford: Oxford University Press.

——. 1980. *Problems in Materialism and Culture*. London: Verso.

——. 1983. *Keywords: A Vocabulary of Culture and Society*. New York: Oxford University Press.

Wilmsen, E.N. 1989. *Land Filled with Flies: A Political Economy of the Kalahari*. Chicago: University of Chicago Press.

Wolf, E. 1969. *Peasant Wars of the Twentieth Century*. New York: Harper Torchbooks.

——. 1982. *Europe and the People Without History*. Berkeley: University of California Press.

Wood, E.M. 1995. *Democracy against Capitalism: Renewing Historical Materialism*. Cambridge: Cambridge University Press.

Woodhead, J. 1945. *The Famine Inquiry Commission*. New Delhi: Government of India.

Woodman, D. 1969. *Himalayan Frontiers: A Political Review of British, Chinese, Indian and Russian Rivalries*. London: Barrie and Rockliff.

Woodyatt, (Maj. Gen.) N. 1922. *Under Ten Viceroys: Reminiscences of a Gurkha*. London: Herbert Jenkins.

World Bank. 1991. *The Forest Sector*. World Bank Policy Paper. Washington, DC: The World Bank.

Wrigley. C.C. 1978. "Neo-mercantile Policies and the New Imperialism". In C. Dewey and A.G. Hopkins (eds). *The Imperial Impact:*

Studies in the Economic History of Africa and India: pp. 20–34. London: The Athlone Press.

Yapa, L. 1993. "What are Improved Seeds? An Epistemology of the Green Revolution". *Economic Geography*. 69 (3): 254–73.

Young, O.R. (ed.) 1997. *Global Governance: Drawing Insights from the Environmental Experience*. Cambridge, Mass.: MIT Press.

INDEX

Allen, G.M. and E.M. Gould Jr. 61
Anderson, Benedict 198*n12*
Atkinson, E.T. 205*n15, n19*

Baeten, Elizabeth 9
Bahuguna, Sunderlal 21, 27–32, 34, 40,
    46, 138, 159–61, 198*nn27–29*, 230*n26*
Bahuguna, Vimala 27
Barthes, Roland 1, 10
Bhatt, Chandi Prasad 21–6, 34, 40, 46,
    159, 198*n14*
Bishnoi community 33
Blaikie, Piers and Harold Brookfield
    61–2
Bourdieu, Pierre 178, 238*n4*
Boyd-White, James *xiv*
Brandis, Dietrich 213*n38*, 215–16*n51*,
    216–17*n53*
Brass, Tom 157, 215*n49*
Braudel, Fernand 178
British East India Company
    control of Garhwal 46, 73–4
    changing relationship with Britain
        76–7, 206*n35*, 206–7*n37, n38*
    dominant policy phases 77–80,
        212*nn28–9*, 214*n43*
    struggles with the British parliament
        79–80
    and opium trade 83
    and tea cultivation in Garhwal 83–6,
        90–93
    promotion of European farming
        ventures 86–7, 93

construction of Ganges Canal 87–90
boundary disputes with China 92
end of administration 113
Bromley, Daniel 104–5

Canada 13, 40
Castells, Manuel 158
Central Asia, trade 46
Central Asian *khanates* 50
Cernea, Michael 104–5
Chakrata
    forest division 7, 97, 209*n1*
    local politics 136–8
    rural household economy 209–10*n2*,
        221–2*n96*
Chamoli district 20–21, 42, 152
Chipko
    as social movement, 1, 193–4
    as myth 2, 9–11, 193
    'stories' 4–6
    'women' 14, 40, 42, 182
    competing symbolisms 15
    meanings of 20–21
    interpretations of 22–39
    as borrowed symbol 40
    emergence 152
    discursive strategies 159–61
    and Mrs. Gandhi 163
    aftermath 164–6, 233*nn50–51*
    and the Uttarakhand movement
        180–84, 233–4*n52*
    as 'parable' of regionality 194
Clark, Timmothy J. 41

Cleghorn, Henry 112–13
Colinvaux, Paul 202n24–5
colonial rule and Himalayan ecological
    'crisis' 53
Cornwallis, Lord 110, 212n29
Cronon, William 16–18, 197n6
Curzon, Lord 68

Dasholi Gram Swarajya Mandal (DGSM)
    22–6, 38, 152
David 'Chipko' 15
Dehra Dun 3–7, 44–5, 85–7, 168
development
    and the Himalayan 'crisis' 52–3
    debates and critiques 138–40
    and 'difference' 141
    and postcolonial politics of democracy
        142–4
    planning in colonial India 145–6,
        223–4n23
    planning in post-independence India
        146–9, 224nn28–9, 224–5n33, 225n35
discursive strategies
    and social movements 158–9
    around Chipko 159–61
    and regional protests 180

EarthFirst! 15
ecosystem models 54–61
Elphinstone, Lord 110, 212n31
England
    tree preservation protests 14–15
    impact of enclosures of commons on
        women 220–21n88
environmental narratives 18–20
Evans, Peter 205n25

Finley, Moses I. 196n10
Forest Conservation Act 1980 163–4,
    231–2n41, 232n43
Forest Grievances Committee 125–6
Forest Research Institute 225n43
forestry
    developments between 1805 and 1848
        106–9
    questions of state ownership 109–12,
        210–11n8
    competing perspectives on
        conservation 112–15, 214–15n46

classifications of the 1865 Forest Act
    114–15
definitions of state control 115–16
modes of controlling extraction
    116–20, 215nn47–9
during the World Wars 126–7
and dilemmas of foresters
    219–20nn83–5, 221n92
post independence developments
    127–32, 224n32
estimates of deforestation in UP
    226n48
changes in prices of forest products
    227n54
Foucault, Michel 206n28
Friedmann, John 238n6
Fuller, J.B. 85

Gandhi, Indira 162–3, 230n31, 231n35
Gandhian principles 22, 27
Ganges, story of 47–8
Ganges Canal, construction of 87–90,
    208nn54–6
Garb, Yaakov 14–15, 197n3
Garhwal
    economy prior to 1815 70–72, 204n6
    under Nepalese/Gurkha rule 46, 73
    developments under the British East
        India Company 46, 73–4, 83–96
    expansion of forestry 120–32
    regional transformations under
        dominant policy phases 132–5
    problems of regional economic
        stagnation 167–8
Garhwal and Kumaon Himalaya (also see
    Uttarakhand)
    imagined landscapes 39–40
    forest vegetation characteristics
        99–100, 210n4
    land use changes in Garhwal and
        Kumaon 210n7
    forest disputes 122–7, 218–19n71,
        219–20nn83–5, 221n92, 227–8n59
    outcomes of development processes
        149–52, 226n51
    effects of Sino-Indian war 150
    changing rural social relations 221n93,
        221–2n96

controversy over the Tehri Dam 234*n53*
geographical history 2, 11–12, 178–9, 197*n10*
Glacken, Clarence J. 202*n25*, 204*n58*
Gould, S.J. 64
Government of India
  interpretation of the Chipko movement 21
  views on the use of forests by local communities 226–7*n53, 227n57*
Gramsci, Antonio 159
Great Game 68, 207*n39*
Green Revolution 151, 225*n39*, 226*n51*
Guha, Ramachandra 22, 35–40, 42, 46, 130, 157, 200*n51*, 200*n55*, 216*n52*, 217–18*n60*, 221*n92*
Guha, Ranajit 212*n29*, 228–9*n12*

Hardin, Garrett 104–6
Hartley, L.P. 6
Harvey, David 238*n6*
Hecht, Susanna B. and Alexander Cockburn 197*n11*, 215*n48*
Himalayas
  geological processes 47
  landscapes of idealisation 48–52, 201*n12*
  interpretations of ecological crises 51–4
  ecosystem models 54–61
  and 'backwardness' 66, 68

identity formation 158–9, 229*nn19–20*
Imperial Forest Service (later Indian Forest Service)
  creation of 106,114
  adoption of Burmese forest systems 108–9, 111–12
  questions regarding state ownership 109–112
  under various government departments 115
Indian Forest Act 1865 114, 122–7
Indian National Congress 145–6
Indian Turpentine and Resin Factory 149, 225*nn41–2*
industrial development 145–6, 223–4*n23*
Islington, tree preservation 14–15

Jameson, Dr. 85
Jaunsar-Bawar 222*n1*
Joint Forest Management in West Bengal 171–4, 192–3, 237–8*n68*

Keay, John 68–9, 201*nn13–14*, 204*n1*
Khadi and Village Industries Commission 22
Kumaon Association 125–6

Los Angeles Times 15

Mackay, Charles 228*n1*
Macpherson, C.B. 104–5, 211*n11*
Malcolm, Sir John 110, 212*nn31–2*
Malthusian explanations of Himalayan 'crisis' 51–2, 201–2*n17*
Mann, Susan A. and James M. Dickinson 215*n47*
McGee, Terry G. 238*n6*
McGranahan, Gordon 104–5
McNeill, William 9, 196*n10*, 202*n20*
Metcalfe, Sir Thomas 110, 212*nn31–2*
Mitra, Subrata 159, 229–30*n22*
Ministry of Environment and Forests 181–2
Mooney, Patrick 215*n49*
Moorcroft, William and George Trebeck 46–7, 201*n15*
Mughal empire 47, 70, 78
Munro, Sir Thomas 110, 212*n31*
myth 1–11
mythistories 196–7*n10*

Naipaul, V.S. 2
narratives 16–18
nationalisation 162, 230*n31*
Nehru, Jawaharlal 27, 146–7,164
Nepal, 46,49
  control over Garhwal 46, 73
  migrants to Garhwal 221–2*n96*, 232*n44*

Omvedt, Gail 157
O'Neill, R.V. 55, 202*n21*
Opium Wars 92

Paige, Jeffrey 156
panchayati raj 229–30*n22*
Partition 231*n32*

Pauri Garhwal 27
peasant movements 156–7, 219n83, 228n3
Peet, Richard and Michael Watts 62, 204n57
Peluso, Nancy 239n15
Peschel, Oskar 112
policies, mercantilist 78
   of staple 80–81
   of protection 81–96
   of provision 120–27
political ecology 61–5, 179–80, 191, 203n51
Popkin, Samuel 156
postcolonial politics of democracy 142–4, 223nn19–21
property, theoretical problems and debates 102, 211n11, 109–12, 212nn29–33

regionality 177–8
regional questions 176–80, 238–9n10
Revenue Administration
   control over forests 114–21
   disputes with Forest Service 122–6
   land settlement policies 134
Ribbentrop, Berthold 107, 111, 130, 213n38, 213n42, 218n63
Ribot, Jesse 103–4, 211n10
Royal Geographical Society 49, 68
Royle, Dr. 84
Rushdie, Salman xiv

Saharanpur 84, 87
Samuel, Raphael 197n10
Sarala Behn 28
Scott, James 156
Shiva, Vandana 22, 32–5, 40, 46, 157, 199n48, 199n50
Shore, John 110, 212n31
Singh, Chetan 205n21
Sino-Indian war of 1962 46, 150, 226n47
social movements
   theories and debates 155–9
   in the subcontinent 176
   as 'regions in protest' 177–8, 180
Subaltern Studies 219–20n83, 228–9n12
substantive democracy 193, 240n20
sustainability 184–93

tea cultivation 83–6, 92–3, 207–8n48
Tehri Garhwal 27, 29, 121–2, 218n70, 234n53
Thompson, M., and M. Warburton 58–61, 202n33
Tibet 47, 49, 72, 85–86, 90–93
Traill, G.W. 72, 205n15
transHimalayan trade 46–7, 50, 69–70, 73–4, 92–3, 132, 238n76
translation xiv, xvi

US Pacific Northwest 13,15
Uttar Pradesh
   Forest Corporation Act 1975 163
   Forest Department 20–21, 99, 100–101, 130, 151–2, 181–2
   Forest Development Corporation 154, 164–5, 232–3n45
   Hill Development Agency 167, 235n60, 235n62
   Private Forest Act 1948 128
   Tree Protection Act 1976 163, 231n38
Uttarakhand (also see Garhwal and Kumaon Himalaya) 36–7
   development issues 138
   Kranti Dal (revolutionary group) 166–7
   tree-felling 234–5n56
   struggles for regional autonomy 167–70, 184–7
   caste politics 169–70, 235–7nn65–6
   regional development alternatives 171–4
   and Chipko 180–84
Uttaranchal 169, 235n64
Uttarkashi district 29

von Humboldt, Alexander 112

Wallich, Dr. 108
Walton, H.G. 94, 204n4, 205n11
wastelands 115, 123, 214n44
Watson, Captain 107
Weber, Thomas 13
Williams, G.R.C. 91–2
Wolf, Eric 156
Wrigley, C.C. 206n33